ROUTLEDGE LIBRARY EDITIONS:
THE FIRST WORLD WAR

Volume 4

GERMAN POLICY TOWARD NEUTRAL SPAIN, 1914–1918

GERMAN POLICY TOWARD NEUTRAL SPAIN, 1914–1918

RON M. CARDEN

Routledge
Taylor & Francis Group
LONDON AND NEW YORK

First published in 1987

This edition first published in 2014
by Routledge
2 Park Square, Milton Park, Abingdon, Oxfordshire OX14 4RN

and by Routledge
711 Third Avenue, New York, NY 10017

First issued in paperback 2016

Routledge is an imprint of the Taylor & Francis Group, an informa business

British Library Cataloguing in Publication Data
A catalogue record for this book is available from the British Library

ISBN: 978-0-415-74924-4 (Set)
ISBN 13: 978-1-138-97517-0 (pbk)
ISBN 13: 978-1-138-02444-1 (hbk)

Publisher's Note
The publisher has gone to great lengths to ensure the quality of this reprint but points out that some imperfections in the original copies may be apparent.

Disclaimer
The publisher has made every effort to trace copyright holders and would welcome correspondence from those they have been unable to trace.

MODERN EUROPEAN HISTORY

German Policy Toward Neutral Spain, 1914–1918

Ron M. Carden

Garland Publishing, Inc.
New York and London 1987

Library of Congress Cataloging-in-Publication Data

Carden, Ron M., 1942–
German policy toward neutral Spain, 1914–1918.

(Modern European history)
Thesis (Ph. D.)—University of New Mexico, 1979.
Bibliography: p.
1. World War, 1914–1918—Diplomatic history.
2. Germany—Foreign relations—Spain. 3. Spain—Foreign relations—Germany. 4. Spain—Neutrality.
I. Title. II. Series.
D621.S7C37 1987 940.3′24′430946 87-7436
ISBN 0-8240-8047-5

GERMAN POLICY TOWARD NEUTRAL SPAIN IN WORLD WAR I

1914-1918

BY

R. M. Carden

GERMAN POLICY TOWARD NEUTRAL SPAIN IN WORLD WAR I 1914-1918

R. M. Carden
B.A., History, Texas Tech University, 1965
M.A., History, New Mexico State University, 1967
Ph.D., History, The University of New Mexico, 1979

This paper presents a description and analysis of German diplomatic policy toward Spain during the First World War. In four stages, from August 1914 through October 1918, Berlin used adroit diplomacy and an effective propaganda network to encourage Spain to remain neutral. Conservative Spanish politicians, including King Alfonso XIII, feared that participation in the war would unsettle Spain's domestic political structure and, therefore, wanted to remain outside of the maelstrom. Nevertheless, the King used the world crisis to further his aim of returning Spain to the status of a Great Power; Germany encouraged the King's dreams.

The four stages of German-Spanish relations included a pro-German phase from August 1914 to September 1916, a time of tension in the fall of 1916 through April 1917, deteriorating relations over interned German submarines from May 1917 through March 1918, and finally sharp Spanish demands for indemnities for ships sunk by German submarines. Conciliatory diplomacy and constant use of German propaganda augmented Spanish forces that argued for strict neutrality, a policy that would benefit Germany.

In the interim, the Allies pressured Spain economically and diplomatically from September 1916 through March 1918 to abandon any hint of a pro-German attitude. Eventually, internal dissension and the need to remain within the British and French economic orbits caused Madrid to decide for a benevolent neutrality in favor of the Entente. Berlin, in the meantime, remained conciliatory, refusing to break relations, although the provocation in Madrid was severe.

Significantly, Spain, a leading European neutral, was not a direct participant in the war, and she was not completely favorable to the Allies until late in the struggle. German diplomatic subtlety and skill, an effective and far-reaching propaganda network, and Spanish pragmatism all accounted for this result. In contrast to her relations with other major neutrals, Germany conducted a friendly policy toward Spain and avoided a break with Madrid.

Policy, German toward
Spain in World War I,
1914-1918.

TABLE OF CONTENTS

INTRODUCTION

Diplomatic histories of the First World War rarely deal with the difficulties of the small European neutral nations. Historians in the United States in particular have concentrated, understandably enough, upon the unique problems created by the neutrality of the U.S. government from 1914 through early 1917. Whatever attention that was paid to European neutrals resulted from by-products of studies relating to some aspect of American diplomacy. In the 1920s and 1930s, the Carnegie Endowment for International Peace commissioned works dealing with the wartime economic histories of Holland, Switzerland, Denmark, and Iceland, but Spain, physically large and strategically situated, was ignored.[1] More recently, unpublished dissertations have examined specialized aspects of Spanish wartime policy vis-à-vis the United States or Spain and the European state system up to 1914.[2] Clearly, little American study of Spanish relations with the European belligerents has been done.

European historians too have not investigated the wartime diplomatic relations between Spain and the Central European belligerents. The majority of the efforts that have been made stem, moreover, from the war or from the 1920s, when little extensive documentation was available.[3]

The leading European historian for Spanish foreign policy for the period of 1914-1918 was Albert Mousset, a major journalist in France, and during the war a member of the French Embassy in Madrid. While he was a prolific writer, his many articles and two major books on Spanish foreign policy did not reflect German and American archival material.[4] Since the 1960s, some German and Austrian dissertations have concentrated upon certain aspects of Spanish relations with the Central Powers, utilizing German and Austrian archival sources, but these studies neglected almost all English language sources and several Spanish ones as well.[5] The only Spanish treatments of Madrid's policies during this period are contemporary accounts, books based upon slight documentary evidence, or specialized articles.[6] Thus, European historians, including the Spanish, have not seriously delved into the story of Spanish relations with the Central Powers, especially Germany, the most significant member of the Triple Alliance.

Certainly, one cannot propose that German-Spanish relations during the war were the most important inter-relations between a belligerent and a neutral, but there are ample justifications for examining German policy toward Spain and for discerning Spanish policy. The Iberian peninsula was strategically located, controlling the maritime approaches to the western Mediterranean and eastern Atlantic. Germany sought to use the many unguarded coves as refuges for her submarines. Spain also provided a listening post close to the enemy camp, making it possible to relay intelligence to Berlin. Also, Spain could function as a vital link with German diplomatic posts in the Western Hemisphere and in Asia. From the Allied side, Spain was important because of the extensive financial interests of French and British businessmen. The peninsula offered an excellent array of foodstuffs and military supplies for France and Great Britain. Spaniards could work in French factories, thereby freeing men for military service on the front. Both the Germans and the Western Powers, therefore, stretched every nerve to maintain Spanish neutrality in a sense favorable to their respective sides, and Madrid used the occasion to manipulate all belligerents to the benefit of Spain.

Originally, the purpose in writing this paper was to describe and to analyze the effects of titanic, impersonal forces upon policymakers in Berlin and Madrid. But the end result has been to reveal a well-known truth to more practiced historians. History is more truly the result of actions taken by fallible humans than pre-determined forces beyond the comprehension of any individual. The actions and policies of specific individuals did, however, coalesce to produce an effect little imagined by any one person, nevertheless, particular individuals did emerge from the documents with a vitality all their own.

Especially interesting was the unique and forceful personality of Spanish King Alfonso XIII, who struggled to control an imperious Prime Minister, Count Romanones, and who shrewdly used his special friendship with Kaiser William II for Spanish profit. Other dynamic personalities who helped to shape events were the German Ambassador in Madrid, Prince Maximillian von Ratibor and Corvey, and the American Ambassador, Joseph Willard. Private citizens from the German, Spanish, and American camps provided further, deeper glimpses into German-Spanish relations. This work is, therefore, in large part, a chronicle of the activities of these individuals and an assessment of the collective effects of their efforts.

The sources for this dissertation were varied, though the most important were the German documents available in the National Archives of the United States. As the work progressed, it was clear, however, that one needed an expanded view of Spanish policymakers. As Robert Whealey of Ohio University has pointed out in a recent article, it is virtually impossible to use the disorganized Spanish archival material for the period under review.[7] Therefore, it was necessary to reconstruct the Spanish position from a multitude of sources. The German documents were helpful in this endeavor; French, Spanish, German, English, and American newspapers provided additional assistance. Furthermore, Spanish, German, English, and American memoirs completed the picture. Perhaps most important, corrections and amplifications of Spanish policy could be derived from U.S. Department of State records, the Willard Family Papers, the U.S. Military Archives, and finally the records of the U.S. Committee for

Public Information.

The prime determinant of Spanish policy and of German attitudes toward Spain was geography. Spain, located on the periphery of Europe, was one of six major European neutral nations. Interestingly, the six divided neatly into two geographical groups of three each. The first group was that of Denmark, Switzerland, and Holland, each of which was physically close to the Reich and which had to yield to their powerful neighbor. The second was that of Norway, Sweden, and Spain. These nations were closer to the shipping lanes, and their commerce traditionally was closely connected with Great Britain. As the war progressed, this outer rim of European neutrals received substantial demands upon their economies from the Allies; these demands centered upon additional ships and supplies for the Entente and less trade with Germany. Berlin retaliated by attacks upon the seafaring commerce of these nations. This latter group of neutrals had, therefore, to discern as clearly as possible the outcome of the war and to avoid antagonizing the winning side. As the economic pressure from the Allies became too great to resist and as the tide of battle turned obviously in favor of the Western Powers, the peripheral countries came within the orbit of the Allied and Associated Powers and consequently neutral allies.

Spain's diplomatic importance derived from yet another geographical fact. Extensive interests and some possessions on the North African coast drew the nation into the prewar diplomatic jousts between the emergent Triple Entente and Triple Alliance. Spain tried to follow an independent policy in the region, playing each side against the other. But Madrid was never able to get recognition as a great power, nor was Spain ever able to obtain additional territory, especially control over Tangier. Nevertheless, the two power blocs made it appear Spain was important on the international scene, and the King and his ministers tried to make the most of their position. Wartime relations between Madrid and the belligerents represented a continuation, although in a more intensified form, of this state of affairs.

The purpose of this paper is, therefore, to describe and analyze the methods Germany used to reinforce Spain's independence thereby preventing Madrid's entry into the war on the Allied side. While the bulk of the documentary evidence reflects the German and American views of Spain, yet it is possible to deduce from the available sources Spanish policy toward Germany and the other belligerents. The King remained a Francophile who shrewdly manipulated the Germans into thinking he favored their side. At the same time Alfonso fended off the embrace of the Entente. The Wilhelmstrasse, meanwhile, utilized a multitude of sources, particularly an effective propaganda network, to influence Spanish public and official opinion. Berlin successfully pursued a policy that kept Spain neutral in a sense favorable to Germany until September 1916, when the tide began to turn toward the Allies. Spain, therefore, stayed neutral during much of the war due to the skills and subtlety of German diplomacy on the one hand and Spanish pragmatism and desire to avoid belligerency on the other.

The background for Spain's independent foreign policy and Germany's subsequent utilization of it in World War I reached back into the nineteenth century. Spanish suspicion of and even antipathy for the Western Powers ran deep, and near the end of the nineteenth century Spain tilted ever closer to the camp of the Triple Alliance. But in the late 1890s Spain reasserted a greater degree of freedom of action, and with King Alfonso XIII's majority in 1902, Madrid sought to counterbalance the emerging power blocs.

FOOTNOTES FOR THE INTRODUCTION

[1]Specifically, these works included Eli F. Hecksher, Norway, Sweden and Denmark and Iceland in the World War (New Haven: Yale University Press, 1930), Marius van der Flier, et al, The Netherlands and the World War, 4 vols. (Oxford: Clarendon Press, 1923-1928). For other specialized studies of American diplomacy toward European neutrals see Thomas A. Bailey, The Policy of the United States Toward the Neutrals, 1917-1918 (Baltimore, Md.: Johns Hopkins Press, 1942).

[2]See especially Vicente Pilapil, "Spain in the European State System," (Ph.D. dissertation, Catholic University of America, 1964), Rita M. Cancio, "The Function of María Cristina of Austria's Regency (1885-1902) in Preserving the Spanish Monarchy," (Ph.D. dissertation, St. Louis University, 1955), Wallace R. Klinger, "Spain's Problem of Alliances," (Ph.D. dissertation, University of Pennsylvania, 1944), Gerie Bledsoe, "Spain and the League of Nations," (Ph.D. dissertation, Florida State University, 1968), Shirley Jackson, "The United States and Spain, 1898-1918," (Ph.D. dissertation, Florida State University, 1967), and finally William R. Barker, "England and the European Neutral-Belligerents 1914-1917," (Ph.D. dissertation, University of Southern California, 1937).

[3]The best guide to contemporary comments upon Spain and the First World War is Albert Mousset, Elements d'une bibliographie et tracts imprimés ou publiés en Espagne de 1914 à 1919 et relatifs à la guerre mondiale (Madrid: Biblioteca nueva, 1919). Perhaps particularly representative of the early works dealing with Spain and the war was Luis Bello, España durante la Guerra, Política y Accíon de los Alemanes, 1914-1918 (Madrid: Editional Europa, 1920).

[4]In addition to the guide mentioned above, Mousset wrote L'Espagne dans la politique mondiale (Paris: Bossard, 1923), Histoire d'Espagne (Paris: Sociétè d'Editions Françaises et Internationales, 1947) and La Política Exteríor de España, 1873-1918 (Madrid: Biblioteca nueva, 1918).

[5]Perhaps the best German language works that bear directly upon German-Spanish relations during the war are Lillian Ferreira de vaz Gelos, Die Neutralitaetspolitik Spaniens waehrend des ersten Weltkrieges (Hamburg: Institut fuer Auswaertige Politik, 1966) and Harald Just, "Neutralitaet im Ersten Weltkrieg," Mitteilungen des Oesterreichischen

Staatsarchiv, XIX (Vienna, 1965), pp. 363-435. Neither of these works, however, fully examines the impact of the German propaganda network upon Spanish-German relations; furthermore, neither considers American nor British influences. One of the best recent works that suggests an approach to German relations with the European neutrals is W. M. Carlgren's Neutralitaet oder Allianz: Deutschlands Beziehungen zu Schweden in den Anfangsjahren des ersten Weltkrieges (Stockholm: Alinquist and Wiksell, 1962). Another useful examination of the relations between a neutral and the belligerents is Olav Riste's The Neutral Ally, Norway's Relations with Belligerent Powers in the First World War (Oslo, Norway: Universitetforlaget, 1965).

[6]The best Spanish account of the period, based mostly upon newspapers, is Don Melchor Fernandez Almagro, Historia del Reinado de Don Alfonso XIII (Barcelona: Montaner y Simon, S.A., 1933). Another significant and more recent work relating to Spanish diplomacy during the war is Rafael Olivar Bertrand, "Repercusiones en España de la primera guerra mundial," Cuadernos de Historia Diplomática, III (1956), pp. 3-45. Also of considerable value for recent scholarship is Maximiano García Venero, Melquiades Alvarez: Historia de un Liberal (Madrid: Editorial Alhambra, 1954).

[7]Robert H. Whealey, "Opportunities and Disappointments in the Spanish Foreign Ministry Archives," Archives, XII (Autumn 1975), pp. 68-73.

CHAPTER I

SPAIN AND THE INTERNATIONAL SCENE TO 1902 AND LEADING PERSONALITIES

Initially, Germany was not in a position geographically or diplomatically to draw Spain into the maelstrom, though a number of diverse factors accounted for continued Spanish neutrality, a policy that would be of enormous value to Berlin. First, Spaniards had long memories and harbored hatreds and resentments toward the leading powers of the Entente, France and Great Britain. Second, Spain had evolved a domestic political structure which, by 1914, had become quite tenuous, and participation in the war could destroy the monarchy and conservative ruling classes. Divisions among those who supported the contending sides in the war reflected internal political cleavages, consequently interconnecting domestic and foreign relations. Third, the Germans were able to counter Allied economic and political influence by means of a very active diplomatic and business community which exploited all factors contributing to Spanish neutrality.

Spanish differences with England stemmed from sixteenth century quarrels over religion and economics. Spain and England became mortal enemies due to violent confrontations arising from religious differences during the Reformation, attacks upon Spanish treasure ships from America, and the defeat of the Spanish Armada in 1588. English attempts to breach Spanish colonial trade regulations had resulted in a series of wars during which Spain lost Gibraltar in 1702. Throughout the remainder of the eighteenth century the two were enemies, though they cooperated after 1808 to drive the French from the Iberian peninsula. But after the Napoleonic Wars, England encouraged the colonies of Spain to separate from the mother country, and by the late nineteenth century, Great Britain, occupied by troubles in South Africa, sat by and watched as the United States defeated Spain. The U.S. took the remnants of the worldwide Spanish Empire at the Peace of Paris in 1898. By the early twentieth century, the British cooperated with France in restricting Spanish possessions in North Africa, thereby intensifying popular hatred for the policies of Whitehall.[1]

Spanish popular dislike of France was possibly keener than that for Great Britain. Memories of the French invasion of 1808 yet lingered, and the brutal slaughter of Spaniards continued to color Madrid's view of Paris. Among the religious, French rationalism and anticlericalism were anathema, particularly after 1905, when France expelled Catholic religious orders. Furthermore, the republican structure of the French government seemed to be a threat to the monarchy of Spain. Finally, French attempts to expand into North Africa, an area that Spain had long thought to be her own domain, further exacerbated relations.[2]

For Spanish public opinion the Entente, therefore, represented hateful images of the past and stirred up fears for the future. Great Britain and France together and separately had stripped Spain of her power and influence, attacked her and threatened to strangle future colonial development. Despite this enmity, Spain had to recognize her unique geographical position and had to deal diplomatically and economically with England and France. When, however, the opportunity arose, Madrid balanced the influence of her powerful neighbors by cooperation with Germany.[3] The Germans, of course, encouraged these inroads into British and French control over western Europe.

Spanish domestic developments up to the eve of the war also created a situation that Germany could exploit. Since the Restoration of the monarchy in 1875, Spain had developed only the forms of parliamentary democracy, not the substance. By 1885, Conservatives and Liberals agreed to alternate control of the country. The architect of the system, Antonio Cánovas del Castillo, a conservative and admirer of Germany, convinced that Spain had not sufficiently developed its economy or class structure to avoid chaos in a true democratic system, manipulated elections to create support for a Liberal or Conservative ministry. Through the device of local chieftains or caciques who were dependent upon the central government for financial support, Cánovas and his Liberal Party counterpart, Mateo Práxedes Sagasta, dictated election results in advance.[4] Spain was also a constitutional monarchy, and the ministers of the government governed in cooperation with the King. The system worked well under Habsburg Queen and Regent María Cristina, who scrupulously observed all constitutional requirements. Domestic troubles were, therefore, at a minimum in the late nineteenth century.

In foreign affairs from 1880 through 1891, Spain followed a pro-German policy. The Restoration monarch Alfonso XII on a visit to Berlin in October 1883 offered Spanish support for Germany should a Franco-German war occur. Kaiser William I told the Spanish King, however, that the latter was a bit young and brash and that he ought to think over his offer. The Emperor told the Spanish monarch that Germany would be quite satisfied with benevolent neutrality.[5] In later years, nevertheless, Spain went further; in May 1887 Spain, under the leadership of a pro-German foreign minister, Vega de Armijo, entered the Triple Alliance indirectly through an agreement with Italy. In the event of a Franco-German conflict, Spain promised to assist the Central Powers by placing five thousand men on the Pyrenees border with France, thereby immobilizing three corps of the French army.[6] In return for her service, Spain was to receive assistance in North Africa, particularly coaling stations for commerce with her far eastern possessions.[7] But the Italians never supplied the required stations, and when the proposal came up for renewal in 1891, the Spanish turned it down.[8] In the meantime, Alfonso XII died, and Spain became friendlier with France when Paris demonstrated support and sympathy for Madrid during the Spanish-American War of 1898.

Meanwhile, in domestic affairs from 1885 through 1902, Cánovas and Sagasta were successful in keeping disturbances to a minimum, but the system of alternating Liberal with Conservative governments began to fragment when María Cristina's son, Alfonso XIII, came of age in 1902.[9] It was this fragmentation that eventually created a political vacuum from which emerged government by personalities. Certain of the personalities involved were susceptible to German influence, thereby aiding Germany in preventing Spain from joining the Entente during the war.

The personality of Alfonso XIII and his determination to rule Spain independently of party leaders partly accounted for Spanish domestic instability from 1902 through 1918. From his early childhood the monarch revealed his love for things military. He regularly played with eight boys dressed in uniforms, and he and his playmates conducted mock battles and drills. In later life Alfonso preferred military uniforms for his daily attire.[10] In a council meeting held just after his installation ceremony, the young King demanded the reopening of military colleges recently closed for economic reasons.[11] Infatuation with the military and supreme self-confidence were the major characteristics of Alfonso XIII, and in the process of asserting his own authority, the King uncovered for all to see the insubstantial nature of the Spanish political structure which was parliamentary in name only.

More effective leadership from the King would have eased Spain into the twentieth century without the extensive domestic turmoil that arose from incipient industrialization. The monarch apparently had no specific ideology other than the preservation of his crown through an alliance with the army. Contemporaries described him as gay and quite convivial but devoid of serious political thought.[12] This unflattering portrait is modified, however, by the German documents. As a diplomat, Alfonso was fully aware of the dangers to Spain were she to be drawn into the European conflict. The Spanish monarch's determination to play a major role in the diplomatic sphere is revealed in an entry in his diary dated immediately after his installation as King:

> I can be a King who will be filled with the glory of having regenerated his country, whose name will pass on in history as an imperishable memento of his reign, but likewise I can be a King who does not govern but is governed by his ministers. . . . I hope to rule Spain as a just King. I hope at the same time to revive my country and make her, if not powerful, at least sought for as an ally.[13]

The desires to rule Spain personally and to make the Spanish voice heard in the international constellation of powers remained the young monarch's goals throughout the war.

Both domestic and foreign observers commented upon the extraordinary interest Alfonso exhibited in foreign affairs. The Prime Minister for the greatest length of time during the war, Liberal leader Alvaro de Figueroa, the Count of Romanones, emphasized the breadth and depth of knowledge about foreign affairs possessed by Alfonso.[14] Albert Pingaud, a French historian who had access to the French Foreign Ministry Archives, constantly referred to Alfonso as the preponderant Spanish voice in foreign affairs from 1902 through the war.[15] Clearly, in Spanish relations with other countries, King Alfonso XIII determined the major lines of Madrid's policies.

Meanwhile, in domestic affairs, Cánovas died at the hands of an assassin in 1897, and Sagasta succumbed to natural causes in 1903. Succeeding ministries attempted to introduce genuine parliamentary democracy but failed to go far enough to suit all segments of Spanish political opinion. Particularly, Antonio Maura, a leader of the Conservative Party, sought to purify the corrupt practices of the Cánovas system, but the Liberal opposition regarded his reforms with deep distrust. The awakening industrial masses joined with certain segments of the Liberal Party to oppose Maura. Neither Cánovas nor Maura took significant notice of the emergence of the class of industrial workers in Spain's cities. The result of such neglect was violence. In July 1909 Maura's policies provoked a general uprising in Barcelona during the "tragic week." Antonio Maura resigned his post and the King appointed a member of the Liberal Party as the Prime Minister. Subsequently, a rift developed between the King and the kind of leadership that Maura offered. After 1909 there was no clear leader for the Conservative Party. Maura thereafter rejected participation in the political system.[16]

During the war, Maura appeared ambivalent toward the Germans. He seemed pro-German and then would waver and speak out in a pro-Entente sense. After new elections and severe domestic disturbances, he reentered the political field in March 1918, when he accepted the post of Prime Minister again in a national government. Maura became, then, a major political personality for Germany to support, despite his occassional ambiguity in international affairs. His conservative outlook seemed to be in accord with German monarchial conservatism, but while there was some superficial similarity between his philosophy and that of the German Foreign Office, Maura merely wanted to keep Spain out of the war; he had no desire to advance any of the goals of the Wilhelmstrasse, a lesson that Berlin learned in the summer and fall of 1918, when Maura vigorously challenged German attacks upon Spanish shipping.[17]

Another personality within the Conservative Party camp became important to the Germans. Due to Maura's intransigence from 1909 through 1918, leadership of the conservatives fell to Eduardo Dato, a capable and effective politician. Dato was the Prime Minister when the war began, and he insisted upon neutrality. He also successfully faced the criticisms of the liberals, many of whom proclaimed that Spain could never escape the grasp of the Entente and that she had to declare herself for the Western Powers. Dato ably resisted these critics, even though he personally favored the Triple Entente.[18] The Wilhelmstrasse, therefore, encouraged Dato's support for neutrality, but the Germans were aware of the Prime Minister's personal tendency toward the British and French, subsequently, Berlin regarded Dato with suspicion.

The divisions among the liberals became much more significant for the Germans; this group especially held political power longer than any other during the war. The most significant liberal leader was Alvaro de Figueroa, the Count of Romanones. He was a declared Francophile and enemy of Germany. As early as August 1914 he published an article in his newspaper Diario Universal proclaiming that Spain had to eschew neutrality and join the Entente which, he believed, would win the war. The greatest number among the liberals followed Romanones, but there were three other segments of liberal opinion.

The right wing faction of liberalism, headed by Manuel García Prieto, advocated strict neutrality in much the same vein as Eduardo Dato. A dissident within Romanones's group was Miguel Villanueva; he believed that a closer relationship with Germany might successfully counteract French activities in North Africa. The Germans supported both Villanueva and García Prieto with some enthusiasm. The left wing of the liberals, led by the Reformist Republican, Melquiades Alvarez, steered a middle course. He and his entourage pointed out the need to avoid Spanish involvement in the war, but if Madrid were forced into the conflict, the Allied side would be preferable for Spain.[19] Among the liberals, only García Prieto and Villanueva could be of any use to Berlin.

Those domestic forces that Germany regarded as their unmitigated enemies, other than Romanones, were the leftists grouped around Alexander Lerroux and the peripheral Left Republicans and Socialists. The extreme left, represented by Lerroux, an Andalusian from the province of Cordova and successor to Manuel Ruiz Zorilla as leader of the Radical Party, appealed to the lower middle classes and to the urban proletariat and advocated immediate entrance into the war in 1914 on the Entente side. The Left Republicans, led by Rodrigo Soriano, supported a policy of benevolent neutrality in favor of the Entente. The Socialists, led by Pablo Iglesias, were pacifistic and antimilitaristic, but they sympathized with the West.[20]

Yet another Spanish political force that Germany actively encouraged was the extreme right, the Carlists, who constantly advocated intervention on the German side. This group, originating in 1834, stemmed from those who, partly due to the Salic law prohibiting female succession to the throne and partly due to opposition to the supporters of the proposed Spanish Queen Isabel II, advocated the brother of Ferdinand VII, Carlos, as the Spanish monarch.[21] A series of three unsuccessful Carlist wars ensued in the nineteenth century, the supporters of the descendents of Carlos reflecting clerical and extreme conservative views. By the time of the First World War, the identity of the actual pretender was less important than the symbolism of keeping the party alive to reject all liberal advances that had transpired in Spain since 1834.

In fact, the Carlist pretender, Don Jaime, favored the Entente, fought for the French, and was captured by the Austrians. The Germans took care that Don Jaime was well treated.[22] But the Carlists supported Germany, and their domestic leader was Juan Vásquez de Mella. In his public pronouncements Vásquez de Mella was circumspect; he admired French culture and hated the British as the despoilers of Gibraltar. He argued, however, for the strictest possible neutrality, a course that could only benefit Germany, especially as the war drew to a close. He hoped Germany would aid in creating a strong Spanish army and navy to match French and British military power. But Vásquez de Mella was more of an orator than a statesman, and most of his activity was restricted to giving speeches in front of appreciative audiences composed of members of the German and Austro-Hungarian diplomatic corps.[23] The contradiction contained within Protestant German support for staunchly Catholic Carlists often amazed western journalists.[24] At least mutual support between the Carlists and Catholic Austria-Hungary was logical.

Clearly, as Spanish politics expanded beyond the relatively simple division between liberals and conservatives in a carefully controlled political environment, Germany had many more opportunities to influence Madrid's foreign policy. Berlin made use of the many possibilities of playing one group off against another; the German Ambassador astutely used his connections with pro-German elements to help bring down Prime Minister Romanones in April 1917. While Spanish politics provided fertile fields in which to cultivate a pro-German Spanish policy, Spanish foreign trade was almost totally within the grasp of the Entente.

Spain closely resembled a colony of the imperial British and French empires in the late nineteenth and early twentieth centuries. French and Belgian capital had built most of the Spanish railroad network; of approximately eleven thousand kilometers of broad gauge railroad tracks in 1914, about 85 percent was under French control.[25] Entente involvement in the iron ore industry was significant; the Belgians controlled mines in Asturias, the French were active at Peñarroya, and the English worked the Rio Tinto mines.[26] In 1913 Entente commerce amounted to one billion and four hundred million pesetas worth of goods, and the balance of trade was in Spain's favor. Germany, by contrast, did less than three hundred million pesetas worth of business with Spain, and most of the trade was in Germany's favor, not Spain's. Altogether, Entente investments in Spain amounted to about four billion pesetas worth and German ones were only about two hundred millions.[27] Obviously, Spain's economy and foreign trade were intimately involved with the

Western Powers.

Berlin, however, was not at a loss to influence the Spanish. German universities had a fairly powerful hold upon the minds of the educated elite. A large German colony composed of businessmen, sailors interned on board their ships when the war began, and refugees from Germany's African possessions helped to extend the influence of the Reich. Personal contact with large numbers of Germans almost neutralized the enormous economic lever of the Entente.

Part of the German influence upon the educated elite may be traced to the work of an obscure philosopher, Karl Christian Krause. Writing in the early nineteenth century, Krause eventually inspired Spaniards who came to study in German universities. Julián Sánz del Rio, visiting Germany in 1843, came into contact with Krause's ideas. The German philosopher argued for ideas that would create a stable, middle-class society. He called for "an intellectualized version of the Protestant ethic of self-improvement, a mystical belief in a God-given natural harmony, and connecting right thinking with good living."[28] These ideas appealed to Spaniards who were impressed by Germany's orderly society which was in such marked contrast with Spanish dissension, typified by civil war and political quarrels. Krausism spread among the educated through the efforts of forceful teachers such as Francisco Giner de los Rios.[29] Later, intellectuals such as José Ortega y Gasset, who had studied at Marburg, furthered Spanish admiration for things German, particularly the sanctity of thought in the great universities.[30] Other Spanish intellectuals expressed their admiration for German scientific achievements, respect for authority, and the intelligence of her people.[31] Not all intellectuals supported the Germans, however, as the eminent Miguel de Unamuno y Jugo was firmly in the Entente camp.

The German colony in Spain was particularly important in carrying out the goals of the Wilhelmstrasse. At the beginning of the war German businessmen and engineers were to be found in all of the urban centers.[32] Initially, the number of resident Germans was about 5,000, but with the influx of refugees from France, Portugal, and Germany's African possessions, the number swelled to about 10,000. A U.S. Embassy report of 1917 put the number of Germans at no more than 40,000 at that late date.[33] Spanish contemporaries suggested the maximum number was closer to 12,000.[34] Regardless of the total number of Germans in Spain, they were highly effective, so much so in fact that visitors described them as "affable individuals located in every town of any size."[35] Their ubiquitousness may be judged by the fact that Englishmen were often mistaken for Germans, and Spaniards would often come up and begin a conversation in German.[36]

Another factor that greatly influenced the Spaniards was the example of Germany's efficient and successful army. In the first few months of the war, Spanish military writers commented upon the rapid advance of the Germans toward the Marne. In later years German military success in Russia, in the Balkans, and in the defeat of Rumania evoked admiration and awe.[37] These spectacular German victories played a key role from 1914 through 1916 in keeping Spain neutral. In those years many leading Spaniards thought Germany would win the war.

Quite clearly there were several diverse factors that tended to keep Spain out of the First World War, particularly popular attitudes toward Great Britain and France, Spanish political divisions, and finally an extensive number of German residents. But King Alfonso XIII had exalted hopes for himself and for his country, and in the years between 1902 and 1914, he tried to get the Allies to recognize the value of an alliance between Spain and the Triple Entente. His efforts failed, however, and when the war began, the Germans could deal with a neutral Spain.

FOOTNOTES FOR CHAPTER I

[1]Charles Cunningham, "Spain and the War," American Political Science Review, XI (August 1917), p. 431.

[2]Ibid.

[3]Ibid.

[4]Raymond Carr, Spain, 1808-1939 (Oxford: Clarendon Press, 1966), p. 347 and ff. Also see Joan Connelly Ullman, The Tragic Week, A Study of Anti-Clericalism in Spain, 1875-1912 (Cambridge, Mass.: Harvard University Press, 1968), pp. 10-14.

[5]Antonio Ramos Oliviera, Politics, Economics and Men of Modern Spain, 1808-1946 (London: Victor Gollancz, Ltd., 1946), pp. 138-139.

[6]Chlodwig, Prinz zu Hohenlohe-Schillingsfuerst, Denkwuerdigkeiten des Fuersten Chlodwig zu Hohenlohe-Schillingsfuerst, 3 vols. (Stuttgart: Deutsche Verlagsanstalt, 1907), II, p. 344.

[7]Mousset, Histoire d'Espagne, p. 515. See also Reemt Reemtsen, Spanisch-deutsche Beziehungen zur Zeit des ersten Dreibundesvertrages 1882-1887 (Berlin: Verlag Emil Ebering, 1938), p. 98. Reemtsen had access to the Spanish Embassy records in Berlin, and in a letter quoted in its entirety in a footnote on page 124, this indirect alliance is described.

[8]Mousset, Histoire d'Espagne, p. 516. Mousset gives a far more detailed treatment of this relationship in his L'Espagne dans la Politique Mondiale, pp. 64-77.

[9]Mousset, Histoire d'Espagne, p. 516.

[10]Vicente Pilapil, Alfonso XIII (New York: Twayne Publishers, Inc., 1969), p. 33.

[11]Salvador de Madariaga, Spain, A Modern History (New York: Frederick A. Praeger, 1958), pp. 289-290.

[12]Pilapil, pp. 33-34.

[13]Alfonso XIII, Diario Intimo de Alfonso XIII (Madrid: Biblioteca nueva, 1960), p. 111 as quoted in Pilapil, pp. 34-35.

[14]Conde de Romanones, Alvaro Figueroa y Torres, Obras Completas, 3 vols. (Madrid: Editorial Plus-Ultra, 1949), III, p. 342.

[15]Albert Pingaud, Histoire Diplomatique de la France Pendant la Grande Guerre (Paris: Editions Alsatia, 1937), pp. 15-16. Pingaud is especially valuable as he had direct access to official French documents for Parisian diplomacy in the war. His work is a useful touchstone to corroborate or to modify Spanish memoirists, especially Romanones.

[16]Carr, Spain, pp. 485-487.

[17]Ibid., p. 488.

[18]Ibid.

[19]Cunningham, "Spain and the War," pp. 435-438.

[20]Oliviera, pp. 171-172 and Gelos, Neutralitaetspolitik Spaniens, p. 108.

[21]Carr, pp. 150-152.

[22]Ratibor to Foreign Office, May 7, 1915, Deutschland 127. Die Spanische Mission in Berlin, T149/79/31. This citation refers to the microfilmed German documents. The list for the citation will always be the correspondents, the date, the name of the folder that the correspondence was located in the German documents, and finally the filming series, in this case T149, the roll no., 79 here, and the number of the film frame, 31 in this instance.

[23]Cunningham, p. 438.

[24]Sanford Griffith, "The German Myth in Spain," Outlook, CXVI (July 4, 1917), pp. 364-365.

[25]Rondo Cameron, France and the Economic Development of Europe, 1800-1914 (Princeton, N. J.: Princeton University Press, 1961), p. 275.

[26]Gelos, Neutralitaetspolitik Spaniens, p. 160, fn. 9. Also see United States, Department of Foreign and Domestic Commerce, Spanish Finance and Trade. Arthur N. Young, Special Agent Series No. 202 (Washington, D.C.: U.S. Government Printing Office, 1920), pp. 138-139.

[27]Cunningham, pp. 439-440 and U.S. Department of Foreign and Domestic Commerce, Spanish Finance and Trade, p. 79.

[28]Carr, pp. 301-302.

[29]Robert W. Kern, Liberals, Reformers and Caciques in

Restoration Spain, 1875-1909 (Albuquerque, N.M.: The University of New Mexico Press, 1974), p. 20.

[30]Madariaga, pp. 100-101.

[31]Cunningham, pp. 425-426.

[32]Ibid., p. 424. In addition see Dr. Boelitz, "Das Deutschtum in Spanien," *Zeitschrift fuer Auslandskunde: Organ des Verbandes Deutschland-Spanien*, I (1919), p. 6.

[33]H. E. Yarnell to Force Commander, Record Group 45, WE-7: Spain, December 31, 1917 (National Archives, Washington, D.C.).

[34]Luis Bello, *España durante la Guerra*, pp. 107-108.

[35]Cunningham, p. 424.

[36]Henry Wickham-Steed, *Through Thirty Years, 1892-1922* (New York: Doubleday and Company, 1925), pp. 116-117.

[37]Cunningham, p. 427.

CHAPTER II

SPAIN AND INTERNATIONAL POLITICS 1902-1914

German-Spanish diplomatic relations during the war had their origins in the policies of young King Alfonso XIII from 1902, when he reached his majority, up to 1914. The core of those policies stemmed from advice received from his mother, María Cristina, a member of the Austrian Habsburg family and Regent who constantly reiterated the need for Spain to stay within the French diplomatic orbit.[1] The great republic to the north, paradoxically enough, would provide stability for the Spanish monarchy in foreign affairs.

The reasons for the Queen Regent's policies were hardly obscure. She probably harbored deep resentment toward Berlin and the Prussians for the destruction of much of Austria's power in 1866 during the Austro-Prussian War.[2] Her brother had fought for the Austrians in that conflict. Also in 1898 France had stood by Spain in the war with the United States.[3] Consequently, in the 1902 constellation of European powers, France, a fellow Latin and ostensibly Catholic nation, provided the best potential ally. Alfonso, therefore, followed a policy that reflected his mother's injunctions.

From 1902 through 1914 Spain sought to ally herself

with the Western Powers. But Alfonso had a relatively high price; he demanded a free hand in Portugal and greater freedom in North Africa, virtually the only part of the ancient Spanish empire left after defeat in the Spanish-American War of 1898. The Western Powers, France and Great Britain, remained close to Spain, but on the eve of the war, the King's scheme to attach himself formally to France failed. Germany was aware of Spain's desires and followed carefully the course of the negotiations for a Franco-Spanish Alliance. The state of internal politics and economic developments, and finally, the failure of a formal alliance with France decided Spain for neutrality, much to Germany's relief.

Alfonso shared his mother's dislike of overbearing Prussian attitudes, and his meetings with Kaiser William II of Germany confirmed the Spanish King's prejudices. The German Emperor, however, actively courted Alfonso's friendship beginning in 1903. The Kaiser bestowed upon Alfonso an honorary rank in the German army.[4] Soon thereafter William II visited Spain accompanied by eight German cruisers.[5] Alfonso later told the French Military Attaché what had happened during this first meeting between the two monarchs. The eighteen year old Spanish King had been told to wear simple clothes and to greet William in a stiff, military manner. He also had been told to use the second person intimate pronoun in French in addressing the German monarch. But when Alfonso met William and began to talk, the young boy burst out laughing, occasioning a lecture from William. The

German Emperor told Alfonso that he should have worn more formal clothing and that he should not forget his manners in front of the German Emperor. William also severely upbraided the Spanish King for using the second person intimate pronoun.[6] Alfonso, thereafter, had no special regard for the Germans, but his mother's Austrian heritage did incline him sympathetically toward the Austro-Hungarian Empire. Later, the Kaiser tendered the young Spanish King extensive advice about international relations, and the lectures were not well received.[7]

The Kaiser further upset Alfonso only a year later. When Alfonso visited Berlin in 1904, the German Emperor treated him with slight deference at a state function, speaking German rather than French.[8] The Germans furthermore were convinced that the eligible Spanish bachelor needed a German princess as his bride. Alfonso tactfully refused the proffered hand of Princess Marie Antoinette of Mecklenburg-Schwerin. He evidently thought that Spain's best interests could not be served by an indirect alliance as such a marriage would imply. Besides, he had already lost his heart to an English royal lady, Princess Victoria Eugenie, Edward VII's niece and former French Empress Eugenie's godchild.[9]

German observers thought King Alfonso wanted an alliance with the English, hence his marriage to Victoria Eugenie.[10] But a recent study of Alfonso's foreign policy prior to the war indicates it was a love match.[11] Yet the English had actively courted the Spanish monarch, having sent King Edward VII's brother, the Duke of Connaught, to Alfonso's assumption of power in 1902.[12] So his mother's anti-Prussian bias and his future wife's obvious English and French sympathies helped to mold Alfonso's policies.

Through 1905 and 1906, Alfonso moved closer to the Entente Powers. He was well received in France on a state visit in May 1905, and a year later his leanings toward England were sealed by his marriage.[13] While the British had apparently thwarted an attempt by Spain in 1902 to assure her possessions in North Africa in a special agreement with France, the Dual Alliance of 1904 created a new set of conditions whereby England ostensibly encouraged a rapprochement between France and Spain. The new Entente divided up colonial claims; Britain gave up hers in Morocco to France as France gave up her claims in Egypt to Great Britain. France now had a free hand in North Africa, and Spanish interests had to be subordinate to those of France.[14] Perhaps the Spanish connection with the English royal house would modify Entente aims in North Africa.

Thereafter, however, the Franco-Spanish agreement of 1905 was not favorable to Spain. Spanish rights were greatly reduced and she could not act even in her own sphere without French consent.[15] Once France and Great Britain cooperated, Spain lost much of her previous power of maneuverability. Alfonso seemed to accept this course perhaps reflecting his family's preferences, thus setting forth his pro-French, pro-Entente view that he was to pursue for the most part completely through the First World War.[16]

The Germans tried to split the alliance of the Western Powers by precipitating the Moroccan Crisis of 1905-1906. The Germans wanted to resurrect colonial animosities between France and England by objecting to French economic penetration of Morocco. They also indicated their interest in helping Spain get Tangier, a North African city guarding the western approaches to Gibraltar. But the alliance held firm, and in a conference France and Britain pressured Spain to accede to their interests, particularly French railroad construction in Spain. Spain thereafter signed an accord with France broadening French economic interests in the Iberian peninsula.[17]

The overwhelming economic and military influence of France and Great Britain was in evidence again from 1907 through 1912. First the Western Powers drew Spain into their orbit by the Cartagena Agreements of April 1907, which seemed to meet Spain's needs and almost meant an alliance with the Entente. All agreed to maintain the status quo in the Mediterranean and along the coastline around Spain and Africa. In addition, each agreed to communicate with one another in the event any circumstance arose that might tend to alter the existing territorial situation in any of the aforementioned areas.[18] Great Britain sought further to augment the Spanish military through shipbuilding projects of the Vickers-Armstrong firm. Spain was thus useful to Great Britain in preventing total French dominance of the western Mediterranean.

Alfonso XIII, however, did not regard the Cartagena Agreements as a genuine alliance. He sought equal power status with Great Britain and France, and he yet yearned for total control over the Iberian peninsula and North Africa. The Western Powers, especially Great Britain, however, shied away from any specific guarantees they undoubtedly knew would flow from a direct alliance. Consequently, Alfonso was denied his heartfelt wish of reestablishing the great power position of Spain.

Germany sought again in 1911 to demonstrate her prowess at Agadir and to shake off the Entente hold upon North Africa and Spain. Due to local disturbances in Moroccan areas held by neither France nor Spain, France sent in troops and thereby enlarged her sphere of influence. Both Spain and Germany objected, the latter sending a warship, the Panther, to the port of Agadir to protect Teutonic interests. As a result of the settlement of the crisis, Spain received compensation for territorial transfers made at her expense; in the Franco-Spanish treaty of November 1912, Spain received 18,000 square miles of Moroccan territory and France received 460,000.[19] The Germans got territories in the French Congo, though the British-French Entente held, and Spain remained a pawn in English foreign policy, acting as a barrier to total French control of the western Mediterranean.

Alfonso tried to play France against England in 1913, though unsuccessfully. The French Ambassador in Madrid reported in March 1913 of Spanish hints at the possibility of a future alliance.[20] The French Military Attaché in Madrid also reported that Alfonso spoke highly of a special agreement with France.[21] Even earlier Alfonso had communicated to the Russians his desire for their aid in an alliance.[22] But as negotiations between the French and Spanish proceeded, the high price, always apparent, became precise. Alfonso offered to guarantee the Pyrenees frontier and to provide troops in North Africa and in Europe in return for a free hand in Portugal.[23] Portugal had been a republic since 1910, and Alfonso feared for the monarchial principle with such a nearby republican neighbor, especially so as the Portuguese King and Crown Prince had been assassinated. In 1910, Spain had asked the views of France and Great Britain on Spanish intervention in Portugal. France was noncommittal, but Great Britain rejected the project because Portugal traditionally had been their protectorate since 1702.[24] Alfonso's first attempt to expand Spanish power therefore failed.

In the spring of 1913, Alfonso tried another tactic on a visit to Paris, offering his services to France in case of a conflict between the two power blocs. In reply in October 1913 on a visit to Madrid, French President Raymond Poincaré discussed the possibility of Spain's becoming a part of the Entente. Prime Minister Romanones mentioned in his memoirs the meetings with Poincaré in 1913, and evidently the Spanish Prime Minister disliked the idea of a formal association with France at that time as his government was shaky. But the King apparently desired a formal alliance.[25]

The negotiations failed because Spanish domestic politics intervened; Romanones's government fell in late October 1913 and the new government of Eduardo Dato opposed closer relations with France. A formal treaty was thus stillborn. All that was accomplished in 1913 was a reassertion of the 1907 Cartagena Agreements.[26]

Once the war began in August 1914 the extent to which Alfonso personally intended to remain at least within the good graces of the Entente was revealed by his comments to Frenchmen. He promised to do all he could to render France service. The King even allegedly told the Spanish Ambassador in Paris, "Only I and the canaille are for France."[27] The Spanish Ambassador further related that the feeling in Madrid was especially pro-German, though in the King's own household the picture was not too clear. The Queen Mother, María Cristina, was reportedly unhappy as she hated the Germans, but she supported the Habsburgs.[28] Indeed, Alfonso even told the French Ambassador in Madrid, "I am not able to serve under your flag, but at least one of my relatives will serve under it."[29] In an interview given an English correspondent in 1924 Alfonso implied that he had told the French that they should rest assured about their common border with Spain along the Pyrenees.[30] The King related to the American Ambassador in Madrid, Joseph Willard, that his personal inclination was to take part in the struggle but that his duty to Spain was paramount and that neutrality must be strictly enforced.[31]

Alfonso, however, began to trim his sails as the war progressed and as it became evident Germany might take Paris and thus place German power on the Pyrenees. Count Romanones noted this change in the King's attitude as the invasion through Belgium swept on into northern France.[32] Alfonso, however, promised France benevolent neutrality.[33]

Indeed, the British Ambassador in Madrid, Sir Arthur Hardinge, commented upon the King's sentiments. The picture drawn is one of a man greatly distressed by the snub he received from Kaiser William II and a person practically and personally oriented toward the Allies.[34] This portrait, while in the main accurate, did not reflect the totality of influences operating upon the King. Particularly, the Germans knew they could rely upon the political results of their military victories.

Through their first-hand view of Alfonso and through the activities of their Ambassador, the Germans were able to keep Spain neutral, especially while the Central Powers were winning battles. Once Alfonso sensed that the balance had shifted, he abandoned his ambivalent policy and openly supported the Allies. To be sure, the west really had no need to involve Spain in the war as they could manipulate her without her being an official ally. To the Germans the chief task was to prevent Spain from becoming a total captive of the Entente. If strict neutrality could not be wrung from the Spanish, then neutrality in more limited form was their goal. Germany could always dangle Portugal and Gibraltar in front of Alfonso, in hope of getting him on its side. Spain also offered an excellent sounding board for Latin American opinion and a location from which to send spies, saboteurs, and propaganda to the U.S.A. and to various South and Central American nations.[35]

Several avenues were open to the Germans to influence the King, and the most obvious was the diplomatic community headed by Ambassador Prince Maximillian von Ratibor. The Ambassador had carefully followed Spain's negotiations with France, thinking Alfonso was bravely struggling against the nefarious designs of the Liberal Party's Count Romanones. To Ratibor the Prime Minister seemed actively to pursue a pro-French commercial policy and to encourage press opinion to advocate an association with France and England.[36] The Germans were privy to the suggestions of a Spanish-French rapprochement in 1913, but Ratibor's informants accurately pointed out that Spain had gotten no firm offer, at least not in the sense Alfonso desired; consequently, Spain was not allied with France directly. The Ambassador was comforted by the position of the Spanish military as represented by their paper, <u>Correspondencia Militar</u>, which opposed an alliance with France.[37]

In June 1914, the German Military Attaché, Major Arnold Kalle, spoke with the Spanish Military Attaché, Luiz Ruiz de Valdivia, in Berlin. The Spanish Attaché explained Alfonso's diplomatic moves the previous year as a recognition of the reality of the Spanish economic situation. Spain was too close economically and physically to France and to Great Britain to risk offending them. Yet if Germany won a future war, France would be defeated and England chastised, and Spain could succeed in her goals in North Africa.[38] Everyone knew that Valdivia was pro-German and that Alfonso was probably soothing the Germans in light of his recent pro-French moves. Kalle nevertheless placed some value on Valdivia's intimation that Spain would not come into a future war on the Entente side.[39]

Ratibor added his observations to those of Kalle. The German Ambassador reported that Spain apparently saw nothing to gain from Germany and a great deal both to gain and to lose from the Entente powers. The Germans realized that Spain had to appear friendly toward France and Great Britain for geographical and economic reasons. Ratibor lived in a world of make-believe, and he saw the French-Spanish conversations primarily the work of Count Romanones, not solely the policy of Alfonso.[40] This was a line that Ratibor would follow throughout the war; indeed, the Germans never wanted to believe that Alfonso could ever be in opposition to a fellow monarchial state. The Germans, and Ratibor in particular, remained convinced that Alfonso was the dupe of the camarilla around him, and with German aid, the King would come to his senses. They were quite wrong; Alfonso directed his own foreign policy within the constraints of his domestic situation and of the geographical location of Spain.

Despite the King's personal inclination toward France and the Entente, he and his ministers declared for neutrality once hostilities began.[41] The King presided over a cabinet meeting held August 5, 1914, in Madrid, saying on that occasion that Spain could "travel on no other road than that of benevolent neutrality."[42] Clearly the monarch wished to continue friendship with France and England, but to do so under the protective umbrella of neutrality.

The outlines of several directions that Spain would take with the belligerents were present in embryo form during the next month.[43] First, there were demonstrations by several groups opposed to one side or the other in the great conflict, thus presaging the split within Spanish public opinion.[44] The Church, military and aristocracy sided with the Central Powers, while Liberals, Socialists, and intellectuals advocated union with the Entente.[45] Second, Spain sought to assure her financial position during the war, suggesting to the United States that special economic agreements were needed to assure Spanish industry of sufficient shipping and cotton.[46] The third point was Spain's desire to collaborate with the U.S. and to act as the peacemaker.

From the very beginning, Alfonso intimated to the United States he expected the Entente to win the war.[47] Liberal opinion was similar; Count Romanones, a leading liberal, expressed his views in a newspaper article that appeared in his organ, _El Diario Universal_, on August 19, 1914. He said neutrality was a suicidal policy, one that would kill

Spain. Thus, he urged Spain to practice a pro-Entente policy continuing the prewar direction.[48] Romanones related in his memoirs that his own editor refused responsibility for the article. But the Liberal leader felt Spain had to declare itself on the Entente side or at least to work for a benevolent neutrality for the Western Powers. The day after the publication of the article, Romanones was told by telegram to come to the royal palace for an interview with King Alfonso XIII. The King asked the motives for the article and, according to Romanones, the monarch said he too was inclined toward the Allies.[49] But the stir the article caused was not restricted to the King; newspaper editors immediately took up the issues raised, and <u>El Imparcial</u>, a leading Madrid organ, emphasized the lack of military preparedness for Spain's entry into the conflict. Spain was not diplomatically isolated as Romanones had implied in his article, but the "reality of the nation" required neutrality.[50] Indeed, in an article by González Hontoria, politician and commentator, the Cartagena Agreements of 1907 and their reaffirmation in 1913 specifically required written notice of change of conditions for the Mediterranean Sea.[51] No such written communications had ever been received, therefore, Spain had no obligation to enter the war.

The press conflict pitted the <u>francófilos</u> against the <u>germanófilos</u>. Sympathy divided among those for strict neutrality, those supporting the Germans, and finally those arguing for intervention on the Allied side.[52] Those who supported

Germany emphasized her disciplined army and society.[53] The socialists emphasized the possibility of economic distress for the workers were Spain to enter the war. Consequently, Pablo Iglesias, Socialist leader, commented to El Imparcial on September 13, 1914, that Spain had to remain neutral. Prime Minister Eduardo Dato suggested a major role might be in the offing for Spain in arranging the peace conference.[54] This hope was to provide one of the major justifications to maintain Spanish neutrality as the war progressed. In order to attain credibility in this role, Spain assumed the diplomatic interests of the belligerents.

The newspaper debate over the propriety of Spanish neutrality continued throughout September and October 1914, but the Cortes, the legislative assembly of Spain, finally confirmed the decision already made by the Prime Minister and the King. On October 19, 1914, Dato repeated that cordial relations would be maintained with both sides and that strict neutrality would be observed. He felt he had to make a clear statement on the issue as Spanish press opinion was lining up on one side or the other.[55] In a ministerial council meeting of October 23, 1914, the King repeated his desire for neutrality.[56] On November 6, 1914, the Cortes, both the Chamber of Deputies and the Senate, approved the position, making official the policy Spain had followed since the end of July.[57] Opinion was still divided in the Cortes, however, as the Left Republicans, led by Alexander Lerroux argued for intervention, yet the debate was conducted without rancor.[58]

Perhaps, as a contemporary pointed out, the possibility of remaining neutral was an open question in August, but after the Battle of the Marne in September the outcome of the war was not clear; therefore, the Cortes confirmed neutrality as the official policy of Spain.[59] Had the results of the war been clear earlier, then Spain could have declared for the appropriate side, thereby gaining support from that side. Indeed, this was Spain's problem, she had constantly to conduct a guessing game to determine which side was going to win so that she would not be left out of any future peace settlement.

Domestic considerations also dictated a declaration of neutrality. The dawn of urbanization and industrialization had created a proletariat that was anarchist or syndicalist hardly caring for the bourgeois war. Republicans were not willing to spill blood on foreign soil when their ideals did not prevail in Spain. Regionalists could not or would not take up arms in any venture for a united Spain. Carlists rejected the political and social ideals of the British and French, admiring instead the Germans and their monarchist principles protecting a narrow segment of society.[60] Therefore, Spain could not openly enter the conflict, but she could exploit the wartime situation to her own advantage.

A clear pattern in Alfonso's policies had thus emerged as early as 1913 and continued throughout the war. The Spanish King, mindful of his domestic situation and geographical location, tried to bargain between France and Great Britain over the North African city of Tangier, even tempting France with special guarantees. This technique of playing each side against the other was used again and again by the Spanish monarch during the conflict. For each pro-German position that Alfonso seemed to take, he extracted concessions; equally for each pro-Allied step he took, he at least sought concessions. But, German threats to sink Spanish vessels and Entente threats to deny Spain needed cotton and coal put the Spanish King between two difficult choices. The evolution of German policy toward Spain revealed the virtuosity of Alfonso in meeting these wartime challenges to his nation's existence and livelihood.

In the course of the war, German contacts and thereby influence with Spain and information about the country came from a variety of sources. Of primary importance, of course, was the German Ambassador, Prince Maximillian von Ratibor and Corvey, who had been at Madrid since 1910. His attitude was one of imperiousness toward Spain and of personal vindictiveness toward liberal politicians such as Count Romanones. The Ambassador apparently was somewhat lazy, arising only at noon, and he suffered from arthritis.[61] His sloth worsened when the Ambassador began to feel that Spanish politics were directed at him personally. When relations between the two countries reached crisis proportions, the Secretary of the Embassy, Count Bassewitz, acted as the German emissary. The Ambassador cultivated close relations with a variety of

Spanish politicians, but his preferences were well known.

Another rather candid assessment of Prince Ratibor appeared in the memoirs of the German minister to Portugal, Friedrich Rosen. He related that Ratibor did not enjoy an especially close relationship with the King or with other members of the government. The King, according to Rosen, deliberately tried to avoid Ratibor, and most communications were through Military Attaché Arnold Kalle. Ratibor, according to Rosen, apparently suffered from asthma, leaving Embassy affairs in the hands of Count Bassewitz.[62] Consequently, the Ambassador did not always provide highly reliable information to the Foreign Office; indeed, at certain junctures, the Secretary of State often consulted other, cooler heads.

Among the somewhat more reliable guides to Spanish activities were the Military Attaché in Madrid, Major Arnold Kalle, and the Spanish minister in Brussels, the Marquis of Villalobar. The Attaché seemed hardly to consult with the Ambassador, and the reason was not hard to find. Kalle was quite accurate in his assessments, and he had direct access to King Alfonso. Kalle conducted his own diplomacy virtually independently of the Foreign Office. Consequently, the State Secretary and the Ambassador had to deal with constant interference from the military in relations with Spain. The Spanish Minister Villalobar was a close personal friend of the representative at Brussels, Baron von der Lancken.[63] When the Germans sought to get a more direct view of Spanish affairs, Villalobar often provided it. Thus, these two sources provided confirmation or rejection of Ratibor's comments. On more than one occasion, Ratibor's reports needed correction.

Yet other private conduits served to give the Foreign Office a more accurate picture of Spanish affairs. Primary among these were the reports of the Kocherthaler brothers. One was Julio Kocherthaler, who lived at Madrid and who traveled throughout Spain. He wrote regularly to his brother, Hugo, who lived in Brussels. These letters were usually lengthy analyses of Spanish conditions, replete with references to personal contacts who provided more in depth information about current problems. On occasion, Hugo Kocherthaler would travel to Berlin for conferences with the State Secretary.

Another individual also provided valuable if somewhat emotionally tinged information. This was a Barcelona businessman, August Hofer, who galvanized the resident German business community to support the Reich during the war. Though Hofer often turned out somewhat unreliable, he initially organized an extensive German news network in the first days of the war. Other businessmen followed his lead, especially the German General Electric Company or AEG (the _Allgemeine Elektrizitaets Gesellschaft_). Lastly, a great business combine, the Madrid based German Overseas Company, sent detailed economic and political analyses monthly to Berlin. From these usually sane reports, the Foreign Office normally could discern the path of Spanish policy.[64]

Other sources of some value were those of the royal houses. The Spanish King's cousin, Don Alfonso Marie of Bourbon, was pro-German and served often as a conveyor of the King's desires. He was the son of Infanta Eulalia, one of Alfonso XIII's two aunts. She was well known as an eccentric, having published a book in France advocating women's rights. She was eventually forgiven by the King for her literary indiscretion, but her son Alfonso Marie and his wife, a Braganza princess believed by the Germans to be steeped in duplicity, were strong supporters of Germany.[65] Indeed, these latter two traveled extensively in Europe, spending considerable time in Switzerland where they contacted the Germans and often relayed King Alfonso's suggestions for peace or for other foreign policy adventures. On occasion the words of Alfonso Marie and his wife were strictly their own ideas.[66]

Perhaps the most valuable royal connection was the brotherly feeling that Kaiser William II had for Alfonso XIII. This was especially useful for the Spanish as the German monarch often acted in favor of Alfonso. It was this relationship that often kept German-Spanish diplomacy on a friendly basis. The Germans adhered tenaciously throughout the war to the idea that Alfonso was personally on their side, and the Kaiser never failed to mention the monarchial solidarity that existed between himself and the Spanish sovereign. The reiteration of this feeling was ironic in view of the fact that Alfonso XIII disliked William II.

In Berlin, the Spanish Ambassador, Luis Polo de Bernabé, and his Military Attaché were pro-German. These two demonstrated that they were not really the representatives of Spain, but rather were the personal representatives of the German State Secretary. Polo toned down many despatches from Madrid and provided the Foreign Office with invaluable hints of future Spanish courses of action. The Military Attaché, Major Valdivia, seemed constantly in attendance at German military headquarters. The Attaché and the German military cooperated to the fullest extent, with the Attaché eventually conveying highly favorable reports of the German military situation to Spain and to Alfonso even in the waning days of the war.

Members of the diplomatic community from France and Great Britain as well as the neutral power of the United States had far better relations with individual members of the various ministries and with the King. French Ambassador Geoffray had been posted at Madrid since 1912, and in the judgment of a contemporary French journalist and member of the French Embassy in Madrid, Albert Mousset, the Ambassador well understood the Spanish temper, discharging his duties with tact and success in spite of Prince Ratibor's turbulence. Joseph Thierry replaced Geoffray and succeeded in negotiating the economic agreement of 1918; he died just before the end of the war.[67]

The British representative was Sir Arthur Hardinge who also had been in Madrid since 1912. In his memoirs he recounted the arrogance of Ratibor and his own ease in speaking with the Queen who was, of course, herself English.[68] Joseph Willard, the American Ambassador, related most easily with members of the five Spanish ministries from 1914 through 1918; and he enjoyed a reputation for careful and straightforeward dealing with members of the government.[69] The King spoke with Willard on occasion, but seemed to prefer the Military Attaché to the civilian Ambassador. This was true for the French as well; Alfonso unburdened himself most easily to someone in uniform.

Other significant diplomats were the Austro-Hungarian and Russian Ambassadors. Prince Fuerstenburg represented the Habsburg monarchy, and he usually found himself with few communications from the Germans and with little to guide him from Vienna. Occasionally he was able to influence Spain through the Queen Mother, herself a Habsburg, but Alfonso's relations with the Germans usually ended up being more important. The Russian emissary, Budberg, was more often an intermediary between Alfonso and the other Entente powers, but with the confused situation in Russia after the Bolshevik Revolution, Alfonso became concerned for the family of the deposed Tsar. Otherwise, the Russians and Austrians were on the sidelines of Spanish relations with Germany throughout the war.

Generally speaking, Alfonso spoke most freely and most often with the Military Attaché of the Embassies posted at Madrid. His Prime Ministers communicated with the accredited Ambassadors. Occasionally, the Queen communicated with the British Ambassador, and the Queen Mother, María Cristina, dealt with the Austro-Hungarian Ambassador. Thus, in following Spanish policy, one must trace through several paths, but the most significant one was that of the King himself.

One of the gravest and perhaps most important involvements of Germany with Spain was in press relations and propaganda. The Germans had an invaluable head start in this field and managed to hold their lead through very difficult sets of circumstances. The evolution of this involvement went back to 1912 and demonstrated the role that Ambassador Ratibor and the official German diplomatic representation in Spain had in mixing into domestic affairs for a wartime purpose. Furthermore, the role that resident German businessmen played was considerable. For the most part it was they who created a successful information and news network. Without this extensive press involvement, it is doubtful that Germany could have influenced Spain to maintain its neutrality at critical junctures in German-Spanish relations, especially in 1916 and early 1917.

FOOTNOTES FOR CHAPTER II

[1]Pilapil, Alfonso XIII, p. 85.

[2]Cambon to Flourens, February 25, 1888, No. 18, Annex II, France, Commission de Publications des Documents relatifs aux Origines de la Guerre du 1914, Documents Diplomatiques Francais, 1871-1914 (Paris: Imprimeric Nationale, 1929), V:1st Series, p. 702. Hereafter cited as DDF.

[3]Cambon to Delcassé, February 8, 1903, DDF, III:2nd Series, pp. 98-99.

[4]Pilapil, p. 86.

[5]Ibid.

[6]Pingaud, Histoire Diplomatique, p. 16 and Prince Berhard von Buelow, Memoirs 1909-1919, 3 vols. (London: Putnam, 1932), II, p. 105.

[7]Radowitz to Foreign Office, March 23, 1904, Johannes Lepsius, et al, eds. Die Grosse Politik der Europaeischen Kabinette, 1871-1914, 40 vols. (Berlin: Deutsche Verlagsgesellschaft fuer Politik und Geschichte, 1924), XVII, p. 364.

[8]Pilapil, p. 89.

[9]Ibid., pp. 93-94. Alfonso may have been the intended groom for Edward's daughter Patricia, but he preferred the King's niece. See for this point Robert Sencourt, King Alfonso XIII, A Biography (London: Faber and Faber, 1942), p. 280.

[10]Adolf Hasenclever, "Zur Geschichte der spanisch-franzoeschischen Beziehungen vor Ausbruch des Weltkrieges," Berliner Monatshefte, X (September 7, 1936), p. 719.

[11]Pilapil, p. 46.

[12]Sencourt, p. 112 and Princess Pilar of Bavaria and Desmond Chapman Huston, Every Inch a King: Alfonso XIII (New York: Dutton, 1932), p. 91.

[13]Pilapil, p. 97.

[14]Ibid., p. 99. Later the English did insist upon taking notice of Spanish interests.

[15]Cambon to Delcassé, June 4, 1904, DDF, V:2nd Series, p. 212.

[16]Ibid.

[17]Cartwright to Grey, February 22, 1906, Great Britain, G.F. Gooch and Harold Temperley, eds., *British Documents on the Origins of the War, 1898-1914* (London: His Majesty's Stationery Office, 1927), III, pp. 270-271. Hereafter cited as BD.

[18]Basis of Notes to be Exchanged between the British and Spanish Governments, March 28, 1907, BD, VII, p. 18.

[19]Madariaga, *Spain, A Modern History*, p. 305.

[20]Geoffray to Jonnart, March 18, 1913, DDF, VI: 3rd Series, pp. 41-42.

[21]Tillion to Etienne, March 22, 1913, Ibid., p. 73.

[22]Pilapil, p. 129.

[23]Ibid.

[24]Ibid. Alfonso had mentioned this considerably earlier; see Grey to Bertie, December 20, 1905, BD, III, p. 160 and Nicolson to Grey, December 27, 1905, BD, III, p. 167.

[25]Romanones, *Obras Completas*, p. 325.

[26]Hasenclever, p. 730.

[27]Geoffray to Viviani, August 1, 1914, DDF, II: 3rd Series, p. 416. The domestic ministerial change from a Liberal to a Conservative Prime Minister reflected differences in Madrid over the wisdom of close economic ties with Paris. Conservative, clerical elements did not trust Romanones's pro-French policy, and, by implication, the policy of the King. See for this point Raymond Carr, *Spain*, p. 396 and p. 486. See also for further explanations of these differences the *New York Times*, March 17, 1917.

[28]Lord Bertie of Thane, *The Diary of Lord Bertie of Thane*, Lady Algernon G. Lennox, ed. (London: Hodder and Stoughton, 1924), I, p. 111.

[29]Pingaud, p. 20.

[30]Hayden Talbot, *An Interview with the King of Spain* (New York: ITT Corp., Bureau of Information, 1924), p. 10.

[31]Willard to Lansing, Confidential, Willard Family Papers, Box 113, August 29, 1914, p. II. Manuscript Division, The Library of Congress, Washington, D.C.

[32]Romanones, Obras Completas, p. 338 and p. 342.

[33]Bertie to Grey, August 3, 1914, BD, X, p. 343. For all practical purposes this was an Entente between France and Spain, though it did not go as far as Alfonso wanted. For an argument that the agreement was no more than an understanding, see Paul G. Halpin, The Mediterranean Naval Situation 1908-1914 (Cambridge, Mass.: Harvard University Press, 1971), pp. 294-295. A German work written before World War II belabored the point of whether or not there was an actual alliance between France and Spain, finally concluding, quite correctly, that there was none. See Paul Herre, Die Kleinen Staaten Europas und die Entstehung des Weltkrieges (Munich: C.H. Beck'sche Verlag, 1937), p. 74.

[34]Sir Arthur Hardinge, A Diplomatist in Europe (London: Jonathan Cape, Ltd., 1927), p. 262. Hardinge gives an excellent account of the arrogance of German Ambassador Ratibor; the view is amply corroborated by the German documents and by the views of other contemporaries.

[35]Friederich Katz, Deutschland, Diaz und die Mexikanische Revolution: Die Deutsche Politik in Mexiko, 1870-1920 (East Berlin: Deutscher Verlag der Wissenschaften, 1964), p. 407. Hereafter cited as Katz, Deutschland.

[36]Ratibor to Foreign Office, February 23, 1913, Spanien 67. Die Auswaertige Politik Spaniens, T149/78/249-251. Hereafter cited as Spanien 67. Auswaertige.

[37]Kalle to War Ministry, April 24, 1913, Ibid., p. 259.

[38]Kalle to Foreign Office, June 17, 1913, Ibid., p. 481.

[39]Ibid.

[40]Ratibor to Foreign Office, June 25, 1914, Spanien 40. Allgemeine Angelegenheiten Spaniens, T149/355/32-33. Hereafter cited as Spanien 40. Allgemeine.

[41]Gaceta de Madrid, July 31, 1914.

[42]Villaurrutia to Madrid, September 1, 1914, as in Don Melchor Fernandez Almagro, Historia del Reinado de Don Alfonso XIII (Barcelona: Montaner y Simon, 1933), pp. 253-254.

[43]Schulthess' Europaeischer Geschichtskalendar, 1914-

1918 (Munich: C.H. Beck'sche Verlag, 1921), for July 31, 1914, p. 512d. Hereafter cited as Schulthess'.

[44]New York Times, August 1, 1914.

[45]Gerald H. Meaker, The Revolutionary Left in Spain, 1914-1923 (Stanford, Calif.: Stanford University Press, 1974), pp. 18-19. See also Halpin, p. 295 and Luigi Albertini, The Origins of the War of 1914 (London and New York: Oxford University Press, 1952), III, pp. 691-693.

[46]Dearing to Lansing, August 15, 1914, United States, Department of State, Papers Relating to the Foreign Relations of the United States, 1914 Supplement, The World War (Washington D.C.: U.S. Government Printing Office, 1928), pp. 63-64. Hereafter cited U.S. Foreign Relations followed by the appropriate year, supplement, and page.

[47]Willard to Lansing, August 23, 1914, U.S. Foreign Relations, 1914 Supplement, pp. 70-71.

[48]New York Times, August 27, 1914.

[49]Romanones, Obras Completas, pp. 337-338.

[50]El Imparcial, August 21, 1914.

[51]ABC, 1915 as quoted in Rafael Gay de Montella, Diez Años de Politica Internacional en el Mediterraneo, 1904-1914 (Madrid: Francisco Beltran, n.d.), p. 72.

[52]La Época, December 28, 1914.

[53]El Imparcial, July 5, 1915.

[54]Ibid., September 23, 1914.

[55]Ibid., October 19, 1914.

[56]Ibid., October 23, 1914.

[57]Ibid., November 6, 1914, and Schulthess', November 8, 1914, p. 514.

[58]Ibid. See also Mousset, Histoire d'Espagne, p. 178, fn.

[59]Bello, España durante la Guerra, p. 103.

[60]Maximiano García Venero, Melquiades Alvarez: Historia de un Liberal, pp. 278-279. See also José M. Cordero Torres, Relaciones exteriores de España (Madrid: Editiones del Movimiento, 1954), p. 305.

[61]Harald Just, "Neutralitaet im Ersten Weltkrieg," p. 430. Taken from Fuerstenberg to Foreign Office, February 8, 1917, Haus-, Hof-, und Staatsarchiv PA rot 896. This article is a series of lengthy quotations from Austrian archives and as such is more like a documents collection. Hereafter this article will be cited as Just, "Neutralitaet."

[62]Friederich Rosen, Aus Einem Diplomatischen Wanderleben, 2 vols. (Wiesbaden: Limes Verlag, 1959), I, p. 28.

[63]Oskar Freiherr von der Lancken-Wakenitz, Meine Dreissig Dienstjahre (1888-1918) (Berlin: 1931), p. 165. This book has some excellent photographs of the American representative in Brussels, Brand Whitlock. An interesting note upon the German Military Attaché Arnold Kalle in Madrid is in a book by Alfred Vagts. Apparently, in the 1920's Kalle served as the chief press officer for Gustav Stresemann, the Chancellor who arranged improved relations with the West for the Weimar Republic. See Alfred Vagts, The Military Attache (Princeton, New Jersey: Princeton University Press, 1967), p. 162.

[64]For samples of these types of reports, see Kocherthaler to Langwerth, December 9, 1915, Spanien 57. Die Spanische Ministerien, T149/356/519 and Deutsche Ueberseeische Bericht fuer Februar 1919, March 4, 1919, Spanien 40. Allgemeine, 281-282.

[65]Bethmann Hollweg to Madrid and to Lancken, August 29, 1915, Weltkrieg Nr. 11q. secr. Unternehmungen und gelungen in Spanien, T149/402/268-269. Hereafter cited as Weltkrieg Nr. 11q. Unternehmungen. In this document reference was made to Alfonso Marie and his wife who was described as "one of the Braganza sisters who have strong tendencies to conspiracies and intrigues."

[66]For information about the close relatives of King Alfonso XIII, see The Statesman's Yearbook, 1914, 51st Annual Publication, ed. by J. Scott Keltie (London: MacMillan, 1914), pp. 1297-1298. For Princess Eulalia's exploits see Princess Eulalia, Memoires of her Royal Highness, the Infanta Eulalia, trans. by Phyllis Mégroz (London: Hutchinson, 1936), pp. 44-45.

[67]Mousset, Histoire d'Espagne, pp. 215-217.

[68]Hardinge, p. 260.

[69]Romanones, Obras Completas, p. 331.

CHAPTER III

THE PRESS AND POLITICS 1912-1916

German propaganda efforts during World War I were not especially well organized; indeed, one might even characterize them as chaotic. Postwar studies and participants in the fragmented communications work of the Imperial Government indicated that Germany may very well have lost the conflict because of a bad press abroad, particularly among neutral nations.[1] Germany certainly did not have a positive image in the United States, a well-known and well-documented view, but the story vis-à-vis other neutrals is not as well known.[2] German propaganda efforts within Europe's physically largest neutral and perhaps most important, Spain, were surprisingly effective and sophisticated, especially at the outset of the conflict. Considering the enormous economic advantages possessed by the Entente powers in Spain, one might regard Germany's success in creating and maintaining in that nation a large body of pro-German and pro-Austro-Hungarian opinion as even more remarkable.

Two people accounted for the successful press campaign, the Ambassador Prince Max von Ratibor and a private German businessman at Barcelona, August Hofer. From the beginning of his service at Madrid, the Ambassador took Hofer's counsel that there was a need for an expanded German information bureau in Spain to counteract French and English influences. Both Ratibor and Hofer worked to overcome indifference and hostility in Berlin for their projects. From 1912 to 1914, Ratibor tried to create this expanded service, but it was not until December 1914 that he was completely successful. From that date through 1916, the foundation that he and Hofer had established was enlarged and improved upon, and it provided the basis for future German propaganda activities. Significantly, Spain remained neutral throughout the war, and the German Information Service for Spain was one factor in that position.

In 1912, German news for Spain arrived and was distributed in a highly unimaginative way. News came from Germany via the Ernst Hirsch Telegraphic Agency after having been screened by the Foreign Office at Berlin. A press officer for the German Embassy at Madrid saw to the necessary translations and distributions throughout the Iberian peninsula and even to Latin America. This press officer was Alexander Bruns, a close friend and confidant of the Spanish monarch, Alfonso XIII.[3] Bruns tried to maintain the pretense he was not actually associated with the German Embassy in the hope his work would be more effective, but his cooperation with the German Ambassador was well known.[4]

The initial suggestions for changing Bruns's rather limited role and the whole structure of the German information services came from a letter Hofer sent to the German

Consul at Barcelona. Hofer outlined what was to become the prototype of German propaganda once the war began. Hofer introduced himself as the director of the type foundry firm, Sucesor d'Neuville, with its headquarters in Barcelona. As he traveled about the countryside, Hofer noticed little news arrived directly from Germany. What news Spain did obtain came through the French Havas News Agency, which reflected a pro-French bias. Hofer even went so far as to count despatches arriving at Spain and discovered for every two or three pro-German reports there were at least ten pro-French. To remedy this difficulty he suggested German efforts be redoubled; a Spaniard should be placed in charge of a pro-German news network in Madrid, and Hofer offered himself as the chief of a Barcelona branch. He argued that his type foundry firm with its five travelers and agents could help coordinate the activities of the new service.[5]

The Ambassador had a guarded opinion of Hofer's proposals. In a telegram to the Foreign Office, Ratibor recognized the propaganda value a Spaniard at the head of a pro-German agency would have, yet he also recognized the power that Bruns possessed and the esteem in which the Foreign Office held the press officer. Ratibor praised both Hirsch and Bruns, but cautiously suggested that an information service which would "broaden the friendly form of Spanish relations" was desirable. Hofer had mentioned a candidate for the directorship at Madrid, a Barcelona newspaperman, Juan Fabré y Olivier; Ratibor repeated this suggestion in his telegram but mentioned he really knew nothing of the man. Nevertheless, Ratibor asked to be authorized to investigate Hofer's suggestions.[6]

State Secretary for Foreign Affairs, Gottlieb von Jagow, was only mildly interested in the proposals emanating from Madrid. He warned Ratibor that no funds for the proposals were available and indicated the current information service was satisfactory. Jagow did suggest Ratibor investigate the men concerned and consult with both Bruns and Hirsch about any conceivable merit in the proposals.[7] But central to Jagow's replies to this query and to subsequent ones was a concern that Bruns might lose his special position of friendship with Alfonso. The Foreign Secretary evidently considered Bruns a useful source of information concerning the King, and the King apparently liked Bruns because the monarch had financed a recent trip to Germany for him. Clearly, the Foreign Office was not impressed in 1912 with any need to change the information service for Spain.

Ratibor, in the meantime, acted upon the suggestion to consult with Bruns, Hirsch, and Hofer for the purpose of finding out what the official newsmen would think about the proposals. Ratibor arranged a meeting with Hirsch and Hofer in Madrid on June 6, 1912. Hirsch was enthusiastic about the ideas, and he and Hofer expressed the hope of supplanting the Spanish subsidiary of the Havas Agency, the Fabra News Service. Both also thought the provincial newspapers were financially unstable and thus ripe for German subvention.

Ratibor was pleased with the success of this meeting, but he still had to deal with the main character in this little drama, Alexander Bruns.[8]

In a second meeting on June 25, 1912, Ratibor managed to get Bruns, Fabré y Olivier, and Hofer together. Surprisingly, Bruns immediately agreed to the essence of Hofer's ideas. He said he made the same suggestion earlier to his former employer, the semiofficial Wolff News Agency in Germany. Bruns, however, was a bit more cautious in his assessment of the possible success of a new information venture. He pointed out it would be especially difficult to supplant the Fabra Agency, which had a great deal of practical news experience. In addition, Fabra was successful because of the proximity of France and because of the ease of translation of great quantities of material from French to Spanish. Turning to his main point, Bruns confidentially objected to any appointment of Fabré y Olivier as the head of the Madrid bureau of the agency. Bruns said Fabré had lived for several years at Barcelona and that it would take some time for him to become accustomed to the political climate of Madrid. Bruns also pointed out Fabré had little knowledge of foreign affairs; this knowledge was necessary in choosing the most effective articles for furthering German policy.[9]

Hoping to get official approval to set up a new, more comprehensive news network, Ratibor telegraphed a complete report of both meetings to Berlin. The Ambassador emphasized the support both Bruns and Hirsch had given Hofer's suggestions; Ratibor particularly emphasized that both Bruns and Hirsch would be retained. Ratibor hinted in the report that Hofer would be led to believe his proposals were accepted in their entirety. Yet, the Embassy would keep the services of the official structure in order to "pick up the pieces" and continue as before if the venture failed.[10]

Throughout Ratibor's communications with Berlin about the subject of propaganda, the Ambassador suggested he was not total master of the German Embassy. He had to be cautious in view of the favor Bruns had with Jagow at Berlin, but clearly Ratibor was using a subtle technique to undermine Bruns. Ratibor's constant insistence upon the retention of both Bruns and Hirsch in the event of failure of the proposal was calculated to calm Bruns and to reassure Jagow. In his assessment of the proposal, Bruns took particular pains to criticize Fabré y Olivier's foreign affairs expertise. Bruns also had emphasized that he was in a better position to view the international scene. The reply soon forthcoming from Berlin underscored the need for caution on the Ambassador's part.

Jagow sent to Madrid a copy of a conversation he had had with Bruns along with a reply concerning Ratibor's suggestions to explore further Hofer's ideas. Bruns had managed to return to Germany and to discuss the new proposals before Jagow could answer the Imperial Ambassador at Madrid. Bruns argued it was absolutely necessary that he remain at the head of the press section at Madrid, clearly protecting himself from Ratibor's subtle movements to oust the press officer. Jagow seemed accommodating but insisted upon an agreement among Bruns, Hirsch, Hofer, and Fabré y Olivier before the new service might begin.[11] Furthermore, a certain degree of security had to be maintained for the service. Perhaps what was of greatest significance was that nothing was said about money to support the project.[12]

In fact, nothing more was said about the idea for several months. Evidently Bruns had succeeded in scuttling the project since he could hope the patriotism of Hofer would not extend to personal financing of a news program. But Bruns faced a challenge to his prestige in the eyes of the Foreign Office. By the end of 1912, Ratibor found a more willing ear at Berlin. In addition, Hofer actually tried to set up his own pro-German news service. So by 1913, the climate for ousting Bruns and for creating a service headed by Hofer was closer to reality.

Bruns's position was damaged by letters arriving in Berlin from South American representatives of the German government. The recipient of these letters was Ludwig Asch, the man in charge of Berlin's Transatlantic Bureau, which fed news to the Hirsch Agency. Asch was supposed to follow Bruns's instructions for transmitting news and newspapers to South America and to Spain. The quantity of such information had fallen off drastically, and the German minister at Valparaíso complained of the paucity. He relayed a long letter from a German citizen in Venzuela. This letter demanded twice the current news volume from Germany.[13] To protect himself from what appeared to be his lack of effort, Asch wrote a letter to the Foreign Office attributing the decline in Latin American and Spanish news traffic to direct orders from Bruns, who had told Asch that the whole program would be changed. Berlin was to slow down the transmissions until the new system could be worked out. Asch complained that he did as he was told, but Bruns never came to Berlin to deal with the proposed new program.[14] Consequently, Bruns's competence as a press officer for Spain and Latin America was in doubt.

Jagow talked with Bruns about the affair and seemed satisfied. Bruns admitted he did precisely as Asch had said but that he had hoped for an expanded service which had been suggested earlier in the discussions with Ratibor. Nothing in the way of support had come from those conversations, and Bruns had neglected to order Asch to resume regular services. Bruns did defend himself by suggesting the Hirsch agency was unreliable; he suggested the telegraph company was not sufficiently serious about its task and might reveal Bruns's connection with the German Embassy at Madrid.[15] These excuses were weak, and though Jagow wanted to keep Bruns as an important liaison officer with King Alfonso, the Foreign Secretary now seemed more willing to listen to Ratibor's suggestions for a new information service; at least Ratibor saw an opportunity to argue for a system that would not depend solely upon Bruns.

The Ambassador suggested himself as the head of a new information service, so he could keep a closer watch upon Bruns. The press officer's unfortunate experience with Asch gave some credence to the idea that a more efficient information service was needed.[16] In addition, Ratibor reported Hofer's personal activities in getting pro-German news in front of the Spanish public. Hofer had financed a publication in Barcelona entitled <u>Ibero-Mundial</u>. Too few had subscribed to his service, and he soon ran up a deficit of 10,000 pesetas monthly.[17] Ratibor evidently hoped Hofer's initiative would impress Jagow, but the Foreign Office remained silent. Subsequently, Ratibor obtained an in-depth report upon Hofer and upon a tantalizing offer to influence the Spanish press more directly.

In March 1914, the Consul at Barcelona, Georg Plehn, reported upon Hofer's activities and personality. Hofer had arrived in Barcelona in 1908 to resurrect an ailing business concern, the Type Foundry Firm, Sucesor d'Neuville, whose home office was at Frankfurt am Main. He had a good reputation among his fellow German nationals, particularly as a patriot. His business required frequent travels throughout Spain, particularly to remote towns selling newspaper equipment. Hofer was in a good position to view the propaganda requirements of the whole Iberian peninsula, but Plehn viewed Hofer's activity negatively. The Consul said Hofer had little tact; he probably could not influence Spanish newspapermen "in the proper way."[18] Plehn recommended acceptance of

Hofer's ideas but rejection of the man as the director of a new German information service for Spain.[19]

Ratibor added his arguments to the Foreign Office for a revamped news service. He pointed out that this was an excellent opportunity to influence rural opinion. No other organization could be so influential. More to the point, Ratibor suggested an advance to Hofer of 2,000 marks from the Embassy's press funds for propaganda purposes, at the same time requiring an accounting and proof in writing of newspapers that Hofer might win over to the German side. Further, Ratibor would oversee a news structure that would include Bruns, Hirsch, and Asch as well as Hofer. To prevent possible impetuous actions on Hofer's part, the Consul at Barcelona could refer any doubtful articles to Bruns before publication and distribution. Added to these suggestions was a report from Plehn about an excellent opportunity to influence the domestic Spanish press through bribery.[20]

The owner of the Barcelona paper La Vanguardia told the German Consul that the Havas Agency did not report balanced news. News favorable to Germany rarely appeared. If any reports came directly from Germany, they were incomprehensible to some of the editors who could not read German. Most Spanish editors could understand at least some French. He urged that the German government create a direct telegraphic link from Spain at Vigo to Germany at Emden. Perhaps, too, the German government could subsidize the costs of telegrams from Germany. Ratibor regarded this communication as a veiled suggestion for a subsidy and as an excellent opportunity to get pro-German views directly into a leading Barcelona newspaper. Indeed, Ratibor reported rather excitedly that this might open the door to influencing other Spanish newspapers.[21]

The reply of the Foreign Office was predictable; Jagow seemed to sense Ratibor's almost desperate attempts to control the Embassy's press activities, and the Foreign Secretary rejected all of the Ambassador's suggestions.[22] First, Jagow praised Bruns as a useful conduit to the King and as a reliable person. Perhaps Plehn's suggestion of Hofer's tactlessness had had an impact upon Jagow. Furthermore, Jagow suggested more information be sent to Bruns and that his service simply be expanded. Jagow also suggested that the owner of La Vanguardia negotiate with Consul Plehn or with Ludwig Asch at Berlin.[23] Clearly, a unified propaganda effort directed by Ratibor and subsidized by the Foreign Office was premature. But Ratibor and Hofer did not abandon their efforts; indeed, both defied the Foreign Office and as war broke out succeeded between September and October 1914 in getting a wide range of official support for the foundations created by Hofer and Ratibor.

In the meantime, the Entente, particularly the French and their ally the Belgians, were not lax. In December 1914 the French created the International Committee of Propaganda and assumed the lead in Entente efforts to influence Spain in favor of the Western Powers. The French colony supported this effort in Madrid by publishing the official French view of the causes of the war, entitled <u>Documentos é Informes</u>. The community also supported another publication intended to influence members of the Cortes, journalists, and leading intellectuals, the <u>Boletín de Información</u>. Throughout 1915 the International Committee redoubled its activities with the publication of numerous brochures such as <u>La Conveniencia española en la guerra actual</u>, <u>A los catolicós germanófilos de España y otro países</u>, <u>Boletín de la Alianza francesa</u>, <u>Bulletin des Français resident à l'etranger</u>, <u>Revista franco-española</u>, and an illustrated weekly, <u>Iberia</u>.[24]

Once hostilities began, Ratibor intensified his campaign to get a propaganda and news service established in Spain. Even though the country was neutral in the conflict, the economic influence of the Entente upon Spain was obvious. Ratibor thus became almost hysterical in advocating measures to influence and direct internal Spanish affairs. The Ambassador encouraged Hofer and other private subjects of the Imperial German government to intervene in Spanish affairs by setting up a propaganda network in direct opposition to von Jagow's wishes.

In September 1914, Ratibor proposed support for an afternoon paper to be published at Barcelona. He requested the expenditure of 5,000 marks to reach an estimated 15,000 readers. A marginal note indicated that the request for the money had been approved; although there was no indication that Hofer was directly involved in this proposal.[25] Indeed, the note indicated the ambassadorial press fund had been increased to 25,000 marks.[26] But within two weeks Ratibor had exhausted his press funds, and he was back in a telegram dated October 8, 1914 asking for more.[27]

Other sources of both information and influence were ferreted out by Bruns. He had succeeded in getting two businessmen, Julio Kocherthaler, who was quite close to insiders at Alfonso's court, and Herr Armbruster of the electrical firm AEG (_Allgemeine Elektrizitaets Gesellschaft_) to work for German interests.[28] From these two, particularly Kocherthaler, much valuable information and influence came into and out of Spain for Germany. For the moment, Prince Ratibor strove to obtain official support for more extensive propaganda efforts.

In a lengthy report of October 12, 1914, Ratibor presented a persuasive case for substantial financial aid to be given local German propaganda activities. Ratibor clearly revealed his role in these efforts; he asserted he thought it was his duty at the outbreak of war to counter news reports from France unfavorable to Germany. Further, he praised Hofer's activities which included translation, printing, and distribution of the German White Books to Spain and to South and Central America. But perhaps more telling in his attempts to convince the Foreign Office of the need to support such further efforts were his descriptions of French activity and of the actions of local newspapers. He stated he had learned "from a good source" that France had allowed 600,000 francs for the winning of Spanish public opinion. Indeed, Ratibor already counted several influential papers as lost to the German side, especially El Liberal, La Correspondencia de España, La Imparcial, and the Heraldo de Madrid.[29] The Germans henceforth habitually referred to these papers as the "Trust," by which they meant papers supported by the French or reflecting the pro-Allied view. While there were some papers with a pro-German view, there was a real need to get papers with wider circulation on the German side. Though La Tribuna, Correspondencia Militar and the ABC were all listed as being pro-German in view, Ratibor felt Germany had to control even more papers.[30]

In a later telegram that same month Ratibor pushed home his point that official support was needed. Hofer already had financed from his own pocket an illustrated weekly, La Neutralidad, but he needed 5,000 pesetas for the task. The winning over of opinion in Barcelona, Spain's commercial center, seemed especially important to Ratibor, and Hofer's work underlined the possibilities for the success of supporting and encouraging Spanish neutrality. Ratibor played upon the sympathies of the Foreign Office, since both the Embassy and private German subjects were doing all they could to work for the German cause, it would be unseemly for the Imperial Government to ignore official support.[31]

But the Foreign Office was adamant, and Ratibor had to turn to more spectacular devices to get financial aid. In a telegram sent on October 20, 1914, Ratibor reported that

La Tribuna's owners promised they would reflect a pro-German stance at a cost of 8,000 pesetas per month for the first four months and then 4,000 pesetas for six additional months. The Tribuna seemed valuable to Ratibor as it would engage in an anti-Portuguese campaign, particularly since Germany expected the pro-British Portuguese to declare war against Germany at any moment. Clearly, too, this move would be useful as Alfonso hoped for a diplomatic reunion between Spain and Portugal. Another newspaper, El País, showed signs of accepting German support for a pro-German stance.[32] This news had a positive effect in Berlin as the Foreign Office sent a one sentence acceptance of the financial conditions necessary to gain both La Tribuna and El País.[33] Once the Foreign Office approved support for these two newspapers, subsequent support for other propaganda activities came quickly in their wake. In a telegram of November 5, 1914, Ratibor argued once again for acceptance of the work at Barcelona and that at Madrid, all of which was being conducted by private German subjects.[34] On November 6, 1914, the Foreign Office replied with a single word: "approved," but insisted that only 3,500 marks could be spent for such purposes.[35]

The remainder of November saw a sheaf of telegrams and official reports from Madrid. First among these was a letter directed to the Information Service at Frankfurt from the verbose Hofer. He asked for large pictures to use as window displays in the offices of German firms. Other choice pictures were to go to the best Spanish illustrated magazines. In view of the low level of literacy in Spain this was a wise move indeed. Movies provided even better propaganda, as the French had earlier discovered, and Hofer felt they would be useful for the Germans too. A hint of the division of tasks within Spain by private German subjects was contained in Hofer's comments. He promised he would not infringe upon the territory of Wilhelm Rautzenberg, the Director of the Propaganda Division of the AEG. Another private propaganda organization was located at Bilbao, the Bilbao Verein.[36] But Hofer, like other German subjects, was not reticent about the costs of his operations. They may have been patriots, but as Hofer pointed out, he had operated with a deficit of 2,000 pesetas and his bills dated from September 1, 1914, almost a month and a week before official support for his activities began.[37]

In addition to Hofer at Barcelona, Wilhelm Rautzenberg at Madrid organized an effective propaganda network that meshed with that at Barcelona. In a report of November 9, 1914, Rautzenberg described in detail how his organization at Madrid supplemented and, in some cases, complemented Hofer's work. Rautzenberg pointed out the positive effect German business firms might have in developing pro-German sentiment throughout Spain. Businessmen in league with local mayors could work together to drive anti-German papers from the coffee houses where newspapers were often read aloud. Large business firms also could use their considerable economic influence through advertisements to modify the pro-Allied stance of the "Trust" newspapers. In a more original vein, Rautzenberg suggested that important stories should be typed to send to significant Spanish newspapers. In this fashion the newspapers would consider the stories meant for them alone. Using another tactic, Rautzenberg suggested German propagandists should highlight the activities of the Social Democratic Party, indicating that Germany genuinely had a concern for the working man rather than noble words. He enthusiastically described German accident insurance, hospitals, and workers' apartments.[38]

Another major point that German propaganda followed closely during the war years was the historic relationship between Spain and the Allies. Rautzenberg suggested that Spaniards needed to be reminded of Spain's fall from great power status through the activities of both France and England, beginning with the War of Spanish Succession in the eighteenth century through French attempts to exclude Spain from North Africa.[39]

Evidently Ratibor, and perhaps Hofer, put pressure upon the Foreign Office through a series of letters and suggestions sent to the Reichstag, particularly to Matthias Erzberger, a Center Party deputy and member of the Information Service. Erzberger, responsible for Catholic propaganda in particular, suggested that Ratibor must cultivate the friendship of the owner of the influential Spanish newspaper, _ABC_. He further suggested that the _ABC_ could be subsidized to reflect a pro-German stance quite easily. Erzberger also mentioned the _Tribuna_ and the possibility that its owner now leaned toward a pro-German position. He even repeated the exact figure which Ratibor had suggested, and which reflected how much money the French sent to influence Spanish opinion, ostensibly to get Spain to enter the war on the Allied side. Negotiations with the Barcelona paper, _Vanguardia_, to become a German mouthpiece, were also mentioned. A pro-German paper in that significant industrial center was highly desirable.[40]

Though the documents do not reveal who Erzberger's correspondent was, the figures used and the newspapers mentioned corresponded precisely with the needs and desires of Hofer, Rautzenberg, and Prince Ratibor. One could surmise that either Hofer or Rautzenberg or someone in their employ could have sent this letter to Erzberger, hoping thereby to gain extra help in a full, thorough-going official support for the German Information Service for Spain. Oddly enough, the letter was not mentioned until December 1914, well after the Foreign Office had agreed to the suggestions made by Ratibor. One can further surmise that the writer hoped that the information would arrive sooner and have an effect earlier than it did. But the Foreign Office thought enough of the Erzberger letter to preserve it in proximity to the other correspondence from Madrid relating to precisely the same subject.

On December 9, 1914, Prince Ratibor reported somewhat

jubilantly upon the progress, completeness, and complexity of the German Information Service for Spain. By that date there were three basic sources other than the official one at Madrid disseminating pro-German news and propaganda throughout Spain. August Hofer acted in a three-part capacity at Barcelona. He was the agent of the German Information Service for Spanish and Portuguese-speaking countries which sent him reports intended for Spain and Latin America. He also acted as an agent of the Berlin Overseas Service that prepared photographs of the war. Finally, he served as a coordinator for German propaganda at Barcelona, publishing an illustrated weekly, La Guerra Mundial, of 6,000-8,000 copies and preparing German and Spanish editions of news despatches as they arrived from Germany by wireless and the mails. These editions were sent to the German Embassy, the 26 German consulates in Spain and Portugal, and to the 160 German Leagues of private German subjects for further distribution. Furthermore, the Spanish edition of the news despatches was sent to the Spanish and Portuguese daily press (400 copies), and 140 to influential private Spanish citizens who evidenced a pro-German interest. Hofer also culled through Spanish newspapers and sent pro-German articles to Italian and Rumanian newspapers to counter Allied propaganda in these countries.[41]

The second major news organization of a private citizen in Spain was that of Wilhelm Rautzenberg. He selected lengthy articles, more like treatises, and sent them to 178 Spanish newspapers in Madrid and in the provinces as well as to ten Portuguese newspapers. Rautzenberg's activities, in contrast to those of Hofer, who provided accurate information to the Spanish public about the war as soon as possible, were supposed to be more scholarly and to provide "background" information.[42]

A third and somewhat less extensive enterprise, though highly successful, was that of Carl Koppel, the director of a clock factory in Madrid and a highly respected businessman in Spain. He wrote a work entitled _Por la Patria y por la Verdad_, a short pamphlet interpreting the origins of the war. Thirty to forty thousand copies were printed and distributed. Koppel promised to continue his short interpretive work with a new account appearing approximately every ten days.[43]

Ratibor was exceptionally pleased with the propaganda network that he had erected in such a short time. He emphasized to the Foreign Office that he was in direct control of all of these activities and that he could halt publication of anything the Embassy officials considered offensive to Spanish opinion.[44] Obviously, the officially accredited representatives of the Reich intervened in the domestic affairs of Spain by direct attempts to use fellow German citizens to persuade Spain to maintain her neutrality.

From the political standpoint, the Germans sought to satisfy Spain in as many ways as possible. From October 1914 through June 1916, the Germans tried to appease Spaniards on three issues. The first of these was that of the Ferrer Statue at Brussels. Conservative elements in Spain requested that this monument to an anarchist be removed; otherwise, the army and other conservative elements threatened to abandon their pro-German stand. In addition, subsidies of Spanish newspapers furthered German influence. Secondly, on an official level, Alfonso tried to use the war to get his cherished foreign policy goals accomplished. He wanted the Entente to give him Tangier and a free hand in Portugal, and when these were not forthcoming from the Western Powers, he turned to Germany for support. He had extracted a statement of German sympathy in late 1914, and subsequent conversations with the German Military Attaché at Madrid gave contemporaries to understand that Spain had obtained a secret agreement to work for the Central Powers, if not to come into the war directly. Rumors of this apparent agreement circulated in the late fall of 1915. The third involvement of Germany with Alfonso's schemes was German cooperation in helping to restrict the political influence of the Spanish Prime Minister Count Romanones.

The Francisco Ferrer incident was opened by a letter from an obscure Spanish priest to the German Foreign Office on October 2, 1914. In a lengthy letter written entirely in Latin (the priest apologetically explaining he did not know German), the "tragic week" disturbances of late July 1909 were recounted.[45] Ferrer had been a rationalist and something of an anticleric. He founded "Godless" schools, the Escuela Moderna (36 schools in all), that were sympathetic to anarchist ideas. In the Barcelona disturbances following the calling up of the army against an uprising in Morocco, Ferrer was accused of having had a major part. He was tried by a military court and executed in October 1909 for allegedly having led the disturbances, although in fact he had done nothing more than write a revolutionary pamphlet. Thereafter, he was regarded by European anticlericals as a martyr. Hence, a statue to his memory had been erected at Brussels in 1913.[46]

Clearly, the priest saw the German occupation of Brussels as an excellent opportunity to remove this monument to heresy. Precisely why a Roman Catholic saw Protestant Germany as the bearer of Godliness can be traced to the good effects of German propaganda. This had been one of the main points made against the "ungodly French" who had restricted the Church. The German Military Attaché, Arnold Kalle, informed the Foreign Office that this would be an excellent opportunity to further German relations with conservative elements in Spain. He reported that a leader of the Carlist faction had asked for permission to enter Brussels and destroy the statue.[47] When an answer was not immediately forthcoming, the Carlists threatened Ratibor and the Austro-Hungarian Ambassador Prince Fuerstenberg with the increase of contraband shipments across the Pyrenees to France. The Carlists even demonstrated their prowess by controlling border smuggling.[48]

The Germans faced a difficult problem. Ratibor noted that any open acceptance of Carlists demands would be an affront to socialist opinion in the Reich. The State Secretary, Gottfried von Jagow, agreed. But the hope of developing friendly groups inside Spain motivated the Germans to seek some means to satisfy the Carlist request. A series of internal discussions followed throughout November and December on removal of the statue. The Carlists had simply wanted to put a bomb at its base and blast away. Authorities at Brussels, however, pointed out that the statue was quite large and any explosion to remove it undoubtedly would take much of the surrounding plaza with it.[49] By early January 1915, von Jagow felt he had the answer.

The State Secretary suggested acid be thrown on the statue in the dead of night. Later, the monument could be removed, and an official announcement could be made. Provocateurs could be blamed and the statue could then be removed to maintain public order. Subsequently, on January 24, 1915, a news report dictated by the Governor-General von der Bissing at Brussels indicated that the statue had been removed following an acid attack.[50] Ratibor was quite pleased with the way the problem had been handled, and he hastened to tell King Alfonso of the role the German government had had in the affair.[51] Thus, Carlist opinion was mollified. But the possibility of a more significant Spanish adherence to the German cause was in the offing; a genuine alliance between Spain and Germany almost became a reality in the summer and fall of 1915.

In the meantime, on December 19, 1914, to further

propaganda efforts, Ratibor asked permission to distribute 10,000 marks as Christmas gifts to specific editors and reporters. The Foreign Office immediately agreed. Subsequently, in January Ratibor reported how he had used this money. Some 4,000 pesetas were given to the Correo Español, 1,000 to El Dabate, 1,500 to the editor of La Tribuna, and Navarro Salvador of the Heraldo de Madrid received 250 pesetas for his pro-German services. The editor of the Correo Español was given an extra sum of 300 pesetas as an award for paying attention to pro-German news. Ratibor stated that the remainder was used to reward newspaper people who served the German cause. Ratibor reported: "I believe that they will work now for our side with doubled enthusiasm. And also they will persuade others to become Germanophiles."[52]

Ratibor and the German Embassy occupied themselves with further negotiations with other newspapers in February and March 1915, attempting to enlarge the stable of pro-German forces, particularly among the Spaniards themselves rather than through private German citizens. El País, a socialist newspaper, indicated a pro-German leaning in the fall of 1914, but subsequent events had made it impossible for the paper to be openly pro-German. An article that praised Kaiser William II appeared at the same time that the Germans removed the statue of the anarchist, Francisco Ferrer, in Brussels. The socialist readers objected to the pro-German view, and El País found itself embarrassed and thus unable to go against the opinion of the remainder of the socialist press. Ratibor noted that he should have gotten El País on the German side earlier.[53]

Negotiations with another significant newspaper turned out much better. The radical Republican paper El Diluvio in Barcelona was approached through the good offices of August Hofer, who arranged a payment of 2,500 pesetas per month in postdated checks. El Diluvio was to publish official German war news and to feature articles about the German working class and German Health Insurance. Both Hofer and the Consul at Barcelona were to select suitable articles for El Diluvio to print. Ratibor realized the difficulty in changing the views of the republican sector of Spanish opinion, and later he suggested that one must wait and see the effectiveness of El Diluvio in bringing about any change at all. But Ratibor felt he had to approach all segments of opinion.[54]

In March La Tribuna's owner asked for an increase in his subsidy. Ratibor seemed perfectly willing to agree to this; he argued to the Foreign Office that since El País would no longer be subsidized, La Tribuna could now get 6,000 pesetas per month instead of the 4,000 now paid.[55] The Foreign Office obviously valued La Tribuna and agreed to Ratibor's suggestion.[56]

While the Germans were unsuccessful in outrightly purchasing other Spanish newspapers, pressure of one kind or another was used to influence the remaining significant newspapers toward a pro-German position. German firms purchased advertisements in both the Imparcial and in the Heraldo, thus pressuring them at least to use more pro-German news reports. In addition, Alexander Bruns was able to funnel pro-German news to the Heraldo via a Swiss journalist.[57]

Meanwhile, two rather large and imposing issues were building among the directors of the German propaganda organizations. The first problem revolved around a conflict between Hofer and Ratibor over priorities within the future course of German news and propaganda distribution in Spain. Another major difficulty involved attempts to purchase all of the remaining important Spanish newspapers, with the Germans going to great lengths to snatch the "Trust" from the Allies after Italy entered the war on the Entente side.

Hofer wrote his normal lengthy report to Berlin in June 1915, but included was a candid assessment of Ratibor and the Madrid German coterie. This report was the climax of a running feud between Hofer and Ratibor about the funds needed to underwrite Hofer's increasingly ballooning efforts. Ratibor had agreed to recommend Hofer receive 3,000 pesetas per month for his work, up over his allotment in the fall, but Hofer was dissatisfied and wrote directly to Berlin complaining about his 1,100 peseta sum.[58] On April 15, 1915, a Foreign Office inner memo had empowered the Ambassador to increase the subsidy for Hofer up to 3,500, but Hofer was to be warned that he had to be satisfied with this amount as no further raises could be contemplated.[59] Ratibor was tardy in making a request for more money for Hofer, his suggestion arriving on April 20, 1915.[60] Ratibor was finally told of the Foreign Office's decision on April 22, 1915.[61]

On June 4, 1915, Hofer wrote directly to the _Zentralstelle_, detailing his program and his future plans and including a scathing indictment of both Bruns and Ratibor. Though the report went directly to the Central Office for Information Services, a copy was sent to the Foreign Office. Hofer ended his exhaustive official report with the comment that he could hardly refrain from discussing the "middleman" for the press in Madrid, Alexander Bruns. Hofer said that Bruns had no really good reputation among journalists in Madrid, indeed, he was thought of as a spy for the Ambassador, Ratibor. On a personal note Hofer reported that Bruns was married to an Englishwoman and that:

> . . . he does not please me personally. I have no proof against him, but I nurture a certain mistrust on account of his English wife. It can be that I delude myself, but in these meaningful times I think it is my duty to say all I think and know.[62]

Hofer went on to advocate his candidate for the overall directorship of the News and Propaganda Service, Fabré y Olivier. Fabré was, in Hofer's view, better oriented as a Spanish journalist and would be inconspicuous in Spanish newspaper circles in both Barcelona and Madrid.[63]

Hofer's dissatisfaction was not totally expressed in this official report which he must have known would go to the Foreign Office. In a private letter of June 4, 1915, Hofer was much more candid about Ratibor and the Foreign Office.

Hofer excoriated the high German diplomats and local Consuls whom he described as behaving irresponsibly. He felt that both ignored his own suggestions and those of others on the local scene, such as the Director of the German Transatlantic Bank, Welsch. Berlin was described as being too stingy, and no one realized the millions that were necessary to maintain Spanish neutrality. Hofer concentrated upon Ratibor with the comment: "What is one to do with an Ambassador who arises at 11 in the morning and is not ready to talk until 12 when others have already gone through one half of their workday?"[64] Hofer knew that the German position vis-à-vis Spanish public opinion was good, but he worried about the fickleness of the Spanish public. Yielding momentarily to melodrama, he proclaimed, "Dear God! What I could do in the press with a million pesetas!"[65] Hofer suggested that since Italy was now definitely an enemy, money must have been freed for use in Spain, Rumania, and Bulgaria.[66]

But Hofer had always complained about lack of money, and the Foreign Office paid little attention to his requests. Ratibor maintained total control over the press service in Spain, and he devoted his energies to purchasing the press "Trust." In a telegram to the Foreign Office on May 28, 1915, Ratibor asked that he be authorized to negotiate a purchase agreement.[67]

A few days later Ratibor reinforced his view that a greater effort now needed to be made. He pointed out that with Italy in the war on the Allied side, England and France could be expected to extend their bribes and propaganda efforts to persuade Spain to enter the war on the Entente side. He reviewed the deals with the Heraldo and the Tribuna and asserted that the Trustblaetter must be won for the German side or at least rendered ineffective for the Entente.[68]

From another direction the Foreign Office was moved from its lethargy by a report from the Oberkommando der Heeresleitung that its Military Attaché had noted increased allied efforts to win over the Spanish press. This report was somewhat more realistic than the one of Ratibor. The Attaché pointed out he did not expect the Allies to be successful in dislodging Spain from its position of neutrality, ". . . further, one has to reckon with bribery of press and leading politicians, thus, one must offer countermeasures with large sums of money."[69]

State Secretary von Jagow told Ratibor on June 2, 1915, that a new sum was at the Ambassador's disposal to purchase important newspapers and to influence important politicians. Jagow further suggested more energetic measures and reports upon Ratibor's progress.[70]

A few days later Ratibor reported that the Allies had a stronger hold upon the Trustblaetter than he had thought. He had tried a different tactic by offering to pay for advertisements supporting the German position, but the cost was prohibitive for the amount of influence the Germans could derive from it. Ratibor listened to the owner of the Tribuna and a suggestion this man had made. Salvador Cánovas

Cervantes, the owner, suggested that some five to ten million pesetas be set aside to purchase the Trust papers at Madrid and then two to three million to unite the Tribuna, the Trust papers, and the papers at Barcelona for a first class information service that could saturate Spain with pro-German views. Ratibor asked for special approval to empower Cánovas to negotiate for Germany, particularly, for Cánovas to win controlling shares of the Barcelona papers Día Grafico and La Tribuna.[71] Otherwise the Germans tried to win rural opinion. On June 25, 1915, Ratibor reported that he had gotten support among the provincial newspapers at Zaragoza, Sevilla, and San Sebastián. He also had prepared fly-leafs for Barcelona, Valencia, Bilbao, and Sevilla.[72]

The military once again intervened; this time a detailed list of suggestions came from Vienna and the office of General Conrad von Hoetzendorff, Commander in Chief of the Austro-Hungarian army. Conrad had discussed the Spanish situation with several visiting Spanish politicians, and was convinced that the Carlist Vásquez de Mella was the most important national Spanish politician to support, in hopes that Vásquez might attach Spain to the Central Powers. He mentioned several newspapers that the Foreign Office at Berlin already knew could be purchased, and some that they apparently knew little about. Particularly, the Spanish politicians mentioned that La Correspondencia de España's owner, the Marquis of Santa Ana, might be brought over to the side of the Central Powers. Conrad urged that most efforts be expended in Barcelona and Bilbao, where the Socialist and Republican views were strongest and where pro-French views were most widely expressed.[73]

The Foreign Office received a report from Julio Kocherthaler in Brussels concerning the suggestions made by Conrad. Kocherthaler's brother, Hugo, was in Spain and wrote to his brother in Brussels about the political situation and the views of Alfonso. The brothers Kocherthaler believed that Spain would remain neutral and that La Correspondencia de España could not really be approached. But other negotiations to control the Spanish press were in the works.[74]

Indeed, the negotiations had progressed quite well for the Barcelona papers. On July 9, 1915, Ratibor reported that the negotiations had ended and that two-thirds of the shares of the Día Grafico and the Tribuna were to be purchased at a cost of 200,000 pesetas. By July 21, the deal was consummated; the General Consul at Barcelona delivered the money to the owners of the two papers.[75]

In the remaining months of 1915, Ratibor concentrated upon countering pro-Allied propaganda of Alexander Lerroux and upon encouraging criticism of Entente military activities. In August 1915, Ratibor reported a request from a Spaniard to obtain German support for undermining the allegedly socialist, pro-Allied Lerroux. A man by the name of Llado wanted to found a socialist newspaper with the express purpose of subtly splitting the Lerroux party through a defense of Spanish policies of neutrality. Ratibor was not favorable to this suggestion; indeed, the cost of German operations in Spain was getting too high. He noted that this venture would cost 16,000-20,000 pesetas per month. Instead, he felt that public opinion in Spain was already sufficiently pro-German, and the use of these other channels would successfully counteract Lerroux.[76]

In other reports in October 1915, Ratibor apparently orchestrated criticism of the Salonica landings. He reported that several newspapers had written sharp articles attacking the Allies for violating Greek neutrality by landing troops in Salonica. But what was of even greater interest was the phrase "the campaign continues." Evidently, Ratibor directed the views private interests were to take and prepared the press campaigns within Spain. The subsidized press was a ready vehicle for such efforts at molding Spanish opinion.

In the meantime, two other major issues occupied German-Spanish relations. One was Alfonso's continued efforts to obtain control over Tangier. The other was a German attempt to establish a tacit German-Spanish Alliance. Throughout 1915 Berlin and Madrid seemed to be coming to terms; although while the negotiations were proceeding, Germany expanded her sabotage activities throughout the Iberian peninsula.

FOOTNOTES FOR CHAPTER III

[1]Walter Nicolai, Nachrichtendienst, Presse und Volksstimmung im Weltkriege (Berlin: Mittler, 1920), p. 87. See also Rudolf Wiehler, Deutsche Wirtschaftpropaganda im Weltkriege (Berlin: Mittler, 1921), p. 34. For a chart detailing the eventual organization of German propaganda organizations for foreign countries, see Wiehler, p. 66. A good discussion of German propaganda activities in neutrals is Will Irwin, Propaganda and News or What Makes You Think So? (New York: McGraw-Hill, 1936), p. 128-130. The standard guide to contemporary materials relating to propaganda during the conflict is Harold Lasswell, Propaganda Technique in the World War (New York: Garland Publishing Company, 1927), esp. pp. 149-150. Each of the above authors emphasized the divided, uncoordinated propaganda efforts of the Germans, particularly since the Foreign Office, military and numerous private interests essentially conducted their own propaganda activities. For a more recent account of the organization of the German propaganda apparatus, based upon documents available only in East Germany, see Katz, Deutschland, pp. 446-447.

[2]H. C. Peterson, Propaganda for War: The Campaign Against Neutrality, 1914-1917 (Norman, Oklahoma: The University of Oklahoma Press, 1939) p. 141-142.

[3]Ratibor to Foreign Office, March 28, 1912, Spanien 46. secr. Subventionierung Spanischer Zeitungen, T149/356/137. Hereafter cited as Spanien 46. secr. Subventionierung.

[4]Hofer to the Zentralstelle fuer Auslandsdienst, June 1, 1915, Ibid., 293.

[5]Hofer to Falcke, March 21, 1912, Ibid., 133.

[6]Ratibor to Foreign Office, March 28, 1912, Ibid., 137.

[7]Jagow to Ratibor, April 3, 1912, Ibid., 138-140.

[8]Ratibor to Foreign Office, June 6, 1912, Ibid., 141-144.

[9]Ibid., 145-147.

[10]Ibid.

[11]Jagow to Ratibor, August 22, 1912, Ibid., 148-149.

[12]Ibid.

[13]Welckner to Asch, November 13, 1912, Ibid., 155-156.

[14]Asch to Hamman, December 13, 1912, Ibid., 150-152.

[15]Jagow to Ratibor, December 24, 1912, Ibid., 156-158. Interestingly enough, Bruns in not mentioned extensively in the documents after this point. Consequently, the real master of German propaganda in Spain was Ratibor.

[16]Ratibor to Foreign Office, January 22, 1913, Ibid., 160.

[17]Ratibor to Foreign Office, November 23, 1913, Ibid., 162-163.

[18]Ratibor to Foreign Office, March 15, 1914, Ibid., 159-160.

[19]Ibid.

[20]Ibid.

[21]Ibid.

[22]Jagow to Ratibor, April 30, 1914, Ibid., 169-172.

[23]Ibid.

[24]Raymond Lantier, "La Propagande Française en Espagne," Revue de Paris (June 1, 1916) pp. 661-670 and Pierre Paris, "L'Espagne et la Guerre," Bulletin Hispanique XVIII (1916), #1, p. 27.

[25]Foreign Office to Bethmann Hollweg, September Report, 1914, Spanien 46. Die Spanische Presse, T149/355/631. Hereafter cited as Spanien 46. Presse.

[26]Ibid.

[27]Ratibor to Foreign Office, October 8, 1914, Ibid., 630.

[28]Ratibor to Foreign Office, October 12, 1914, Ibid., 636.

[29]Ratibor to Foreign Office, October 12, 1914, Ibid., 632-636.

[30]Ibid.

[31]Ratibor to Foreign Office, October 14, 1914, Ibid., 637-639. The exact quote therein reads, "... Geldmittel ..., die ich zur Aufrechterhaltung und Verbesserung des deutschen Nachrichtendienstes sowie fuer Unterstuetzung von Unternehmungen verwenden wuerde, die eine Beeinfluessung der spanischen oeffentlichen Meinung in unserem Sinne zum Ziele haben.

[32]Ratibor to Foreign Office, October 20, 1914, Spanien 46. secr. Subventionierung, 173.

[33]Foreign Office to Ratibor, October 22, 1914, Ibid., 174.

[34]Ratibor to Foreign Office, November 5, 1914, Ibid., 178.

[35]Foreign Office to Ratibor, November 6, 1914, Ibid., 176.

[36]Hofer to Nachrichtendienst, November 7, 1914, Spanien 46. Presse, 642-644.

[37]Ibid.

[38]Rautzenberg to Nachrichtenbuero, Frankfurt am Main, November 9, 1914, Ibid., 656.

[39]Ibid., 663.

[40]Ratibor to Foreign Office, December 9, 1914, Spanien 46. secr. Subventionierung, 217-218.

[41]Ibid.

[42]Ibid.

[43]Ibid.

[44]Ratibor to Foreign Office, January 26, 1915, Ibid., 252-253.

[45]Benitho T. Alonso to Foreign Office, October 2, 1914, Spanien 40. Allgemeine Angelegenheiten Spaniens, T149/355/377. Hereafter cited as Spanien 40. Allgemeine. In addition, see the following quote from a contemporary observer of the effectiveness of German propaganda among the common clergy in Spain: "The war, you see,' explained the diminutive curé with the expansive gesture, 'is the will of God against iniquitous France. The most righteous Emperor of Germany is His instrument in this bitter task.' At my rather quizzical smile he added, reprovingly, 'And a most loyal son of the Church.' I ventured to remonstrate that the Kaiser is commonly believed to be Protestant. But the curé passed the palm of his hand along the paling before him, as though

smoothing out the wrinkles of earth, and corrected me by explaining that his Majesty was 'obliged to fulfill the outward formalities imposed by the state, but that in private he perfomed the rites of the Church.'" taken from Sanford Griffith, Outlook, CXVI (July 4, 1917), p. 392.

[46]Carr, p. 485.

[47]Kalle to Foreign Office, November 17, 1914, Spanien 40. Allgemeine, 395.

[48]Fuerstenberg to Berchthold, November 18, 1914, Ibid., 387-388. See also confirmation of this point in the Austrian documents in Just, "Neutralitaet," p. 371.

[49]Jagow to Ratibor, December 15, 1914, Spanien 40. Allgemeine, 396.

[50]Lancken to Langwerth, January 1, 1915, Ibid., 408.

[51]Ratibor to Foreign Office, February 13, 1915, Ibid., 422.

[52]Ratibor to Foreign Office, February 20, 1915, Spanien 46. secr. Subventionierung, 252.

[53]Ibid.

[54]Ratibor to Foreign Office, March 19, 1915, Ibid., 262.

[55]Foreign Office to Ratibor, March 20, 1915, Ibid., 262.

[56]Ratibor to Foreign Office, March 21, 1915, Ibid., 268.

[57]Ibid.

[58]Hofer to Zentralstelle, June 1, 1915, Ibid., 288-294.

[59]Foreign Office to Ratibor, April 15, 1915, Ibid., 265-266.

[60]Ratibor to Foreign Office, April 20, 1915, Ibid., 272.

[61]Foreign Office to Ratibor, April 22, 1915, Ibid., 272.

[62]Hofer to Zentralstelle, June 1, 1915, Ibid., 288-294.

[63]Ibid.

[64]Private letter of Hofer to Herr H., June 4, 1915, Ibid., 287.

[65]Ibid.

[66]Ibid.

[67]Ratibor to Foreign Office, May 28, 1915, Ibid., 274.

[68]Ratibor to Foreign Office, May 31, 1915, Weltkrieg Nr. 11q. Unternehmungen und Aufwiegelungen, T149/402/187-188. Hereafter cited as Weltkrieg Nr. 11q. Aufwiegelungen.

[69]Treutler to Foreign Office, June 1, 1915, Spanien 46. secr. Subventionierung, 278.

[70]Jagow to Ratibor, June 2, 1915, Ibid., 279.

[71]Ratibor to Foreign Office, June 12, 1915, Ibid., 283-284.

[72]Ratibor to Foreign Office, June 25, 1915, Ibid., 297-298.

[73]Conrad to Falkenhayn, December 30, 1915, Ibid., 300-302.

[74]Lancken to Langwerth, August 27, 1915, Ibid., 307.

[75]Ratibor to Foreign Office, July 9, 1915, Ibid., 303.

[76]Ratibor to Foreign Office, August 16, 1915, Ibid., 307.

CHAPTER IV

A GERMAN ALLIANCE AND GERMAN SABOTAGE

1914 - 1915

Against the backdrop of intensive Reich propaganda and German success on the battlefield from 1914 through the summer of 1915, Alfonso tried to extract guarantees of a free hand in Portugal and control over Gibraltar. Ambassador Ratibor had offered Alfonso a free hand in Portugal on October 15, 1914, but the Spanish reply had been noncommittal.[1] The German hope was to counter pro-English tendencies in Portugal. Romanones reported in his memoirs that he had almost daily contact with the Prime Minister, Eduardo Dato, therefore the Liberal leader was in a position to know about the offers from Germany, and he too indicated Ratibor had offered Spain an indirect alliance.

In a recent study of Spanish neutrality during World War I some additional light had been shed upon this apparent offer. The State Minister Marquis of Lema received Ratibor in October 1914 and was sounded out about Spanish attitudes if Portugal were to enter the war on the Allied side. In the course of the conversation Ratibor intimated if the British fleet were destroyed, then Spain would be able to carry out its desires regarding Portugal and

Gibraltar.[2] But Lema, who was pro-British, replied that Spain would not modify its firm position of neutrality (a position which had not yet been confirmed by the Cortes) and the possibility of Portuguese entrance into the war would not substantially change the Spanish position.[3] Later Ratibor intimated that the German offer would not be available forever.[4] Polo de Bernabé, the Spanish Ambassador in Berlin, tried to persuade his superiors that the possibility of defeat for British seapower was great and that Spain should accept the German offer.[5] But the Spaniards never overtly or covertly stated their acceptance of the offer.

Interestingly, Albert Mousset, a member of the French Embassy and journalist, related almost the exact terms of the suggestions, dating them November 4, 1914. This revelation was in an article written in the spring of 1915. Mousset said that Ratibor had made an offer to Dato, promising the Spanish Gibraltar and freedom of action in Morocco and Portugal.[6] Clearly there were few secrets in Madrid, but the knowledge among the Entente powers of the German offers aided Alfonso in trying to turn the situation to the advantage of Spain.

In the spring of 1915 Alfonso continued his efforts to exploit the war. In interviews with the Russian Ambassador and with the French, he hinted at the offers made by Ratibor. He recounted his services to France since the war had begun, particularly his guarantee of the Pyrenees, and he suggested Spain should not be forgotten at the peace table when the war ended.[7] Specifically, Alfonso wanted Tangier in return for Spanish entry into the war.[8] But the French were adamantly opposed, suggesting that the British were never willing to discuss the transfer of Gibraltar to Spain in return for a guarantee of a favorable Spanish attitude.[9] The British, initially accepting the idea of transferring Tangier to Spain, did come around to the French view, and on March 5, 1915, the Ambassador of the United States, Joseph Willard, wrote the Secretary of State, William Bryan, relating that the British felt Gibraltar could best be protected by the Spanish zone in Morocco and by an internationalized Tangier.[10]

Interestingly, the Germans broadcast their intentions toward Spain through the semiofficial Die Koelnische Zeitung and through the Correo de Alemania, a Spanish language newspaper published in Berlin. Summaries of articles therein appeared in the Literary Digest of late March 1915. As reported by the American magazine, the Germans suggested Spain should get back Gibraltar, were she to join the Central Powers. Furthermore, the Germans said Spain would also receive Tangier, thereby making her the leading power in the Mediterranean.[11]

One must also keep in mind the negotiations then proceeding in Rome between the Germans and Italians on one side and the Entente and the Italians on the other side. Though Spain was not as strategically located as Italy, the opportunity to negotiate in order to gain diplomatic strength from benevolent neutrality was none the less strong. In

Spain's case, geography was a determining factor. The fact that she was surrounded by the Entente meant Spain could be coerced economically much more easily than Italy. Since the Central Powers were much closer to Italy, her position in the war could be decisive. When Italy signed the secret Treaty of London and came into the war on the Entente side by May 1915, the Western Powers had no real need for Spain's active participation in the conflict. The western Mediterranean now was an Allied lake.

Spaniards were particularly bitter that Italy might have been promised territory in return for her entering the war. The Minister of State, Marquis of Lema, told Ambassador Willard that recent newspaper articles demanding the transfer of Tangier to Spain represented the aspirations of the Spanish government as well.[12] In a speech delivered at the end of April, the leading Conservative politician, Antonio Maura, demanded Tangier. Romanones, the Liberal leader, also backed the idea of Tangier's transfer.[13]

As the Allied Dardanelles campaign proceeded, Spain feared Constantinople might fall to the Western Powers, thus destroying the Ottoman Empire and altering the power balance in the eastern Mediterranean. To restore the balance Tangier should be given to Spain in the west.[14] Spain, then, saw herself in danger of diplomatic isolation as the war changed the political power balance. King Alfonso therefore turned to Germany and Austria-Hungary, partly to frighten the Entente and partly to provide himself with a firm ally.

Proof of this ardent wooing of the Central Powers came from the Austrians, who learned of Alfonso's desires to get what was interpreted as the support of the Central Powers for an extended Spanish presence in North Africa. The private secretary of the former Spanish Ambassador in Vienna appeared at the Ballhausplatz to communicate this desire. The King of Spain, through the good offices of this gentleman, relayed that Madrid would be quite pleased if public opinion were to force him to associate with the Central Powers. Alfonso, ostensibly, believed the army would support such a reorientation of Spanish policy. In addition, the entire nation believed no better opportunity would ever exist to regain the lost province of Gibraltar. A propaganda campaign for that purpose would, therefore, be welcomed by Alfonso.[15]

On July 19, 1915, Alfonso spoke with the Military Attaché Kalle at length about German-Spanish relations. The King emphasized the need for German economic aid to help Spain escape the "yoke" of England and France. He referred specifically to the need for the Krupp armaments firm to help Spain construct weapons and munitions factories.[16] Kalle listened attentively, and in consultation with an engineer who represented Krupp, Alfred Helbig, Kalle sent a memorandum to Alfonso about a month later, detailing future German economic and diplomatic aid.

Kalle's memorandum was a masterpiece of subtlety. Spain was not directly promised anything, but the possibilities might be considerable if Spain followed neutral policies that were benevolent toward Germany. Kalle merely mentioned the "desirability" of returning Gibraltar to its "rightful" owner, Spain. He also mentioned the need to strengthen Spanish defense capabilities. German capital was to have a favorable position in Spain, and German help would be forthcoming for the construction of a naval yard. An independent Spanish navy would result in an independent Spanish foreign policy. Kalle emphasized that German money and expertise would be behind the navy. Kalle even lectured Alfonso on the corrupt Spanish political system. Evidently he was referring to the cacique system, a peculiarity of Spanish politics in which elections were arranged and parties took turns ruling the nation. Kalle suggested internal changes and a pro-German foreign policy would free Spain from dependence upon Great Britain and France.[17] No precise agreements came from this memorandum, as always Alfonso wanted to use the Germans to counter the Entente; the rumor of an impending agreement was more valuable than a genuine alliance. The Spanish monarch turned to another method of getting more specific assurances from the Germans.

The King's cousin, Don Alfonso Marie of Bourbon, the son of Infanta Eulalia, had visited the German front in eastern Europe in late August 1915 and had talked with German General Falkenhayn. The Spaniard was not bashful about Spanish hopes for German support once the war was over. He suggested directly that Germany support Spanish claims to

Oran in Algeria and to Gibraltar. On a more fantastic note, Don Alfonso suggested that the Germans give Spain ten million pesetas to establish a newspaper in southern France with the purpose of stirring up separatist sentiment and, hopefully, a revolution. The ultimate purpose of the scheme would be for France to retaliate, occupying the Balearic Islands, thereby giving King Alfonso and the conservatives an excuse to strike out against France.[18] The Foreign Office was interested in the first few suggestions, but the latter was rejected as too bizarre.

Through several channels, the Foreign Office sought to determine if Don Alfonso's suggestions represented the policy of the King. Undersecretary Arthur Zimmermann asked the German representative at Brussels, von der Lancken, if the Spanish really were interested in some means of going to war against France. Hugo Kocherthaler relayed to Lancken that there was no evidence Spain really wanted to use such a devious method of getting into the war.[19] Indeed, there was no real desire to participate in the conflict. State Secretary von Jagow belittled the bizarre plans of Don Alfonso, remarking that he was the son of Princess Eulalia who was known for her eccentricities. Jagow did, however, indicate he wanted to hear directly from Ratibor about the King's view of the suggestions of Don Alfonso. The Ambassador to Madrid soon complied with Jagow's request for information through a report from the Military Attaché.[20]

King Alfonso discussed his cousin's advances with

Kalle on September 14, 1915. Alfonso said that his cousin had no commission to arrange any particular scheme with the Germans. The King did go on to say, however, that he felt there should be an opening of further discussions about Tangier, Morocco, Agadir, and Gibraltar. Kalle did not indicate his response to this suggestion. Ratibor relayed information about the interview Kalle had with King Alfonso, and the Ambassador seemed more interested in the propaganda the Spanish apparently wanted, especially the spectacular suggestions made by Don Alfonso about attempts to foment rebellion in the south of France.[21] Clearly, King Alfonso wanted to keep German promises alive, but the Germans did not go beyond their offers of October 1914 and August 1915.

The question of whether there was a formal alliance with the Germans is, therefore, difficult to answer. Contemporary news reports about the German offers of 1914 appeared intermittently until October 1915.[22] The diplomatic activity of Don Alfonso may also have been communicated to the western press in August and September of 1915.

There is some evidence that Alfonso trimmed his sails and eased back into the Entente orbit from September through October 1915. French newspapers had begun to criticize Madrid for alleged attempts to ally with Germany. Consequently in September Melquiades Alvarez went to France and held lengthy conversations with Theophile Delcassé. The Spanish Reformist Liberal leader emphasized Spanish interests in the Mediterranean, stressing his hope for an Entente victory.[23] The American Naval Attaché also took note of French pressure and the Spanish response.[24] Further, King Alfonso XIII told French Ambassador Geoffray that Spain yet desired a place at the peace conference at the end of the war. He sweetened the request by praising French military leadership, comparing General Joffre with Napoleon.[25] The King also hinted that the Entente might benefit from Spanish entrance into the war.[26] Evidently Alfonso wished to reassure the Allies that Spain had not secretly joined with Germany. Alfonso's comments to representatives of the Western Powers in September and October, therefore, indicate there was no formal alliance with Germany, indeed the Spanish economy was doing quite well without direct involvement in the conflict.

Economic benefits from the war had become quite lucrative. The British blockade of 1915 had cut off Germany and Austria-Hungary from trade with Spain, but exports to the Entente nations soared. The total balance of trade in 1914 was minus 154 million pesetas, but by 1915 the balance was plus 275 million pesetas. The advances for the remainder of the war were equally impressive.[27] The gold reserves of the bank of Spain doubled between 1914 and 1916; in 1914 the reserve had been 543 million pesetas, and by July 1916 it had risen to one billion thirty-two million pesetas.[28] Obviously, for the Germans, a need existed to counter this enormous economic advantage of the Allies.

Part of the means to counter the Allies lay in the German espionage and sabotage network, begun by the summer of 1915. Professor Doctor Philip Stein pointed out to the Foreign Office the significance of pyrite mining from the Rio Tinto mines in the Huelva district. He further noted the constant troubles between the workers and English ownership. The mine workers naturally leaned toward strikes and industrial sabotage; therefore, Germany should encourage further strikes and other work stoppages.[29] Ratibor, alert to this possibility, enthusiastically approved the idea, suggesting that at a cost of 700 to 800,000 pesetas per month he could hire satisfactory strikers who could tie up the mines for three months.[30] Embassy officials advocated the plan, and the Ambassador kept up a spate of telegrams urging a decision throughout July 1915, insisting that a decision must come soon as favorable conditions might rapidly disappear.[31]

But the War Ministry did not think much of attempts to foment strikes; the reason was that even a three month work stoppage would be virtually valueless as substantial supplies of sulphur and other materials were stored up. Instead, the transportation network should be destroyed. Strikes might be useful to create conditions under which attacks upon transportation services could be made without casting suspicion upon the Germans. Such destructions could be seen as natural results of workers taking their revenge upon the companies.[32]

Ratibor spent the next month determining the costs of beginning strikes and then destroying the rail network that carried the ore to ocean-going ships. He decided that it would be better to organize strikes among dock workers so as to prevent exports of the minerals to England; otherwise, suspicion undoubtedly would fall on the Germans.[33] The cost, however, would not be small, about one million pesetas, Ratibor reckoned.[34] The War Ministry accepted Ratibor's suggestion and gave 350,000 marks for the job, which they expected to be completed within one month.[35] Ratibor thereafter organized a special company, the Faehndrich Gesellschaft, to carry out the task. The company was to distribute the funds for the strikes.[36]

The work was not successful as Ratibor reported in early October. Management at the wharves worked men five days rather than the previous three, and further strikes would be much too costly. Workers were also better satisfied with their conditions and pay; therefore, possibilities of restricting mineral exports were dim.[37]

With the failure of the attempt to restrict exports of minerals, the War Ministry used a different approach. Money was advanced to Military Attaché Kalle for espionage in factories and export harbors.[38] Navy Attaché von Krohn also was given much of the money originally intended for the strikes on the wharves.[39] Throughout November and December 1915, the War Ministry supplied Kalle with explosives to sabotage Spanish factories, always with the proviso that the Embassy and its personnel should never be compromised. Kalle particularly wanted to destroy a factory making hand grenades, the Union Española Fabricas de Superfosfato in Sevilla and

Valencia. Factories in Portugal were also on his list.[40]

German activities were not, however, secret. German espionage was shaken by the discovery that their discussions to destroy Spanish transport were well known and were published by Lerroux's El Radical on December 17, 1915. The English newspaper, the Daily Mail, also published accounts of the proceedings. This was only one of several instances in which the German code and hence German activities were known to the English.[41]

The relatively smooth relations between Germany and Spain received a severe setback in December 1915. Prime Minister Eduardo Dato failed to control rampant inflation introduced by the war. Prices rose, and the laboring classes had few necessities. Dato could not deal with the situation and had to resign. Count Romanones then formed a new government at Alfonso's request.[42] The Count had been a member of the Cortes for over twenty years and had served as a member of the Municipal Council of Madrid, the Mayor of Madrid, the Minister of Public Instruction, Public Works, and had been Prime Minister until October 1913. He had a reputation for sharp business dealings and had amassed one of the largest fortunes in Spain. He also had considerable investments in France and in shipping companies trading with England. The American Ambassador Joseph Willard regarded him as an intelligent, adept politician, though unscrupulous. Willard adjudged the new Prime Minister as pro-Allied, though Romanones had reiterated the policy of strict neutrality.[43]

State Secretary von Jagow advised Ratibor to remain silent on the choice of Romanones as Prime Minister.[44] As the British and French had put great pressure upon Alfonso to appoint Romanones, whose pro-Entente leanings were well known, the King sent an emissary to Ratibor on December 9, 1915 to sound out the attitude of the Imperial Government toward Romanones.[45] Ratibor merely said he had no instructions on the question.[46]

Alfonso still wanted to assure the Germans that with Romanones at the helm Spain had no desire to enter the war. On December 10, 1915, the King's personal secretary explained to Ratibor that Dato had rejected a commission to form a new government, and other Conservatives such as Besada had turned down a similar offer. The Conservatives were in too great a disarray to form any new government. Alfonso then had no choice but to turn to Romanones. The King further assured the Germans that Romanones would be kept under control. As proof, Alfonso pointed out that Miguel Villanueva, a pro-German, was to be the Foreign Minister.[47]

The King's account of the circumstances surrounding the formation of a new government was quite correct, judging from U.S. Ambassador Joseph Willard's accounts. The American Ambassador said that Alfonso revised Romanones's list of cabinet members, hoping that the Count would object and refuse to form a government, thus leaving the path open for a Conservative coalition to return to power. The King feared complications if such a strong pro-Allied government came to power. Romanones, however, accepted the monarch's changes. But the inclusion of Miguel Villanueva to placate the Germans was not quite correct; Willard described him as a man of strong, independent will who desired Spain to remain aloof from the belligerents.[48] Villanueva was, therefore, often seen as being pro-German, but he was more truly pro-Spanish.

Ratibor was most skeptical of Alfonso's assurances. The Ambassador saw the beginning of the end for Spanish neutrality; Romanones undoubtedly would introduce benevolent neutrality for the Entente. Germany could now expect even greater quantities of contraband to be shipped across the Pyrenees to France.[49] By the end of December, Ratibor's messages became even more heated, suggesting that Germany had to act in the face of the threat contained in Romanones's appointment.[50] This comment presaged the attitude that Ratibor consistently exhibited toward Romanones. The reliability of Ratibor became definitely suspect when the Ambassador spoke of the Spanish Prime Minister. From this point onward, German-Spanish relations drifted apart.

During Romanones's tenure as Prime Minister, Alfonso XIII sought to restrain him and to regain control over foreign affairs. Indeed, the picture of foreign relations was complicated by an internal struggle between the King and Romanones as well as by an attempt by Alfonso to avoid open adherence to the Entente cause. The story, therefore, of German policy after December 1915 was one of concessions to deflect the influence of Romanones.

FOOTNOTES FOR CHAPTER IV

[1]Conde de Romanones, Las Responsibilidades políticas del antiguo regímen de 1875 a 1932 (Madrid: Renacimienta, n.d.), p. 81.

[2]Lema to Polo de Bernabé, no date, placed after October 5, 1914, Spain, Ministerio de Asuntos Exteriores, 73 Legation 3055 as quoted in Gelos, Neutralitaetspolitik Spaniens, p. 30.

[3]Ibid.

[4]Lema to Polo, October 14, 1914, Ibid.

[5]Polo to Lema, November 19, 1914, Ibid., pp. 31-32.

[6]Albert Mousset, "L'Espagne dans la Conflit Actuel," La Grand Revue (April 1915), p. 188. In an extremely well-written dissertation dealing with Spain and the League of Nations after the war, Gerie Bledsoe suggested there was a definite offer of an alliance in 1915. See Bledsoe, "Spain and the League of Nations," p. 4.

[7]Pingaud, Histoire Diplomatique, p. 24 and footnote 55.

[8]Ibid. More direct proof and corroboration of the French view of Pingaud is available in Russian documents translated into German and published in the thirties. See Budberg to Sasanov, January 19, 1915, M.M. Pokrovsky and Otto Hoetzsch, eds., Die internationalen Beziehungen im Zeitalter des Imperialisimus, Dokumente aus den Archiven der Zarischen und Provisorischen Regierung (Berlin, 1934), VI, 1st Halbband, p. 36 and p. 38. And see Sasanov to Budberg, April 14, 1915, Ibid., 2nd Halbband, in footnote 4.

[9]Pingaud, pp. 27-28 and footnote 56.

[10]Willard to Bryan, March 5, 1915, Willard Family Papers, Box 113, Manuscript Division, Library of Congress, Washington, D.C.

[11]Anonymous, "Tempting Spain," The Literary Digest (March 27, 1915), p. 680.

[12]Willard to Bryan, May 14, 1915, Willard Family Papers,

Box 113, Manuscript Division, Library of Congress, Washington, D.C.

[13] El Imparcial, April 30, 1915 and April 19, 1915.

[14] Ibid., March 16, 1915 and Pingaud, p. 25.

[15] Just, "Neutralitaet," p. 388 as taken from Burian, telegram to Hohenlohe, June 16, 1915, Haus-, Hof-, und Staatsarchiv PA rot 895.

[16] Kalle to General Headquarters, August 13, 1915, Spanien 61. secr. Die Beziehungen zwischen Spanien und Deutschland, T136/SA Reel 34/no frame number. Hereafter cited with the reel designation and then a frame number, if there was one. Also, the Germans sought to aid Spanish military preparations through munitions purchases in the U.S. These purchases, therefore, did double duty. They provided Spain with supplies and deprived the Allies of sources of supply in the United States. For this point see Franz von Papen, Memoirs, trans. by Brian Connell (New York: Dutton, 1953), pp. 39-40.

[17] Kalle Memorandum to Alfonso, September, 1915, Spanien 61. secr. Die Beziehungen, SA Reel 34/no frame number.

[18] Bethmann Hollweg to Madrid and to Lancken, August 29, 1915, Weltkrieg Nr. 11q. Aufwiegelungen, 268-269.

[19] Lancken to Foreign Office, August 29, 1915, Ibid., 272.

[20] Jagow to Treutler, September 3, 1915, Ibid., 274-275.

[21] Ratibor to Foreign Office, September 14, 1915, Ibid., 289.

[22] New York Times, October 15, 1915.

[23] García Venero, Melquiades Alvarez, pp. 287-288.

[24] Office of Naval Intelligence, September 27, 1915, 5766-C-10-C, Record Group 38, National Archives, Washington, D.C.

[25] Pingaud, p. 26.

[26] Ibid.

[27] Walter Soeffner, "Die Deutsch-Spanischen Handelsbeziehungen von 1871-1926," (Ph.D. dissertation, University of Leipzig, 1926), p. 90 as cited in Gelos, Neutralitaetspolitik Spaniens, pp. 88-90.

[28]Madariaga, pp. 322-323.

[29]Zentralstelle fuer Auslandsdienst to Langwerth, June 4, 1915, Weltkrieg Nr. 11q. secr. Unternehmungen und Aufwiegelungen in Spanien, T149/402/195.

[30]Ratibor to Foreign Office, June 20, 1915, Ibid., 225.

[31]Ratibor to Foreign Office, July 15, 1915, Ibid., 238.

[32]War Ministry to Foreign Office, July 20, 1915, Ibid., 247-248.

[33]Ratibor to Foreign Office, September 4, 1915, Ibid., 277.

[34]Ibid.

[35]War Ministry to Foreign Office, September 9, 1915, Ibid., 284.

[36]Ratibor to Foreign Office, September 19, 1915, Ibid., 295.

[37]Ratibor to Foreign Office, October 3, 1915, Ibid., 316.

[38]War Ministry to Foreign Office, October 19, 1915, Ibid., 321.

[39]War Ministry to Foreign Office, October 26, 1915, Ibid., 323.

[40]Kalle to Nadolny, November 27, 1915, Ibid., 337.

[41]War Ministry to Foreign Office, January 20, 1916, Ibid., 356.

[42]Manuel de J. Galvan, "Spain and the World War," The New York Times Current History (October 1917), p. 59.

[43]Willard to Lansing, December 9, 1915, Willard Family Papers, Box 113, Manuscript Division, Library of Congress, Washington, D.C. For a more colorful description of Romanones, see Ernest Boyd, "Cosas de España," Foreign Affairs (January 1926), p. 328. Boyd's depiction is as follows: "A small, lame man with a dislocated hip, ... a huge, crooked nose, on which are several warts, and a toothless mouth, he looks like a picture by Goya. Add to all that an amazingly brilliant mind, full of kindness and malice, and you have Conde de Romanones."

[44]Jagow to Ratibor, December 5, 1915, Spanien 57. Ministerien, 501.

[45]Ratibor to Foreign Office, December 8, 1915, Ibid., 511.

[46]Ratibor to Foreign Office, December 9, 1915, Ibid., 513.

[47]Ratibor to Foreign Office, December 10, 1915, Ibid., 515-516.

[48]Willard to Lansing, December 9, 1915, Willard Family Papers, Box 113, Manuscript Division, Library of Congress, Washington, D.C.

[49]Ibid.

[50]Ratibor to Foreign Office, December 31, 1915, Spanien 61. secr. Die Beziehungen, SA Reel 34/80.

CHAPTER V

GERMAN CONCESSIONS TO SPAIN

DECEMBER 1915 - SEPTEMBER 1916

By February 2, 1916, Minister of State Villanueva made an interesting suggestion to Ratibor, and the Ambassador discussed it with Alfonso. The proposal revolved around alleviation of severe shipping problems afflicting Spain as a result of the war. The Ambassador, following Villanueva, suggested that German ships interned in Spanish harbors might be turned to good use. These vessels might be transferred to Spain to ease the effects of the German blockade declared the previous February 1915. Ratibor suggested that the vessels could be used in the American trade to relieve Spanish shortages of coal. Ratibor was willing to accept the proposal because Villanueva said such an offer would strengthen his position with his colleagues on the ministerial council.[1] Clearly, the implication was that the German view could easily counter Romanones within the cabinet with such a generous offer.[2]

The reason for such keen concern over Spanish tonnage was the loss of ships occasioned by submarine attacks and the diversion of vessels to the carrying trade for the Entente and not for domestic needs. The lack of cotton and coal for Spain's industries was being felt most severely.[3] A Committee of the National Labor Association in Barcelona urged the government to seize interned German and Austrian ships to supply the deficiencies.[4] Apparently only twenty days' supply of coal was left for industry in manufacturing centers.[5] Indeed, in March 1916, newspaper opinion was quite specific: interned ships had to be used to save Spain from starvation and turmoil.[6] Public pressure was, therefore, quite enormous, and Villanueva had made a suggestion reflecting his patriotism and not just indicating a pro-German attitude.

In the meantime, however, the Spanish government had not given up its attempts to arrive at a closer understanding with the Entente and to obtain Tangier. Spanish Ambassadors in Paris and London brought up the question of the transfer of Tangier as the price for Spanish aid in the war, but the result was the same as before: rejection. Perhaps the Allies now hoped that losses on the high seas and diversions of tonnage to Entente use would lead to a rupture with Germany, and the West would have to give up nothing to have Spain as a benevolent neutral.[7] Yet Romanones made overtures to the British and French, and King Alfonso XIII tried to placate the Germans, partly to counter the effects of public opinion and partly to counter Romanones.

In February 1916, Alfonso made a remarkable suggestion to Kalle; he wanted Germany to send a special delegation to Spain by means of a submarine. He felt that such an act would make an enormous impression upon Spanish public opinion and would demonstrate German prowess in eluding the enemy. An additional remark revealed the true intent of the suggestion; he said, "Above all, I would like to see Romanones's face when he hears of it."[8]

The Germans needed no further explanations to see what was taking place. Romanones evidently was reflecting his earlier position. He wanted Spain to favor France and England to a greater extent, perhaps even to go to war on their side. The King's suggestion was intended as a means of impressing upon Romanones the tremendous admiration Spain had for Germany. A submarine visit to Spain under difficult circumstances would bring out this feeling. Yet another goal perhaps was in the King's mind when he picked up the thread of the conversation in late February 1916.

The King may have made the original suggestion for a transfer of German ships. In a lengthy conversation with Kalle, the King reiterated one of his favorite points. He said that Spain could never be free of England unless some means were found to cast off English fetters. He said turning over German ships to Spain would be an excellent way to do this. Alfonso hastened to guarantee personally that the ships would never be used for England's benefit. But Kalle was cautious, and the Military Attaché said that other, firmer guarantees would have to be made other than a verbal promise. Spain also would have to control more closely the contraband trade with France. In his private reports to Berlin, Kalle was much warmer than he had been with Alfonso. The Military Attaché emphasized that Alfonso was the one true friend Germany had in Spain. Acceptance of the King's suggestion would strengthen the monarch against Romanones.[9]

Domestic political events seemed to overshadow Alfonso's scheme. Villanueva left the cabinet and became president of the Chamber of Deputies. Romanones may have forced the apparent pro-German out of office so that the Prime Minister could conduct foreign affairs directly. Romanones thereafter assumed the portfolio of State Minister.

Alfonso represented the move as a surprise.[10] The Germans were suspicious, however, and Ratibor recommended that this latest event be used as an excuse to refuse Alfonso's request.[11] The Germans hoped to press for a forced reinstatement of Villanueva. Even Romanones personally assured Ratibor that Spain was yet determined to maintain neutrality, but the Germans remained quite skeptical.[12]

Alfonso may have participated in the removal of Villanueva, thereby creating a reason for the Germans to be less sanguine about Spain. But also Romanones could have taken the step to consolidate his government and to push for a pro-Entente neutrality. More than likely the King did not have a direct hand in the departure of Villanueva. Subsequent quarrels with Romanones and the King's desire for a neutrality that would not invite German retribution would argue for acceptance of Alfonso's argument that he was surprised at the change in Villanueva's position.

Following the receipt of the advice of both the Ambassador and the Military Attaché, State Secretary von Jagow dealt with both the veiled and direct suggestions of Alfonso. Jagow instructed Ratibor to say that Germany was willing to accede to a transfer of ships, but proof would be needed to assure that the vessels would not be seized by the English. Jagow wanted Ratibor to avoid a sharp tone, however, and to convey the subtle point that Germany was greatly concerned about Villanueva's dismissal.[13] Evidently, Alfonso might be induced to take a harsher attitude toward Romanones. Alfonso might thus get his ships if Romanones were controlled.

The very next day, the Spanish Ambassador to Berlin, Luis Polo de Bernabé, delivered a sharp note from Romanones's government. The Spanish insisted Germany immediately stop the sinking of Spanish ships and recognize the need of Spain for ship space.[14]

The Germans were convinced that Alfonso was playing a double game. He seemed to pretend to the Germans that he wanted to trim Romanones's power and to demonstrate his independence from the Entente, while at the same time he and Romanones may have been working together to get a transfer of German ships for Spanish use. The Germans also seemed to think that both Alfonso and Romanones were doing the bidding of the English and French.

The King and Romanones tried to correct this view. Alfonso discussed the dismissal of Villanueva further with Ratibor. The King insisted that the removal of the pro-German had been due to purely domestic causes. Romanones also vouched for that explanation.[15] In regard to Entente pressure, Alfonso privately showed Ratibor despatches from the Spanish Embassies in London and Paris. Both had expressed objections to Spain's assumption of German interests in Portugal, especially as Lisbon seemed on the verge of a rupture with the Central Powers. Alfonso said he hoped this would show how far Spain was willing to go to counter Entente desires and to aid Germany.[16]

Interestingly, the British deplored Portuguese entry into the war. Indeed, Winston Churchill regarded Spain of much greater value strategically and militarily than Portugal. But due to economic problems at Lisbon, England advanced credits part of which were conditional upon the Portuguese supplying ship space. The only source of such bottoms was the German vessels interned in her ports. All seventy-six alien vessels were requisitioned on February 24, 1916, and by March 9, 1916, the German Minister in Lisbon, Friedrich Rosen, was instructed by the Wilhelmstrasse to deliver an ultimatum, thus precipitating war. The British actually cared nothing for Portugal but only wanted her aid in the carrying trade.[17]

In the meantime, the question of the extent of cooperation between Alfonso and Romanones was not yet answered. In addition, Alfonso's assurances to the contrary notwithstanding, the Entente may have been behind the demand for ship transfers. Despite such suspicions, Ambassador

Ratibor argued that some sort of ship offer ought to be made to Spain. He reasoned that a transfer might have the salutary effect of maintaining a pro-German view within Spain. Though the exact genesis of the ship transfer request could not be ascertained, Ratibor felt that Alfonso really was trying to express his independence of France and England and was trying to counter Romanones.[18] Subsequent events proved that this assessment was correct. Meanwhile economic conditions inside Spain worsened and Alfonso became insistent upon some concessions from Germany.

Polo delivered a note to Berlin at the end of March 1916, detailing economic problems stemming from the loss of ship space. The King and Romanones insisted upon the transfer of German ships to Spain. The vessels would be used only on the Spanish-American trade routes and only Spanish products would be exported. Spain also promised to get England to respect these vessels on the high seas.[19] Jagow, however, was not impressed by the suggestions. He cited a Spanish financial journal which described Spanish maritime transport; apparently, Spain was carrying coal not only for herself but also for Italy. So in Jagow's view, Spanish ship bottoms were satisfactory for domestic needs.[20] Clearly, the Germans seemed unwilling to listen to their Ambassador and their Military Attaché. The Foreign Office did not desire to accede to Spanish demands.

Through the month of April several developments occurred, leading to a change in Germany's position. A series of sinkings of Spanish ships and the loss of life of several Spanish notables placed greater importance upon coming to terms. Later, King Alfonso engaged in several masterful strokes of personal diplomacy, negotiating directly with Kaiser William II. Thus, the Foreign Office was overruled by late April, and Germany sought actively to win Alfonso's support through spectacular concessions.

During the first week of April 1916, the Germans torpedoed the French channel steamer, Sussex. The eminent Spanish composer Enrique Granados and his wife were killed in the attack.[21] Two other Spanish vessels the Vigo and Santanderino were struck within the next several days.[22] Romanones asked the Americans for a joint protest against the sinkings. The Germans soon became aware of how seriously Alfonso regarded the sinkings and loss of life. Of course, the incidents also offered greater opportunities to persuade the Germans to accede to Alfonso's earlier request of ship transfers.

Ratibor telegraphed a report of the King's response to the sinkings. Apparently the monarch was greatly disturbed. The Ambassador reiterated his suggestion that ships should be transferred to calm the situation and to keep Alfonso on the German side.[23] In an interview with Kalle the King made a veiled threat that if satisfaction over the sinkings were not forthcoming, then a break in German-Spanish relations would be in the offing.

Back at the Wilhelmstrasse, Jagow began to give way.

He wanted a thorough investigation of the two Spanish ships sunk, but he did concede that Germany might offer to export coal through Dutch ports.[24] Ratibor was delighted at this apparent softening of Berlin's position. He proceeded to elaborate upon the suggestion, proposing that Germany give Spain one ship to import coal from Germany. The Ambassador hoped this would silence pro-Entente pressures inside Spain, particularly those pressures leading to demands for seizure of all German vessels.[25] Finally, on April 19, 1916, the Foreign Office authorized consideration of sending coal to Spain providing Great Britain and France would permit the vessels to enter Spanish harbors.[26]

At this juncture, Alfonso engaged in personal diplomacy with Kaiser William II. The Spanish King asked to speak with the former German minister to Portugal, Dr. Rosen, who was traveling through Madrid on his way back to Berlin. Since Portugal and Germany were at war, the meeting was a natural one as the King apparently wanted a report upon conditions inside Portugal. Besides, Alfonso had always had a special regard for Portugal since that nation had lost its monarchy and since the possibility of Iberian union was uppermost in his mind. But once the conversation began, it was obvious to Rosen that the meeting had another purpose.

The King ignored the Portuguese situation and launched into a lengthy discussion of German-Spanish relations. Evidently, Alfonso intended the suggestions he might make to be communicated to William. The King criticized Germany for failure to aid Spain in the prewar years, particularly as Spain needed industrial development assistance. Alfonso was clearly suggesting that he would welcome economic assistance after the war. Further, Alfonso asked Germany to stipulate precisely her requirements for peace so that he could transmit them to the Entente. Alfonso had fond hopes of being the peacemaker of Europe. Lastly, Alfonso returned to the subject of Spain's need for ship space, referring to the large number of German ships in Spanish harbors. Alfonso also asked Rosen to convey the monarch's full trust in Emperor William.[27]

Alfonso's hopes were well-founded. William read the report from Rosen and commented at length upon it in the margin. The Emperor said he could count on Alfonso to use any ships transferred solely for Spanish needs.[28] Thus, William now leaned toward a transfer of some vessels to Spain.

Alfonso turned to another tactic in Madrid. He suggested to Kalle that Romanones was subsidized with Entente gold and that the Prime Minister was intriguing with Spanish newspapers to arouse considerable popular passion over the sinking of the _Santanderino_. Furthermore, Alfonso admitted that Great Britain had put enormous pressure upon Spain to carry contraband in return for the British carrying coal to Spain.[29] The King thus played upon German suspicions and susceptibilities to get them to help him restrict Romanones's political power and to broaden Spanish carrying capacity, removing the possibility of English threats to Spanish economic life.

In view of these reports from Alfonso, reports placed in juxtaposition among the documentary evidence, one is forced to conclude that they represent the basic reason for a rather remarkable decision in Berlin on April 25, 1916. The documents do not reveal a discussion among the military and the Emperor on the question of appeasing Spain, but by April 25, 1916, the military informed the Foreign Office that a submarine would be sent to Spain and that the commander would carry a handwritten note from the Emperor.[30] The note was to deal with a favorable settlement of the ship question and with an assurance to Alfonso that he might play an important role in any future peacemaking effort.[31] The only discussions that took place on this issue revolved around whether it was a good idea to tell the King beforehand of the imminent arrival of a German submarine. Ultimately, the King was informed on May 3, 1916, and in the radio message the concessions were listed.[32] Clearly, the King was to be given support in his struggles against Romanones and the Entente.

The personal note of William's contained several concessions, though there were some notable _quid pro quos_ involved. William offered Spain ten ships to meet her immediate economic needs. William explained current German attempts to end the war, referring to the German note of December 9, 1915, wherein Germany announced that it was ready to discuss peace offers that permitted her to keep easily defended borders. The Emperor pointed out that the Entente had not recognized the reality of an impending German victory and so the war continued. In a one sentence statement William asked Alfonso to encourage the Entente to accept the German views of peace. William thus seemed to meet most of the requests Alfonso had been directing at Berlin since February.[33] But stringent conditions for the ship transfer were contained in a subsequent message to Polo in Berlin. The vessels were to be used between neutral ports only and never for any of Germany's enemies nor ever against Germany. The ships were to be returned to their owners after the war.[34]

Alfonso also negotiated with the Austrians in April 1916. But Vienna refused to consider transferring any of her twenty-four interned vessels to Spain. In this as in other matters, Berlin had acted without consulting Vienna, and on May 31, 1916, Vienna had to modify her position, offering Spain two Austrian ships in a gesture of support for Berlin's ardent wooing of Madrid.[35]

Alfonso responded favorably to the German notes, and in late May of 1916, the Germans saw their policy of concessions go into operation. In a speech from the throne Alfonso reiterated his previous commitment to neutrality toward all of the belligerents and his desire to maintain friendly relations with the Allied nations.[36] He also traded upon his newly found "power" to bring an end to the war. In a communication to U.S. Ambassador Joseph Willard, the King asserted he had greater influence with the Germans than President Wilson and proceeded to outline the unfavorable war situation of France and England. The thrust of his remarks was that he felt he should represent the Central Powers, while the U.S. represented the Entente in a new round of negotiations to get all sides to the peace table.[37] Alfonso, therefore, saw himself as the representative of the Germans and perhaps as a representative of the monarchial principle.

In the meantime, Germany sought to placate the Spaniards publicly and to set the stage for further cooperation with the King. On May 14, 1916, Germany apologized to Spain for the torpedoing of the Sussex and the loss of the famous Spanish composer, Enrique Granados.[38]

In addition, the Embassy at Madrid gave its unstinting aid to a representative of the local German colony, Engineer Alfred Helbig, to acquire options upon Spanish mines and control over the Spanish railway network.[39] Helbig used the resources of the Embassy to communicate his negotiations with various economic interests in Spain; but he was often countered by Julio Kocherthaler, the Foreign Office's informant about domestic conditions of Spain. Kocherthaler felt that extensive involvement in Spain's economy could not be enough to offset the Entente, consequently, he dampened enthusiasm in Berlin for Helbig's schemes. All Helbig could get in 1916 was a promise by the Krupp von Bohlen firm to take an option on iron ore mines around Almería.[40]

A plan also was afoot to issue a formal invitation for the King's cousin, Don Alfonso, to come to Germany. However, King Alfonso was known to be cool toward his relative's obvious ardent pro-German feelings; consequently, Ratibor urged caution.[41] The King was evidently displeased with such a suggestion, and a lengthy exchange of telegrams resulted in the Germans deciding to invite lesser pro-German figures to the Reich.[42] All of this was in preparation for the coup de grâce to be issued to the Allied Powers in the latter part of June. The general impression sought to be created was that Spain now belonged totally in the German camp. The visit of a German submarine to Cartegena harbor would demonstrate this conclusively.

The U-35, commanded by Lieutenant-Commander Arnauld de la Periere, arrived at Cartagena in the early morning of June 21, 1916. Contemporary opinion saw the visit as a sign that Alfonso was initiating new peace moves with the Kaiser.[43] Also, contemporary Spanish papers expressed skepticism over the alleged use of a special submarine to convey thanks to Alfonso for kind treatment of German refugees from the Imperial colony of the Cameroon, the official reason for the visit.[44]

Perhaps the true purpose of the submarine visit can be deduced from a telegram Ratibor sent the Foreign Office soon thereafter. Ratibor reported that the visit surpassed the highest expectations in impressing Spanish public opinion. The pro-German press was described as ecstatic and the anti-German papers were forced to take full notice of Alfonso's welcome for the German warship.[45] The other purpose of satisfying Alfonso by demonstrating to Romanones the strong pro-German feelings of Spain also seemed to be accomplished. Ratibor reported to Berlin that the King was highly pleased and that he sent his "warmest" thanks to William.[46]

The effect of underscoring Spanish pro-German feeling was perhaps too pronounced as the Entente lost no time in protesting the visit. Germany learned of a strong protest note from England to Spain as early as July 3, 1916. The Spanish replied evasively, and the Germans believed that the British might soon introduce a blockade against Spanish ports.[47] A few days later, Ratibor learned through the Minister of Justice that the British threatened to occupy Spanish harbors if Spain did not protest to Germany that the U-35 visit was a violation of Spanish neutrality. This trusted informant also intimated that the British would instigate strikes and strike threats to make the Spanish more tractable in coming around to British terms.[48] This pressure seemed to have effect when on July 15, 1916, Alfonso personally asked that no more U-boats be sent to Spain. He gave as his reason a desire to avoid conflict with the belligerent powers.[49]

Internal communications with the Foreign Office in Berlin indicated that the Germans at first reacted harshly, declaring that they would support Spain in the event of a British attempt to close Spanish harbors or to blockade them.[50] Ratibor in the meantime became belligerent, arguing that more U-boats should be sent in order to force Spain to a decision and perhaps bring Spain into the war on the side of the Central Powers.[51] But even Ratibor really did not believe that a break would occur between Spain and England. The best that Germany could hope for was to force Spain to make a public rejection of British demands, thus driving Romanones away from the Entente camp.[52]

Von Jagow soon authorized Ratibor to tell Alfonso that Germany would send no more U-boats, thus calming the Entente. At the same time Germany stood ready to defend the coastal regions of Spain if events should so require.[53] This statement seemed to give some backbone to the Spanish reply to Britain.

The Germans learned from the Minister of Justice that Spain told Great Britain that the visit of the U-35 was in accord with the duty of neutrals and that not all U-boats were warships.[54] But the Spanish only appeared to be within the German camp. This was to be the beginning of a major crisis in German-Spanish relations as the Entente put pressure upon Spain until the fall of 1916, when Germany was driven to the brink of breaking relations with Spain.

The remainder of the summer of 1916 presented the Germans with additional evidence of a slow but certain drift of Spain toward the Allies. Intensified Entente propaganda and commercial regulations unfavorable to the Central Powers culminated by September in a campaign by Count Romanones to force Germany to break relations, thus accomplishing the Prime Minister's goal of putting the entire Iberian peninsula within the Entente camp.

On July 27, 1916, the Cortes passed a law stating

that ships could not be sold unless the Spanish government gave its consent. Furthermore, foreign capital investment could not amount to more than 25 percent of the total of a ship firm's capital. Specific names of stockholders were now required rather than simply a generalized statement of the holders of shares in ship firms.[55] Clearly, Spain attempted to demonstrate to the Entente a desire to control the ship transport business in order to make it easier for the British to ferret out pro-German firms. In this way, the war increased the Spanish government's control over business and industry and later facilitated a strict accounting of the movements and cargoes in Spanish bottoms.

In early August 1916, Ratibor began a series of reports upon rising anti-German comments in Spanish newspapers.[56] Ratibor felt that such press campaigns had the approval of the Spanish government, and he urged a strong note from Berlin protesting the new development.[57] But the Foreign Office preferred to use a more subdued approach that seemed to have worked earlier. Jagow replied to Ratibor that there would be no formal note; rather, the Military Attaché should approach the King and "use aristocratic feeling and appeal to the Spanish people."[58]

Ratibor was not put off so easily. He reported a conversation he had with Romanones who communicated intense pressure from the French Ambassador to Madrid and through the Spanish Ambassador to Paris to restrict German propaganda and to permit activities by the French. The French apparently also wanted Romanones to put similar pressure upon Polo in Berlin to restrict German propaganda. Consequently, Ratibor renewed his suggestion in a strong note that demanded restriction of slanderous attacks upon the Kaiser in brochures coming from France and England.[59]

Alfonso, in the meantime, rejected the Military Attaché's attempts to use friendly persuasion. Alfonso said he could not control anti-German comments in the Spanish press; indeed, the Germans had to recognize unique Spanish means of expression and thought.[60] At the same time, Alfonso accepted any German military help that might be proffered in the event of an attack by the Entente powers.[61]

In the interim, a German commercial submarine, the Deutschland, had planned to sail to Spain, but Allied pressures forced the Spanish to request that the vessel not appear in Spanish waters. The Germans acquiesed in order to give the Spanish some leeway in dealing with the British and French. On August 8, 1916, the Deutschland was ordered to avoid northern Spanish harbors on its voyage back to Europe from America.[62]

Despite German attempts to ease Spanish replies to the Entente, evidence was mounting that Romanones planned to end friendship with Germany. While he wanted no direct alliance with the Entente, he did actively seek benevolent neutrality toward the Allies. Romanones began consultations with Ambassadors from France, Italy, and Portugal on the eve of Portuguese entrance into the war.[63] In his memoirs

Romanones recalled a visit in August 1916 from Jules Cambon who urged the Spanish to break relations with Germany.[64] The British even joined in this pressure, perhaps suggesting Spain enter the war as a belligerent.[65] The French, however, were more insistent, sending their Minister for Foreign Affairs Pichon to talk with both Romanones and Alfonso about entering the war.[66] The details of these meetings are not available, but Romanones said in his memoirs that in a council meeting of August 23, 1916, the Spanish discussed a sharp Allied note objecting to "unneutral" activity in Spain, especially the visit of the U-35. The pressure to force a break with Germany had begun.

In reviewing the events from July through August 1916, one cannot help but conclude that the Entente was determined to turn Spain completely away from the Central Powers. Possibly the Allies put pressure upon Romanones and Alfonso to get a declaration of benevolent neutrality. Romanones was perhaps willing to do so as he stated in his memoirs that he urged the cabinet on August 23, 1916 to assist the Entente. But Romanones's account of the proceedings in August is suspect. He also related that Alfonso had told the Count to proceed as he saw fit to "preserve the interests of the country."[67] The King would hardly give his Prime Minister carte blanche in a matter as grave as this. But the pressure from the West was great and Alfonso may have decided to bide his time.

Perhaps the King may have decided to let Romanones

pursue his inclinations, hoping that divided political sentiment in Spain would eventually correct any precipitous involvement in the war. Then too the war was undermining conservative power that supported the monarchy; there were more demands to abandon the corrupt political system and to permit the urban working class to participate in the political process. Perhaps the shift of initiative in foreign affairs from Alfonso to Romanones was a symptom of the decline of royal power.

On August 27, 1916 the Reformist Republican Party leader, Melquiades Alvarez, went to Lisbon at the head of a commission to express approval of Portugal's declaration of war against the Central Powers. This party also was reported campaigning for closer relations now between Spain and the Entente.[68] Ratibor reported a few days later that Spanish censorship was ruthlessly pruning German news sources. The Ambassador saw hints that Romanones was gaining an impressive hold over the King. Alfonso now spoke of the "natural victory of the Allies."[69] Allied journalists, politicians, and academicians poured into Spain. Entrance of cartons of pro-Allied propaganda material was accepted and distribution was aided by the Spanish government.

In this report, Ratibor began what was to become his basic argument through the succeeding months. He suggested that means had to be found to publicize the offer of ten ships to Spain made in the U-35 visit to Cartagena earlier in June. This seemed to him one of the few effective ways to counter

Allied influence in light of apparently anti-German comments by Antonio Maura, the leader of the Conservative Party which was supposedly pro-German. The Spanish party structure was too confused with leadership quarrels to be of much assistance at this juncture.[70]

The strong pro-Allied stance of the Spanish government was visible in the handling of British demands to declare all U-boats warships. The Spanish reply rejected the need for such a declaration, however, with the July 1916 decree and with subsequent requests to the Germans not to send any more submarines to Spain, Romanones in effect carried out British desires.[71]

In a conversation with Kalle on August 31, 1916, King Alfonso, who up to this point had seemed to be staunchly pro-German, began to take an Entente position. Alfonso intimated that the apparent pro-Allied stance of the Romanones cabinet was due to the military and diplomatic developments of the summer of 1916, but if things did not get worse on the battlefield, then there would be no real abandonment of neutrality. Despite Alfonso's transparent attempt to placate the Germans, Kalle got the impression that the King now viewed the war as unfavorable for Germany.[72]

The change in Alfonso's attitude closely paralleled military events in Central Europe. Rumania signed the secret Treaty of Bucharest on August 17, 1916, and came into the war on the Entente side. The outcome was not totally clear until December 1916, when Rumania suffered complete defeat at the hands of Germany and Austria-Hungary. But in the summer of 1916, Germany simply appeared to have recently gained two extra enemies, Portugal and Rumania. These facts along with a renewed Russian effort on the Eastern front seemed to presage evil days for the Central Powers.[73]

Meanwhile, from January 1915 through the summer of 1916, German espionage expanded. The documents are replete with code names and descriptions of devices meant for use in France and Spain. No clear, coherent story emerges from this list of names and boxes of German "pencils" and "milk testers," codewords for explosives, but one spy, named Arnold (the name probably was only a password), figured prominently in the exchange of wireless messages. He was the master spy and saboteur in Spain. He directed manufacture of bombs, destroyed Portuguese military factories and depots, and directed attacks upon French hydroelectric plants across the border and upon French rail lines. He also was to halt Spanish iron ore transport out of Bilbao, Santander, Cartagena, Huelva, Algiers and Tunis.[74]

German consideration of Spanish feelings was evident in sabotage activity. Arnold wanted permission to attack Spanish ore ships, but the War Ministry gave its approval only if the vessels sailed under "false" flags, and attacks had to be outside Spanish territorial waters.[75] After organizing the German espionage and sabotage units in Spain and Portugal, Arnold traveled to Latin America, especially Buenos Aires, Argentina, to deposit large sums for further

German espionage work throughout Latin America.[76] Arnold continued his travels, eventually going to Havana, Cuba.[77] Though the documents do not say so in so many words, it is evident that the Germans sought contacts with Latin America and the U.S.A.; these contacts provided means of sending supplies to the sabotage units in Spain and communication with German Embassies and ministries in North and South America cut off from the continent of Europe by the British blockade.

The political story from September 1916 to April 1917 is one of repeated attempts by Romanones to force a break in relations between Germany and Spain, though not a declaration of war, and attempts by Ratibor and the Foreign Office to forestall such a development. For the most part the story is one of German success, inasmuch as Romanones was eventually forced out of office, at least partially through the propaganda activities of the Germans and through the diplomatic efforts of the Foreign Office.

Several significant conclusions may be drawn from the conduct of Germany policy toward Spain from 1914 through August 1916. The first was the obvious attempt to appease segments of Spanish opinion. The relatively insignificant Ferrer Affair, at least insignificant from the German standpoint, took several weeks of German effort. No one in the world apparently was fooled by the claim that a band of provocateurs had thrown acid on the Brussels statue of Francisco Ferrer. German occupation troops in Belgium were exceptionally efficient, and such an attack would quickly have been put to rest. Clearly, the Germans desired to maintain the split in Spanish opinion and to keep all of the support they could from the conservative, traditionalist elements.

Too, the German Foreign Office recognized the influence of Alfonso in providing continuity and direction in Spanish foreign affairs. The Germans were aware of the prewar attempts by Alfonso to get control over North Africa and Gibraltar. Consequently, they promised to aid Spain diplomatically and economically in the future. What is of greater moment, however, was the recognition that Alfonso did not desire any direct participation in the war. Only a silent position, not even benevolent neutrality, was asked by Ratibor as early as October 1914 and reiterated in August 1915 by the Military Attaché. This recognition of Alfonso's desire for Spain to play a passive role in the actual fighting was a consistent feature of German policy.

German motives in the Cartegena Affair of June 1916 were not so easily discernable. One obvious result was a closer relation with Alfonso. The King could counter the strenuous efforts of Romanones to push Spain toward a benevolent neutrality for the Entente. But in another sense, Germany sought to gain a propaganda victory with its spectacular submarine visit. In this and future developments inside of Spain, German actions and promises may not have been entirely sincere. The excitement of public opinion was probably a more significant goal than actual aid to the Spanish. For example, Germany hardly saw Alfonso as a real negotiating agent for the Central Powers as they gave him to understand in the summer of 1916. Furthermore, any actual transfer of German ships under the rather stringent terms set would have been next to an impossibility. Consequently, German policy became clearer. The Foreign Office was more concerned with appearances and with propaganda than with any substantive aid to Spain. The task was one of a delaying tactic. The more promises one could make, the later one could postpone Spain's entry on the Entente side as Italy had done in May 1915.

Clearly, the concessions Berlin had made to Alfonso in the spring and summer of 1916 had only succeeded in evoking a harsh Entente response. After the submarine visit to Cartagena, the British and French took a renewed interest in Madrid, and the Spanish King soon realized that his Prime Minister had powerful friends in London and Paris. Thereafter, German-Spanish relations took a decided turn for the worse, and it required all of Berlin's skills to avoid a break with Spain.

FOOTNOTES FOR CHAPTER V

[1]Ratibor to Foreign Office, February 2, 1916, Spanien 55. Kronpraetendant Don Carlos und Seine Familie, T149/356/14-15. Hereafter cited as Spanien 55. Kronpraetendant, followed by the frame number.

[2]Just, "Neutralitaet," p. 373, taken from Fuerstenberg telegram of January 25, 1916, Haus-, Hof-. und Staatsarchiv, PA rot 895 Krieg 7, und Fuerstenberg telegram of March 15, 1916, Haus-, Hof, und Staatsarchiv rot 895.

[3]Spain, Instituto de Reformas Sociales, Seccion Segundo, Informes de los Inspectores del Trabajo sobre la Influencia de la Guerra Europea en las Industrias Españoles, 1912-1918, Tomo Primero (Madrid: Imp. de la Sucesora de Minnesa de los Rios, 1918), pp. 17-24.

[4]Great Britain, Series 1, Daily Foreign Press Review January-February 1916, January 19, 1916 (London: H.M. Stationery Office, 1916), no page numbers.

[5]El Mundo, January 22, 1916.

[6]Ibid., March 22, 1916.

[7]Pingaud, Histoire Diplomatique, pp. 28-29.

[8]The exact quote is, "Ich moechte vor allem das Gesicht von Romanones dabei sehen." Kalle to General Headquarters, February 12, 1916, Spanien 61. secr. Die Beziehungen, SA Reel 34/84.

[9]Ratibor to Foreign Office, February 25, 1916, Spanien 61. Die Politischen Beziehungen, 357/27-28.

[10]Kalle to General Headquarters, February 27, 1916, Ibid., 357/34.

[11]Ratibor to Foreign Office, February 27, 1916, Ibid., 357/35-36.

[12]Ratibor to Foreign Office, February 29, 1916, Ibid., 357/40.

[13]Jagow to Ratibor, March 1, 1916, Ibid., 357/38-39.

[14]Polo to Jagow, March 2, 1916, Ibid., 357/44.

[15]Ratibor to Foreign Office, March 7, 1916, Ibid., 357/51.

[16]Ratibor to Foreign Office, March 12, 1916, Ibid., 357/60.

[17]John Vincent-Smith, "Britain, Portugal and the First World War, 1914-1916," European Studies Review, IV (1974), p. 235 and footnote on p. 232. For the British attitude toward Portugal and the value of Spain in comparison with Portugal, see Churchill to Grey and Asquith, August 3, 1914, in Martin Gilbert, ed., Winston Churchill, Companion Volume III, Part 1 (August 1914-April 1915), (Boston: Houghton-Mifflin, 1973), pp. 13-14 and Cornelia, Lady Wimborne to King Alphonso XIII of Spain, January 17, 1915, Ibid., p. 424.

[18]Ratibor to Foreign Office, March 12, 1916, Spanien 61. Die Politischen Beziehungen, 357/60.

[19]Polo to Jagow, March 31, 1916, Ibid., 357/68.

[20]Jagow to Polo, April 6, 1916, Ibid., 357/82-84.

[21]New York Times, April 6, 1916.

[22]Ibid., April 7, 1916. In addition see Willard to Lansing, April 12, 1916, U.S. Foreign Relations, 1916 Supplement, The World War, p. 229.

[23]Ratibor to Foreign Office, April 13, 1916, Spanien 61. Die Politischen Beziehungen, 357/87.

[24]Jagow to Ratibor, April 15, 1916, Ibid., 357/92.

[25]Ratibor to Foreign Office, April 18, 1916, Ibid., 357/93.

[26]Johannes to Ratibor, April 19, 1916, Ibid., 357/89.

[27]Rosen to Bethmann Hollweg, April 20, 1916, Spanien 61. secr. Die Beziehungen, SA Reel 34/90-99.

[28]Ibid.

[29]Kalle to Foreign Office, April 21, 1916, Ibid., SA Reel 34/100.

[30]Treutler to Foreign Office, April 25, 1916, Ibid., SA Reel 34/104-105.

[31]Treutler to Foreign Office, April 26, 1916, Ibid.,

SA Reel 34/107.

[32]William to Alfonso, May 3, 1916, Ibid., SA Reel 34/ 119-120. The fact that the message was sent by wireless was of significance. The Allies were able to decipher all German radio messages since the British had broken Berlin's code as early as 1915. See Barbara Tuchman, The Zimmermann Telegram (New York: Bantam, 1971), p. 19. Later in 1918 the negotiations between Germany and Spain over the disposition of German ships in Spanish harbors were followed avidly and in detail by France and Great Britain as shown by the documents used by Louis Guichard in his book The Naval Blockade 1914-1918, trans. and ed. by Christopher R. Turner (New York: Appleton, 1930), esp. pp. 246-251.

[33]Jagow to Polo, May 9, 1916, Spanien 61. Die Politischen Beziehungen, 357/108-111.

[34]Ibid.

[35]Just, "Neutralitaet," p. 384, taken from a telegram of Ugron to Hohenlohe of April 1, 1916, Haus-, Hof-, und Staatsarchiv, PA rot 895 and pp. 385-386, Foreign Ministry to War Ministry, May 31, 1916, WK AOK 26205.

[36]Ratibor to Foreign Office, May 11, 1916, Spanien 61. Die Politischen Beziehungen, 357/117.

[37]Willard to Lansing, May 11, 1916, U.S. Foreign Relations, 1916 Supplement, pp. 28-29. See in addition a more complete quote from the State Department decimal files in Shirley Jackson's "The United States and Spain, 1898-1918," (Ph.D. dissertation, Florida State University, 1967), p. 164.

[38]New York Times, May 15, 1916.

[39]Jagow to Gruenau, May 4, 1916, Spanien 61. secr. Die Beziehungen zwischen Spanien und Deutschland, T136/34/127-128.

[40]Grusonwerk to Alfred Helbig, June 9, 1916, Spanien 61. Die Politischen Beziehungen, 357/148.

[41]Ratibor to Foreign Office, May 12, 1918, Spanien 55. Das Spanische Koenigshaus, 721.

[42]Jagow to Ratibor, June 9, 1916, Spanien 61. Die Politischen Beziehungen, 357/136.

[43]New York Times, June 23, 1916.

[44]Ibid., June 24, 1916,

[45]Ratibor to Foreign Office, June 24, 1916, Spanien

61. secr. Die Beziehungen, SA Reel 34/151.

[46]Ratibor to Foreign Office, June 25, 1916, Ibid., SA Reel 34/155.

[47]Ratibor to Foreign Office, July 3, 1916, Ibid., SA Reel 34/162-163.

[48]Ratibor to Foreign Office, July 14, 1916, Ibid., SA Reel 34/165.

[49]Kalle to Foreign Office, July 15, 1916, Ibid., SA Reel 34/168.

[50]Jagow to Gruenau, July 16, 1916, Ibid., SA Reel 34/166.

[51]Ratibor to Foreign Office, July 16, 1916, Ibid., SA Reel 34/172-173.

[52]Ibid.

[53]Jagow to Ratibor, July 19, 1917, Ibid., SA Reel 34/176.

[54]Ratibor to Foreign Office, July 26, 1916, Ibid., SA Reel 34/205.

[55]Ratibor to Foreign Office, July 27, 1916, Spanien 61. Die Politischen Beziehungen, 357/180.

[56]Ratibor to Foreign Office, August 2, 1916, Ibid., 357/192.

[57]Ibid.

[58]Jagow to Ratibor, August 5, 1916, Ibid., 357/192-193.

[59]Ratibor to Foreign Office, August 6, 1916, Ibid., 357/199.

[60]Kalle to Foreign Office, August 9, 1916, Spanien 61. secr. Die Beziehungen, SA Reel 34/212.

[61]Ibid.

[62]Deutsche Ozean Rheederei, GmbH to Foreign Office, August 8, 1916, Ibid., SA Reel 34/211.

[63]New York Times, August 16, 1916.

[64]Romanones, Notas de Una Vida in Obras Completas, pp. 349-350.

[65]José Pijoan, "Spain Before, During, and After the War," _19th Century_ IX (October 1921), #536, p. 667.

[66]Ibid.

[67]Romanones, _Obras Completas_, p. 355.

[68]Ibid., on August 27, 1916, p. 7.

[69]Ratibor to Foreign Office, August 20, 1916, Spanien 61. _secr. Die Beziehungen_, SA Reel 35/237-239.

[70]Ibid.

[71]Ratibor to Foreign Office, August 20, 1916, Ibid., SA Reel 35/234.

[72]Kalle to Foreign Office, August 31, 1916, Ibid., SA Reel 35/3.

[73]See Ernest May, "Diplomatic History of World War I," in Vincent J. Esposito, ed., _A Concise History of World War I_ (New York: Praeger, 1964), pp. 275-276. See also A.J.P. Taylor, _The Struggle for the Mastery of Europe_ (Oxford: Clarendon, 1954), pp. 550-551.

[74]Nadolny to Kalle, May 29, 1916, Weltkrieg Nr. 11q. _Aufwiegelungen_, T149/402/378.

[75]Nadolny to Kalle, June 19, 1916, Ibid., 384.

[76]Huelson to Gesandter Buenas Aires, August 4, 1916, Ibid., 406.

[77]Ratibor to Foreign Office, August 15, 1916, Ibid., 409.

CHAPTER VI

GERMAN-SPANISH TENSION

SEPTEMBER 1916 - APRIL 1917

From September 1916 through April 1917, Spanish-German relations went through two crises. One lasted from September to November 1916 and the other began in late December 1916 and reached its culmination in April 1917. Both crises stemmed from Allied pressure upon Spain to break relations with Germany and from Count Romanones's desire to put Spain solidly into the Entente camp. King Alfonso, aided by the Germans, however, successfully avoided a clear, pro-Allied position. The first crisis began in September 1916 with intensified Allied pressure on Spain, followed by a frantic German campaign, led by Ratibor, to get rid of Romanones. In addition, the Foreign Office sought to placate Spain through offers of economic aid and safe-conduct passes for Spanish fruit ships through the forbidden zone around the British Isles. Unofficially, the Foreign Office attempted to get the Admiralty to treat Spanish ships with great care, indeed, to avoid any torpedoings so as not to give Romanones an excuse to convince Alfonso of the need for a break in relations with Germany. Through another channel, that of the Military Attaché von Kalle, Germany also sought to regain

Alfonso's confidence by providing him with reports of German war progress, proving that Germany was winning. For the most part, all of these efforts were successful, and by November 1916 German-Spanish relations were slightly warmer than in September and October.

Ratibor learned through Niceto Alcalá Zamora, a rightist Liberal and later Minister of Public Works, that the Spanish held a special ministerial council meeting on September 6, 1916. The meeting was in response to an Entente note delivered around the fifth of September. England apparently sought to force Spain on the Entente side. The Austrians learned of what appeared to be an Entente offer of Tangier to Spain if the latter came into the war on the Allied side. Prince Fuerstenberg, the Austrian Ambassador in Madrid, reported Spain was tempted by the offer; he also indicated Spain would have to make several unspecified concessions to Entente demands to take advantage of the proposal.[1] There was some truth to these suspicions; in conversations with the English, French President Raymond Poincaré learned that the British were seriously considering ceding Tangier to Spain.[2]

The Entente demanded that Spain seize all German ships in Spanish harbors.[3] Ratibor further learned that in the council meeting Romanones planned to complain to Germany about ship losses in the submarine warfare to meet the renewed Entente pressure.[4] Alcalá Zamora related also that in the meeting Romanones tried to convince the participants that the best future policy for Spain would be to try to force Germany to break relations. Romanones himself did not want a declaration of war against Germany, but merely a break. He apparently feared that Spain would soon become like Greece, in the process of eventually coming under total Entente control. The general course could only be to ignore German protests about Spanish attitudes and actions, thereby hoping to provoke German action. Alcalá Zamora, however, did relate that several council members still opposed intervention in the war.[5] Ratibor hoped to cut off the line of attack that Romanones suggested using. The German Ambassador repeated his suggestion of publicizing the offer of ten ships made earlier during the Cartagena visit of June 1916.[6]

Further reports poured into Berlin detailing the drive in Spain to force a break in relations. When Rumania declared war on Germany in August 1916, several policymakers within Spanish political circles began to feel that Germany was on the verge of losing the war; particularly in view of the Portuguese declaration of war on Germany in March 1916.[7] Kalle, usually a reliable guide to Spanish affairs as he seemed to have cooler judgment than Ratibor, wrote that Romanones had definitely reoriented his policy toward the Allies. Alfonso seemed genuinely concerned about the military situation and desired German military information. Kalle adjudged the political situation as quite serious.[8] In addition, Ratibor excitedly reported that Spain seemed to respond in a positive way to renewed British demands that even commercial submarines be viewed as warships (although he was unaware that the Imperial Government had earlier told Spain via Polo that there would be no commercial submarines sent to Spain).[9] Clearly, the rather cozy relationship of German Embassy personnel with the Spanish government was coming to an end.

On September 8, 1916, Ratibor proposed a list of actions that the German government might use to counter Allied pressures. This list provided basic lines of German policy through November 1916, proposals that turned out successfully. Ratibor suggested publication of the previous offer of German ships to ease the shortage of Spanish coal-carrying bottoms, the publication also of offers of German coal via Dutch harbors with Allied consent, the sparing of Spanish ships in the immediate future, and finally official reports about the military situation to reassure Alfonso of ultimate German victory.[10]

In the meantime, Kalle had another interview with Alfonso. The King stated that he rejected energetically all Entente suggestions that Spain unilaterally seize German ships for those sunk by the Germans. Alfonso, indeed, sought to smooth out the apparent change in policy by emphasizing the enormous Allied pressure imposed upon Spain. Alfonso then referred to the economic position of Spain and his country's need for Allied economic concessions.[11] Alfonso hinted also about pressures from France about Spanish Morocco.[12]

Alfonso, walking a tightrope between the Germans on the one side and Romanones and the Allies on the other, had only reluctantly chosen Count Romanones as Prime Minister in 1915, and as the subsequent events in 1916 demonstrated, Alfonso desired to show Romanones that the King's policy of neutrality and ostensible friendship toward the Germans would be followed. Unfortunately for the King, the pressure of the Allies and their desire to use Romanones to force Spain to a break with Germany directly challenged not only Alfonso's policy but also his power.

Another factor complicated the picture. This was the position of Antonio Maura, who desired to take advantage of the Allied pressure now expended upon both Alfonso and Romanones. The Germans thought that Great Britain had tried to win Maura to their side by promising help in elevating him to the post of Prime Minister. In light of the apparent failure of French propaganda to turn Spain toward the Allied camp, British attention should naturally focus upon Maura, who had been a conservative in his early career but a "Maurista" by 1916; he sought a kind of dictatorship that would have challenged Alfonso XIII. The Germans did not have to wait long for proof of an apparent change in Maura from a pro-German to an apparent pro-Allied position.[13]

Indeed, Maura delivered a speech on September 12, 1916 insisting that Spain could no longer remain isolationist; and since France and England had not been hostile to Spain, they were the logical partners to aid Spain's future development.[14]

In light of the fact that almost all of Maura's followers had heretofore been pro-German, apparently out of opposition to Romanones's pro-Allied stance, the Germans were initially puzzled and outraged. But the gist of Maura's position was clear. He too had swung toward the Entente and was advocating a benevolent neutrality toward them.

The Marquis of Villalobar in Brussels suggested an explanation for Maura's action. The Marquis saw Maura as the King's pawn. Perhaps Maura delivered his speech in order to frighten Romanones about Maura's ambitions and possibilities for the future. Thus, the King could in the future turn to Maura as a replacement for Romanones; one which would please the Allies but yet be more manageable than Romanones, and because of Maura's previous pro-German position could be acceptable to the Germans as well.[15] State Secretary von Jagow, however, saw the speech as the result of a decision at a meeting held a few days before among Alfonso, Romanones, and Maura.[16]

Villalobar later offered yet another explanation of Maura's apparent change of position, the explanation that Jagow thought was accurate. In light of the démarche from Great Britain about excessive pro-German feeling within Spain, the King, Romanones, and Maura discussed the matter. Villalobar felt that the King may have asked Maura to deliver the speech as a sign to the Entente of pro-Allied feelings; thereby taking the sting out of Entente complaints.[17] Subsequently, in the light of further communications from the minister at Bern, the Germans convinced themselves they should not be too surprised at Maura's comments. Schubert at Bern reported that the speech referred primarily to conditions in peacetime and that Maura was merely pointing out the plain geographic facts of Spanish life. To Schubert Maura's speech simply meant that in view of Spain's geographical position, she could not possibly side with Germany, as England and France certainly would prevail in a contest of arms.[18] Thus the Germans talked themselves out of taking Maura's change very seriously.

In the midst of the rapid developments from September 6-12, 1916, Ratibor and Kalle insisted that Romanones would force Spain to go to war against Germany. Ratibor had asked for authority to do all he could to remove Romanones as early as September 9, 1918.[19] Ratibor particularly was convinced that Romanones intended to lead Spain into the Allied camp at all costs. Jagow too suspected that the example of Rumanian Prime Minister Bratianus was too much for Romanones and that the Spanish Prime Minister sought to copy the Rumanian tactic and enter the war on the Allied side. Jagow asked for Villalobar's assessment of Romanones's intentions.[20]

Reports from Villalobar and the Austrian Ambassador Fuerstenberg in Madrid agreed that Romanones was at the very least quite dangerous and at the most the major obstacle between Spain and Germany.[21] Jagow at first followed the panic-stricken suggestions of Ratibor that the Ambassador be empowered to do all that was necessary to cause the fall of Romanones's cabinet.[22] But later, due to pleas from both Kalle and Villalobar, Jagow backed off and suggested less threatening approaches to the possible removal of the Spanish Prime Minister. Specifically, Jagow suggested certain individuals might influence the Queen Mother, a Habsburg Princess, to advocate his removal. By September 15, 1916, Jagow suggested that the Embassy should not appear to mix into domestic Spanish affairs and that a subtle approach was necessary.[23] But the division between the military leadership and the civilian intervened as German Quartermaster General and virtual dictator, Erich Ludendorff, insisted upon the use of more funds to empower Ratibor to bring Romanones down.[24]

In light of subsequent events in the spring of 1917, it seems clear that Ratibor did use his propaganda weapons to wage a campaign against Romanones, partly at the behest of the German military. Jagow too acceded to the demands of the military in a telegram of September 23, 1916 in which Ratibor was officially authorized to do all he could to set Romanones aside, but the Ambassador was to avoid compromising the Embassy or injuring the pride of Alfonso by trying to mix deeply into Spanish affairs.[25]

Perhaps what is of real significance in the frantic exchange of telegrams between Madrid and Berlin about Romanones was the evolution of Alfonso's own attitude toward the Prime Minister. The German documents provide considerable proof that Alfonso did not want to force Germany to break relations as Romanones suggested. Indeed, Alfonso had seemed to ride with the developments of military events and wanted to appear pro-German when Germany seemed militarily successful. Too, Alfonso could hardly afford to accede to all of the Allied demands, since he would lose his freedom of action, which was useful in the struggle for power between Romanones and Alfonso that had developed since Romanones's appointment as Prime Minister in December 1915.

In a lengthy report to the General Staff, Kalle related that Alfonso knew what Romanones wanted. Alfonso saw Romanones convinced that Spain would end up on the Allied side by accepting Allied demands for ship seizures in light of continued German sinkings. As Spanish public opinion in 1916 would not accept a declaration of war against Germany, the only path left was to force Germany into breaking relations. Kalle said Germany had to use the press, pro-German demonstrations, and bribery of politicians to get Romanones removed. He implied the German government had to make clear to the Spanish public Romanones's policy.[26] The Austrian Ambassador in Madrid, Prince Fuerstenberg, said Alfonso intimated that the fall of Romanones would be welcome.[27]

In order to placate the Spanish, Jagow worked to get the High Command to avoid sinking Spanish merchant vessels, particularly before the upcoming meeting of the Cortes. On September 16, 1916, Jagow asked the Admiralty to avoid giving the French and English any cause to excite Spanish opinion through sinkings.[28] Polo conveyed Alfonso's wishes that no more attacks be made, thereby relieving the King from Allied pressure and from support that might be given Romanones in conducting his anti-German policy.[29] The Admiralty, however, was not willing to follow entirely the Foreign Office's suggestions, and was only willing to order submarine commanders to treat Spanish crews with particular care and to avoid decisive action in Spanish territorial waters.[30]

Unfortunately, the sinking of the fruit ship Luis Vives on September 25, 1916 just before the opening of the Cortes on the twenty-seventh of September set off another frantic series of messages between Jagow and the High Command. The Admiralty and the High Command took a legalistic approach to the problem of the Luis Vives, insisting that the vessel was taking contraband foodstuffs to Liverpool thereby falling under the rules which permitted its destruction.[31] Indeed, the Admiralty justified this action at length by pointing to tremendous profits that Spanish merchant firms received as a result of carrying trade for the Entente.[32] But Ratibor still protested that the German government had to avoid sinking any Spanish vessel.[33] To the Ambassador in Madrid further sinkings merely gave the pro-Entente newspapers an opportunity to prove the valuelessness of German promises, thereby easing Romanones's task.[34] By the end of the month Ratibor considered the situation so grave that he insisted upon new concessions for Spain.[35]

Jagow met the emergency in two ways. First he managed

to persuade the Admiralty to issue orders to halt all sinkings of Spanish vessels.[36] Secondly, he dealt with Alfonso through Polo in Berlin and Ratibor in Madrid to ease the economic pressure of the German U-boat war upon Spain. Germany insisted publicly that the sinkings were justified and followed to the letter the requirements of international law, but privately they moved quietly to make concessions.[37]

By the first part of October the Admiralty, despite these private concessions, seemed less interested in sparing Spanish feelings and maintaining Spanish neutrality than in previous months. The Admiralty agreed to restrict submarine warfare around Spain only before the meeting of the Cortes.[38] But from October 1916 onward Jagow and his successor, Arthur Zimmermann, had great difficulty in getting the High Command to cooperate with the Foreign Office. But for the moment they were successful, and throughout October Jagow and then Zimmermann made concessions in the fruit carrying trade. These actions were useful in defusing the immediate crisis that threatened to lead to a break in relations.

In the interim, however, the Allies forced Spain to forbid the entry of belligerent submarines into Spanish harbors without prior approval. If submarine commanders did not comply with this decree, then they would be interned.[39] Faced with such intense Allied pressure, Alfonso certainly should welcome German concessions in the fruit trade and aid in other economic areas.

The base from which the Germans were able to operate

centered upon investments in the electrical, chemical, and mining industries. Two electrical firms, the AEG or Allgemeine Elektrizitaets Gesellschaft and the Siemans works controlled electrical supplies for the tramways in Sevilla.[40] With Belgium under German control, the Brussels electrical firm of Societe financiere de Transports et Entreprises Electriques came under German influence. This firm ran the tramways in Barcelona and Bilbao.[41] German chemical firms, Hoechst Dyes Works and the I.G. Farben company, had invested in Spanish industry.[42] So too had the Krupp von Bohlen Steel Works, which had about 100 million pesetas of investment in iron mines around Bilbao and Santander, particularly in the Orconeca Mine near Bilbao.[43] The Foreign Office encouraged the Krupp firm to show more interest in establishing war factories in Spain to strengthen Spanish defense.[44]

By early November 1916, Ratibor successfully organized German economic interests to promise Spain greater aid; he created the German-Spanish Mine and Industrial Study Company. Its management was Engineer Alfred Helbig and President Zimoseck of the German firm Wimmer and Company. Ratibor requested the Foreign Office to obtain the capital and cooperation of the major German banks, the Krupp works, and the electrical concern of Siemans-Schuckert for feasibility studies in iron, lead or zinc mining as well as aid to construct harbors and docks. The company would have as its major task a study to provide the basis of a German-Spanish commercial treaty.[45] Krupp accepted participation in the new Society and contributed 50,000 pesetas for its success.[46]

On December 2, 1916, several interests had joined the German-Spanish Company, increasing its capital to 300,000 pesetas.[47] But what Krupp and the other interests gave somewhat reluctantly in November, they enthusiastically took away in December. Krupp served notice on December 4, 1916, that it would be glad to participate in Spanish industry in peacetime, but the problems of the war were too pressing; therefore, Krupp backed off from immediate help to Spain.[48]

From January through June 1917, Engineer Helbig's activities came to nothing. He lined up a large number of iron ore concessions, possibilities of participation in iron mining consortiums, and purchases of railroads, but German industry was reluctant. By June 25, 1917, several German firms informed the Foreign Office they were not interested just then in massive investments in Spain.[49] Practically, German attempts to counter Allied economic involvement were failures.

Meanwhile, on the diplomatic front, Jagow, on October 1, 1916, told Polo in Berlin of the willingness of Germany to grant safe-conduct passes to Spanish fruit ships. British acquiescence in the plan was expected, and the Spanish were to get British approval to permit the passage of an equal number of Spanish ships to German harbors.[50] Publicly, however, the Spanish government said nothing about the offer. Ratibor and Jagow hoped that it would help to galvanize public opinion against Romanones.[51] The whole offer was made to overcome the adverse publicity earned from the sinking of the Luis Vives.[52] Local press reports of German attitudes toward fruit exports twisted the German intent, reporting that Germany desired to deny fruit exports to England if England did not permit imports to Germany.[53]

To influence Spanish opinion, German Undersecretary Ernst Langwerth von Simmern, in an interview with a New York correspondent, told the world of Germany's good intentions toward Spain.[54] Hopefully, Spanish censorship would not act harshly toward reports from New York, thereby getting the German view before the Spanish people. Indeed, by October 17, 1916, the Correo España published an account of the fruit ship offer, thus proving the expectations of the Foreign Office that they could get their views before the Spanish public in an indirect manner.[55] This success was preceeded by an earlier one in which the Germans successfully got their June 1916 offer of ten ships and of coal deliveries before the public. Through a Swiss newspaper, the Tages-Anzeiger fuer Stadt und Canton Zuerichs, a report appeared as though it had come from London. By September 29, 1916, La Época published an account of the offer and the reaction of Romanones to it, though he was very evasive in his replies.[56]

Throughout October and November, the Allies continuously increased their propaganda activities. This appeared to the Germans as a virtual press war. Beginning as early as late August and through September 1916, Ratibor reported increased calls for Spanish intervention in the war, particularly from important Barcelona papers such as La Publicicad and the Madrid El Imparcial.[57] French efforts in August and September were directed toward getting Spanish support in criticizing German removals of large numbers of the Belgian civilian population to work in German factories.[58] By October, Ratibor reported even more press attacks against the U-boat war of Germany.[59] In November, the English displayed the Raemaker caricatures of the Central Powers and of their leaders and soldiers. The display showed Germans and Austrians as murderers and the Kaiser as the bloodthirstiest of them all.[60] The Spanish eventually removed this offensive display, but refused to punish the exhibitors as Ratibor and the Foreign Office demanded.[61] To fight back in this heightened press war, Ratibor's press fund was augmented, and the Ambassador requested more German propaganda material.[62]

In the meantime, Romanones had to deal with the German ploy of offering safe-conduct passes for Spanish fruit ships. Indeed, one could argue that Germany never really expected Great Britain to agree to the proposal. The Germans probably wanted to get their views before the Spanish public and were really playing to the grandstand. Another goal of their policy was the maintenance of the good offices of the King. The Germans had remained convinced of the friendship of Alfonso. By October they felt their efforts were successful as Alfonso continued to avoid a break in German-Spanish relations.[63]

Further proof of German duplicity appeared in

October 1916. On the twenty-second of October the Germans knew that the Spaniards had sounded out the British on letting Spanish fruit vessels go to Germany, and the English had rejected the idea. Ratibor suggested that any renewal of the proposal by the Spanish would hardly have any better effect.[64] Jagow instructed Ratibor to go ahead and prepare to issue passes to Spanish vessels in hope of pressuring them to negotiate with the British on the question.[65] Romanones tried to call the German bluff by openly demanding issuance of licenses to Spanish ships, but the Germans were only too glad to follow through.[66] While the Germans really hoped the British might accept their scheme, the primary focus was to influence public opinion and to maintain Spanish neutrality.[67] The British ultimately rejected the idea of safe-conduct passes issued by the German consuls.[68]

The Germans sensed that their efforts had been successful by November and December 1916. Concessions toward Spanish fruit ship traffic and publication of German concessions of the previous summer and promises of future economic aid tended to deflect Romanones's campaign to drive Spain toward breaking relations with Germany. Indeed, information from several different quarters indicated to the Foreign Office that their policy was succeeding; although there were yet "clouds in the political sky."[69] Ratibor also reported that the situation had eased somewhat, but debates in the Cortes over Spain's financial difficulties could give Romanones an opportunity to further damage German-Spanish relations. Ratibor suggested that the Marquis of Villalobar be informed that the Germans thought things had taken a turn for the better and that he communicate with King Alfonso to warn the monarch of future intrigues from Romanones.[70]

Throughout December the Germans sought to maintain what they saw as an advantageous position. First, Villalobar agreed to come to Berlin to discuss new approaches to maintain King Alfonso's friendship, and secondly, the Kaiser wrote a personal letter to the Spanish King, telling him about the latest German peace offer. Indeed, the course of events from Villalobar's visit through the Spanish rejection of an American offer to mediate among the belligerents at the end of 1916 strongly suggests a further success of German diplomacy.

When Villalobar arrived in Berlin on December 16, 1916, a long list of grievances against violations of Spanish neutrality had already been drawn up to provide him with arguing points.[71] In addition, Foreign Secretary Zimmermann discussed recent German suggestions for peace. The State Secretary bade Villalobar communicate this démarche to Alfonso. Interestingly, Zimmermann said he would have preferred to delay making the peace offer until he and Alfonso could have discussed it. But the recent success in Rumania did not make possible any further delay.[72] Clearly, Zimmermann sought to play to Alfonso's well-known and cherished hope to serve as a mediator in the conflict.[73]

This diplomatic foray was accompanied by communications

among Europe's royalty about Spain's grave position in the midst of the war. The Archduchess of Austria, Isabella, talked with the Kaiser on the occasion of Franz Josef's funeral, telling him that Alfonso was pro-German and that he was worried about possible coastal defense in case Spain had to enter the war on Germany's side. The Kaiser gallantly assured the Archduchess that Germany would provide Spain with coastal defense.[74] The Archduchess further told William that Alfonso really would have desired to come to Vienna but could not because of "problems and unrest at home."[75] The Kaiser used the conversations with Isabella as a springboard to write directly to Alfonso.

The letter William sent Alfonso on December 13, 1916 was significant for two reasons. The Germans assured Spain of continuing good relations between the two, and William told Alfonso of the German peace proposal of December 12, 1916 hinting that if it were rejected Spain would not be spared the consequences. William reminded Alfonso of Germany's favorable military position and congratulated him upon a continuous policy of neutrality.[76] Thus, the letter was an attempt to enlist Spain on the German side in a new peace offer and to deflect Spain's joining with the U.S. in a peace offensive.

Though Spain had earlier suggested that the United States should cooperate with Alfonso XIII in bringing about peace, she now rejected Wilson's peace note.[77] In an official communication from Spanish Ambassador Riaño in Washington to U.S. Secretary of State Robert Lansing on Sunday, December 31, 1916, the Spanish rejected the note, saying they thought only they had been asked to participate in bringing about peace.[78]

Alfonso's pride may have entered into the picture. He had always seen himself as the leader of a European peace conference, and his comments to U.S. Ambassador Joseph Willard in June 1916 revealed that the Spanish monarch hoped to act as the representative of continental Europe in a peace conference. Too, the recent German press campaign and Kaiser William's note, intimating that in their peace proposals Alfonso might play a major role, may have influenced the Spanish reply. Spanish newspapers generally applauded the answer to Wilson's note, suggesting that any participation in such efforts would be counter to Spanish dignity.[79] Current opinion in Spain was that only they and not other neutrals should work with the United States to reach a European accord.

The Germans continued to heap praises on Alfonso. The Berlin correspondent of the ABC, a clerical and pro-German paper, said,

> Wilson having failed, the figure of Don Alfonso XIII looms larger before us, and upon it all eyes are fixt (sic) against the day in which all the belligerents will be disposed to listen to words of reconciliation. Besides in Germany it is thought that in a European conflict the neutrals of Europe are more entitled than those of other continents to talk of peace, and most entitled of all a monarch enjoying all the prestige conferred by history and tradition, by the qualities of the nation over which he rules, its lineage, and its attitude toward the conflict. If we look for such a monarch our eyes fall naturally upon Alfonso XIII.

The correspondent went on to quote a "high diplomatic personage" whose views were said to be:

> The false steps made by President Wilson has impresst (sic) Germany with a feeling that Spain alone has the authority to intervene at the right moment, and that Madrid is the most appropriate capital for the conferences, which not only have to make peace, but also to change the present theories of international politics and to shape a new law of nations. Madrid is destined to be the cradle of a new era of European civilization.[80]

Clearly, the Germans spared no pains in trying to impress the Spanish. Alfonso undoubtedly wanted to hear that he and Spain would be the centers of a new order in Europe.

Perhaps one cannot go so far as to draw the same conclusion from this sequence as a correspondent from London's Daily Telegraph in Madrid, that the Spanish were threatened to reply in a sense favorable to Germany, but one can conclude that Alfonso was trying desperately to counter the pro-Entente policy of Romanones.

The visit from Villalobar, William's letter, and military reports brought to Madrid by Major Valdivia, the Spanish Military Attaché in Berlin, all evidently pointed toward Alfonso's pro-German stance.[81] The apparent positive acceptance of these subtle pressures along with Alfonso's constant assurance to the Germans in October that Spain would never give up its neutrality, indeed, that Spain would fight only on the German side if she fought at all, actually pointed toward a struggle between Alfonso and Romanones. The Germans subtlely offered Alfonso a role in a possible future peace, gently reminding him of the consequences were the belligerents not to accept German peace terms, and finally put forth their objections to Romanones.[82]

Meanwhile, throughout December 1916, Spanish newspapers complained of the frequent German attacks on Spanish shipping. Of particular interest was the virtual blockade of the Canary Islands.[83] During the first week of December, five ships were sunk in the vicinity of the Canaries.[84] The apparent settlement of shipping problems through the offers of safe-conduct passes was not really working; El Imparcial observed that Germany could not provide markets to Spain as she could for Sweden, Norway, Holland, Denmark, and Switzerland and that Germany should do all she could to avoid sinkings.[85]

On December 26, 1916, the Conservative organ of former Prime Minister Eduardo Dato, El Época, declared that the possibility of a complete halt of trade with Great Britain existed; the consequences of such a development could only be grave internal disturbances throughout Spain.[86] The government of Count Romanones finally dealt with the increased sinkings, meeting on Thursday, December 27, 1916; this meeting coincided with President Wilson's suggestion that Spain join the U.S. to offer to negotiate an end to the war.

No official note to Germany resulted from the cabinet meeting in late December, but Romanones issued a declaration proclaiming Spanish determination to defend her neutral rights. The Prime Minister reviewed all sinkings to date, from the destruction of the San Isidoro in August 1915 to the latest attacks in December 1916. He demanded the observance of the London Declaration of 1909 in which sea warfare included provisions to care for crews of attacked vessels. He further emphasized that Spain would take energetic measures in the future, including seizing interned German ships to avenge Spanish losses.[87] Romanones, therefore, announced a hard line for Spanish policy.

Surprisingly, the British saw Spain's reply to Wilson's note as a rejection of German encouragements to play a role in a peace conference. Possibly, the British were correct as the Entente was pushing Spain to enter the war; Alfonso rejected the U.S. offer so not to appear too eager to follow the German line, particularly as the new British Prime Minister Lloyd George apparently had joined the French in plans to bring Spain into the war. Alfonso was now faced with considerable pressure for a pro-Entente benevolent neutrality.

Part of the reason for Romanones's challenges to Germany may have been the hope England would back him to the hilt. In December 1916 David Lloyd George seemed to have had plans to aid Spain in a war effort against Germany. An English officer, Sir Charles Petrie, has related his training activities for officers in the British army, officers who were to act as a liaison between the Spanish and the British. Petrie said that the activities began in December 1916 and continued for about three months thereafter. Eventually, the officers were sent back to their regular units. Though Petrie did not indicate the exact time for returning them to their units, the implication is that the British dropped the whole project after Romanones fell from power in April 1917.

The evidence from September 1916 through April 1917 for British support of a belligerent attitude for Spain is circumstantial, but Great Britain and France probably very strongly tempted Romanones. It is yet an open question whether the Entente truly hoped to get Spain to declare war upon Germany. More than likely, Romanones's oft repeated desire to harass the Germans into breaking relations with Spain was the goal also sought by the Entente.[88]

From December 1915 until April 19, 1917, Romanones sought to force Spain completely into benevolent neutrality toward the Entente. In the meantime, Ratibor used every means at his disposal to discredit Romanones, including a bitter newspaper campaign. But in the final analysis, a more significant battle revolved around the differences between Alfonso and Romanones. By April the King managed to regain control over Spanish foreign affairs, and the Germans rejoiced, but by late April, with the U.S. entrance into the war, the tide was already turning. What had looked like a German diplomatic victory became the beginning of a thoroughgoing benevolent Spanish neutrality for the Allied and Associated Powers.

In January 1917, Romanones sought to remove German influence in two ways. First, in an active press campaign and censorship, the Prime Minister tried to undermine the Germans' hold over Spanish public opinion. Secondly,

Romanones, in this case aided by Alfonso, tried to authorize arming Spanish merchant vessels. As early as January 2, 1917, two pro-German newspapers were persecuted for "libelous" statements about Romanones himself.[89] Romanones also sent a message to Berlin threatening that Spain would be forced to ask for the recall of Ratibor if his propaganda activities were not stopped, complaining of Ratibor's excessive meddling in domestic affairs. In the note used to inform Ratibor of this threat, the Foreign Office urged its Ambassador to avoid mixing into Spanish affairs.[90] Even Ludendorff suggested more caution in conducting German propaganda in Spain.[91] Romanones instituted censorship of news reports that arrived via radio and rejected Ratibor's pleas to set aside the negative ruling on German information.[92] Furthermore, English war photographs were to be exhibited.[93] By January 20, 1917, judicial proceedings were begun against five pro-German papers, <u>España Nueva</u>, <u>Correo Español</u>, <u>Commentarios</u>, and <u>El Diario</u> of Madrid, and <u>El Socialista</u>.[94] Ratibor suggested that he should redouble his activities in the press, and by February 5, 1917 extra funds were put at his disposal.[95]

Through the remainder of February and into March 1917, Spanish policy toward the press leaned more and more toward the Entente side. By February 13, 1917 all "one-sided" information about the war was to be presented to the Ministry of the Interior for censorship.[96] All atrocity reports were suppressed, especially those of the Germans, and from March 5, 1917 onward all such reports had to come from official government communiques.[97] By early March, Ratibor was complaining that the only things being published from Germany were selections made by Sir Arthur Hardinge, the British Ambassador in Madrid.[98] Ultimately, Ratibor had to use secret radio sets to get information to publish in the German subsidized press.[99]

In the meantime, Ratibor became convinced that Alfonso was not aware of the true state of German-Spanish relations. The German Ambassador insisted that Polo had not sent accurate reports to Madrid; furthermore, Alfonso allegedly now was at the mercy of Romanones who had gotten Polo to alter the despatches from Berlin. Ratibor rather plaintively asserted that he was not being kept informed about replies given Polo anyway.[100]

This report should be seen in light of the continuing quarrel that developed between Ratibor and Romanones personally. Apparent threats to ask for Ratibor's recall and his conviction that Romanones personified all evil contributed to an especially bitter and acrimonious atmosphere. Indeed, a few weeks later, Villalobar suggested that Ratibor's rancor towards Romanones was playing into the hands of the Allies; Ratibor should desist at once in such a personal press campaign against Romanones.[101] Nonetheless, Ratibor was intent upon a personal campaign directed to remove Romanones.[102]

The Allies had replied in kind to the stepped up German propaganda. By February and into April 1917 Ratibor was complaining of the intensity of anti-German comments. He insisted that the only way to influence the Spanish government was through their Berlin Ambassador, Polo de Bernabé.[103] By April Ratibor reported an influx of Entente officials and propaganda provocateurs into Madrid and Barcelona. To the Ambassador the whole of the Iberian peninsula seemed to be swept by a massive pro-Allied policy.[104]

While Ratibor tried to hold off the Allies through his press connections, the Allies exerted other pressures upon the Spanish. In early January 1917 Spanish officials, in concert with the December 28, 1916 statement of Romanones, began discussions about arming Spanish merchant ships.[105] The German response to the Ambassador was swift; such vessels would be regarded as warships and treated as such. "Put in the press there that armed freighters are regarded as cruisers aids and would be treated as warships."[106] Indeed, Alfonso seemed to be succumbing to the pressures of Great Britain. The Marquis of Cortina, a close friend of Romanones and later Minister of Public Works, began negotiations with the English as early as the middle of January on a host of issues, only one among them the subject of arming merchant vessels.[107]

Yet, it is clear that Alfonso was trying to keep the total embrace of Great Britain, France, and later the United States at arms' length while also placating the Germans. The King tried to conduct his own foreign policy seeking to play England off against the United States in the first few months of 1917. After German declaration of unrestricted submarine warfare around the British Isles, Alfonso personally conveyed his assurances to Ratibor that Spain was remaining neutral.[108]

Spain took a decisively moderate course in replying to the German note of January 31, 1917 which announced unrestricted U-boat attacks. In her formal, quite mild reply to the German announcement of unrestricted submarine warfare, Spain later emphasized neutrality as her ultimate goal.[109] Alfonso told United States Ambassador Willard as early as February 6, 1917, that Spain definitely would not break off diplomatic relations nor would it declare war even if more Spanish ships were sunk and lives lost. Alfonso stated that Spain was the only neutral of importance left; it was necessary for her to remain out of the war to represent the interests of neutrals. Willard saw this as another indication of Alfonso's oft repeated desire to play the role of an honest broker at a future peace conference.[110] Romanones, in a public interview about the Spanish reply to the German note, also emphasized that the note was conciliatory, revealing Spanish desire for German friendship.[111]

By February Alfonso participated in negotiations with the Austrians to end the war. In a private letter to the King, Emperor Karl asked Alfonso to select a moment when he thought all the neutrals would join with Spain in calling for a peace conference. The Emperor's own Foreign Secretary Czernin did not believe this was a propitious time to begin such negotiations, but the Hapsburg ruler felt that Alfonso's royal status and his Mother's Austrian heritage would have a positive effect.

On February 27, 1917, Alfonso answered Karl's entreaties. It was clear that Alfonso was leaning more toward the Entente; in his reply the Spanish King said he would be glad to further Austrian wishes if Germany could be gotten to relinquish Alsace-Lorraine and to create a position for it similar to that of Luxumburg. He continued, suggesting that with such a "trump" in his hands he could assure Austria of a continental peace, with the possible exclusion of England.

Evidently, Alfonso felt he worked better advocating French interests; too, he must have felt he could not risk calling a peace conference without considerable concessions to the Allies. Indeed, one could conclude that Alfonso had already decided for the Allies in December 1916 when the Marquis of Cortina went to England for special economic negotiations. These parleys culminated by December 1917 in the mutually ratified Cortina Agreements which virtually put Spain into the Allied camp as a "neutral ally."

Alfonso was yet popular as a go-between for peace negotiations as evidenced by an approach the Germans made through Villalobar in September 1917. The new State Secretary at Berlin, Richard von Kuehlmann, wanted Villalobar to act as an intermediary with the English in Brussels, to determine the extent to which the English were willing to negotiate peace in the fall of 1917. Unfortunately for the Germans, Villalobar was not trusted by the Spanish Foreign Minister Lema in Madrid. The French learned of this special embassy, and complained that Germany was trying to drive a wedge between the Allies. Presumably, Lema had informed the French. Consequently, nothing came of this attempt at negotiated peace using Spanish intermediaries in 1917.[112]

In February 1917, Germany showed her gratitude for the conciliatory Spanish policy by making concessions on the question of the return of Spanish fruit ships from England. Zimmermann instructed Ratibor to tell Spain that vessels with German passage permits could return if they did so by February 9, 1917 at the latest. Furthermore, to assuage Spanish economic problems from the submarine blockade of Great Britain, Germany sought to buy stocks of apples, olive oil, and oranges. These stocks were to be stored until they could be transported to Germany.[113]

Spanish economic losses mounted throughout February and March 1917. Ten Spanish ships were sunk since January, making a total loss of 40,000 tons since submarine war began in 1915. Further, the lack of coal for industries at Barcelona provoked a domestic crisis.[114] Romanones even remonstrated with Polo that the latter was not satisfactorily representing Spanish interests, especially in regard to ship losses. Romanones cited the case of the sinking of the _San Leandro_ in which Polo allegedly did not protest vigorously.[115] By late March living costs had increased while wages remained relatively low, and a movement to introduce strikes at Barcelona and other leading industrial centers hung like a pall over the government.[116]

Ratibor was convinced the English and French were

directly behind efforts to disturb Spanish economic tranquility.[117] Romanones's government had suspended constitutional guarantees and tightened news censorship by March 31, 1917 just as the rumors of a general strike circulated.[118] Spain also tried to encourage more Spanish ship traffic to alleviate economic difficulties. The Ministry of Commerce insured all ship firms against losses at sea with the requirement that 85 percent of the loss would be paid immediately with the remainder waiting upon construction or purchase of other ships to replace those sunk.[119]

The Germans had little sympathy for Spanish ship losses and consequent economic problems. Food supplies were short and living costs high because of enormous increases in exports to France and England.[120] Economically Spain was desperate. Once the U.S.A. was in the war, Madrid sought to play the United States off against Great Britain for ship space and needed coal and cotton.[121]

In the midst of economic confusion caused by unrestricted submarine warfare and by threatened strikes, German-Spanish relations were severely strained by discovery of substantial quantities of German propaganda material and explosives near Cartagena. On February 18, 1917 local authorities arrested a man who claimed to be an American but who turned out to be a German agent. The agent had dug up some chests containing propaganda materials and high explosives as well as canned goods, private letters, and instructions to German espionage units in Spain and in Latin America.[122]

Alfonso was remarkably calm about the incident, blaming the Military and Naval Attachés for the incident, since he apparently wished to show Ratibor that the Ambassador was not suspect.[123] In a lengthy audience Alfonso had with Ratibor on March 1, 1917 the King assured Ratibor of the friendly feelings Spain had for Germany and promised to handle the matter through the courts in a conciliatory manner. Alfonso regaled Ratibor with a recital of the chests' contents. Ratibor pleaded ignorance of the situation and Alfonso answered that he hoped all future German activities would be centered in the Ambassador's hands. Alfonso further emphasized that the Military and Navy Attachés were responsible for such violations of Spanish neutrality.[124] A formal protest note was soon presented at Berlin.[125]

A frantic search was begun within the German government to discover exactly what the chests contained. A report from the Admiralty to the Foreign Office detailed the contents and revealed that some decidedly secret information was within the propaganda placards, books, and so forth. But the vital elements were written in code, and were thus indecipherable to the Spanish. Clearly, the military had not fully informed the Foreign Office of its activities.[126]

The immediate problem Germany now faced was keeping the Navy Attaché von Krohn at his post. Krohn was convinced that Romanones would use the incident to get him expelled. Evidently, Krohn had acted in an illegal manner, violating Spain's sovereignty for quite some time, but this was the most spectacular incident that had come to public attention.[127] Romanones no longer believed Ratibor's comments that the diplomatic office was uninformed about the U-boat that delivered the materials.[128] Even the Navy Attaché at Madrid now suggested letting up on the submarine war to accommodate Spain.[129]

In the official reply, Foreign Secretary Zimmermann sought to convey German apologies for having violated Spanish sovereignty. In addition, Zimmermann emphasized that Ratibor had had nothing to do with the incident. The State Secretary explained that deliveries of propaganda material via submarine were necessary in view of the British blockade of Europe. Furthermore, explosives were to be used only to destroy German property such as ships captured by the Allies.[130]

A few days later, Polo, in a conversation with Zimmermann, expressed surprise at the German answer. Polo pointed out it was remarkable the German government was not aware of an act of such importance done by their own navy. Even the destruction of ships in a neutral harbor, after all, would be contrary to Spanish law. Polo emphasized that von Krohn must have known of all naval movements and thus had overstepped his authority as a member of the German diplomatic community in Spain. If von Krohn were to continue his activities, then the Spanish government would immediately demand von Krohn's recall.[131]

Officially, Spain told Germany that the answer of

March 19, 1917 was "inadequate."[132] Still the Germans persisted in asking for the return of the chests.[133] Not surprisingly, the Spanish never did hand over the materials to the Germans, and the matter was allowed to drop.[134]

The significance of this Cartagena affair was twofold. First, it was an indication Spain disliked the espionage activities going on within the Iberian peninsula. Later, this dislike and distrust expressed itself in demanding the recall of von Krohn and other Embassy personnel in 1918. Secondly, the incident was illustrative of Romanones's hard-driving policy to put the Germans on the defensive and of Alfonso once again to walk a tightrope between Romanones and the Germans. By the middle of April 1917, Romanones tried to push Spain completely down the path toward an alliance and a declaration of war against Germany, but domestic problems intervened and he fell from power.

From Ratibor's position, particularly in a retrospective review of the events of April 1917, it was his own policy and activity within the propaganda network that succeeded in bringing Romanones down.[135] There was some truth in the German Ambassador's self-congratulatory comments. As Romanones said himself on tendering his resignation, the force of public opinion was such that he could not lead Spain onto the Allied side, and the Germans had helped to mold public opinion. But the causes for Romanones's fall, from a foreign policy standpoint, were more complex.

Romanones had begun his concerted push toward a pro-

Entente policy earlier. On January 9, 1917, he threatened to resign, citing German intrigue and continued losses of Spanish shipping, but King Alfonso asked him to remain.[136] Indeed, the London Times suggested there had been a quarrel between Romanones and the King over the Prime Minister's declaration of December 1916, when he had threatened to break with Germany over future sinkings.[137]

Meanwhile, the German press campaign made his task more difficult. Romanones wrote to several newspapers, protesting the violent denunciations then appearing in the pro-German organs.[138] Even El Imparcial argued that the Germans could hardly expect a friendly Spanish government by attacking Spanish ships and the Prime Minister at the same time.[139] The source of the attacks were well known as a quote from El Imparcial made clear; this leading newspaper carried some verses on the fall of Romanones on April 19, 1917, with the last two lines reading, "Qué olor, Qué olor / Qué olor a Ratibor."[140]

Romanones's domestic problems were intensified by attacks upon Spanish shipping by the press campaign, but the causes of his difficulties went deeper. The government had been unable to get a new budget approved since 1915. Romanones had proposed one that distributed funds to public works and to education, but conservatives in the Cortes saw the proposals as excessively liberal. Taxes upon surplus war profits were attacked by Bilbao and Barcelona shipowners. Proposals to impose land taxes on the nobility were also rejected.

Indeed, the greatest imposts were yet upon the masses of the poor. With dissatisfaction over rising costs of living and with demands for recognition of the political needs of the industrial working classes, the Spanish political structure was becoming unstable.[141] Clearly, any adventures in foreign policy could lead to revolution at home.

After the sinking of the San Fulgencio and the Tom in April 1917 and after the United States declared war on Germany, Romanones met with his cabinet and the King in what apparently was a stormy session. The King had earlier remarked to Romanones that he had never expected Germany really to carry out unrestricted submarine warfare.[142] With the policy now proclaimed Spain suffered more than ever before. Romanones, in the cabinet meeting, proposed a new program of four points: first, to notify Germany that her declaration of unrestricted warfare implied a break in relations, second, that Spain had to adopt means to protect Spanish shipping against repeated German attacks, third, Spain had to take energetic measures against resident Germans who were abusing Spanish hospitality, and last, Romanones proposed a resumption of prewar policies of more intimate relations with the Allies.[143]

Other sources provide insights into the cabinet debates of April 18 and 19, 1917. In a recent biography of Santiago Alba, finance minister in Romanones cabinet, a direct quote of some of the arguments is available. Alba reportedly had inveighed against any radical departure in Spanish policy, suggesting that abandonment of neutrality had to be submitted first to the Cortes.[144] A contemporary report in the London Times emphasized the role played by the President of the Chamber of Deputies, Miguel Villanueva y Gómez, who was alarmed by the possibility of war with Germany.[145] From another quarter the seriousness of Romanones's intentions was clear; U.S. Ambassador Joseph Willard related that Romanones was planning to threaten Germany with severing relations if the submarine war were not halted.[146] In a report of the U.S. Naval Attaché in September 1918, a more colorful description of the session was given. This report emphasized the violence of the debate between Romanones and the King with the latter reportedly exclaiming "Bah, do you still believe that these Allies are going to win out?"[147] Clearly, neither the King nor the cabinet were willing to go as far as Romanones wanted.

During the April discussions, Ratibor mounted an especially active propaganda campaign against Romanones, reporting the situation was still unclear but he hoped his efforts would lead to Romanones's fall. Ratibor further intimated that he was doing Alfonso's bidding, thereby strengthening the royal policy of neutrality.[148] "Situation yet quite unclear, should my efforts actually lead to the fall of Romanones. Thus, I ask promptly, so far as possible, to comply with all expressed wishes of his Majesty the King.[149]

La Época, Dato's conservative journal, explained the result of the cabinet meeting succinctly. To this paper

Romanones was able to believe Spain had understood neutrality in precisely the way he had understood it. But his policy of closer relations with the Allies could not be maintained without involving Spain in what she feared the most: entrance into the war. Spain now was in great danger from the Allies who might regard Spain as reneging on promises made by Romanones.[150] Conservatives were glad Romanones was out of power, partly because of his domestic policies that they feared and partly because he might lead Spain into a war that could have disastrous results in rearranging the Spanish social structure.

Alfonso had struggled with a policy that he thought unwise since 1915 when Romanones came to power. Alfonso always assured Germany of Spain's friendship and good wishes even in the darkest days of September and October 1916. Earlier, Alfonso had tried to undermine Romanones through the German submarine visit at Cartagena. A similar firm stand in 1917 against Romanones and domestic political considerations had thus resulted in Romanones's fall. With Romanones out the King turned to the right wing of the Liberal Party, giving Manuel García Prieto the task of forming a new government, which promptly declared Spain's intention to remain neutral.

Spanish domestic difficulties became much worse in the summer of 1917 as the basis of stability of the system was seriously undermined. Romanones remarked to Melquiades Alvarez, one of the Liberal leaders, that there was no longer a clear distinction between liberals and conservatives and that the unique system of the turnante de gobernación could no longer prevail. The liberals had not supported Romanones to the extent he had expected, therefore, Spain would be in the grip of personalities and shifting coalitions. The Conservatives had earlier rent their unity when Antonio Maura refused to cooperate with other conservative leaders and to assert positive direction and control over the right wing of Spanish politics.[151] Clearly, the war contributed to the dissolution of the Spanish political structure, and provided the basis of a near revolution in the disturbances of the summer of 1917.

In June 1917 Ratibor reported via diplomatic pouch the German view of the April events. There were several factors involved; Ratibor indicated that the Prime Minister's decline was tied in with inflation and the rise of the Spanish officers' *juntas*.[152] As early as April 17, 1917 Romanones was upset over demands made by the military, which felt it was not being satisfactorily considered in Romanones's budgets. Villanueva tried to get the King to remove Romanones and to call another man, Manuel García Prieto, a right-wing liberal who would be more acceptable to the military and who perhaps could modify their demands. The Germans used this situation to their advantage; Ratibor visited other political leaders, especially Vásquez de Mella, a Carlist and Traditionalist who could count on support within the army. Thus, pressure from the Germans from this direction was useful in countering Romanones's policy of support for the Entente.[153]

The Germans thought that on April 18, 1917, the debate within the ministerial council shifted from the military to the question of continued neutrality. In the press several former government ministers were outspoken in their support for neutrality. Don Alfonso of Bourbon talked with the King on the critical day of the nineteenth, convincing the King that the recent loss of the _San Fulgencio_ was not as serious as it seemed, indeed, domestic problems with the military and rising inflation were more serious. On that same day Romanones came face to face with accumulated opposition. The military and the King joined in rejecting Romanones's bid to end Spanish neutrality. Ratibor saw German success due to his propaganda activities and to his cultivation of good relations with several Spanish politicians such as the pro-German and right-wing liberals, Miguel Villanueva, Niceto Alcalá Zamora, and Santiago Alba. Though Ratibor expected Romanones yet to intrigue, he would no longer be feared. The King, the Conservative Party and his country seemed to have disavowed Romanones.[154] The Germans, therefore, saw the governmental change resulting from their efforts.

The new government, headed by Manuel García Prieto, was regarded by the Germans as weak, but which would have a positive "coloring" for Berlin. The Ambassador advised that domestic political concerns would be uppermost in Spanish minds with the rising influence of the _juntas_.[155] By early

June 1917 Ratibor suggested that Germany could not hope to intervene into Spanish politics due to quarrels among political leaders, the King, and the army.[156] Indeed, the disintegration of the monarchy under the pressures of war greatly puzzled the Germans who were convinced that domestic Spanish disturbances were due to the involvement of the British and French.

From September 1916 through April 1917, therefore, the Germans felt they had succeeded famously. With Romanones's determined effort to force a break between Spain and Germany, a great deal of propaganda activity ensued. Further promises of economic aid were forthcoming, and by October 1916, Romanones's efforts had failed. But the English may have entertained ideas of bringing Spain into the war when Lloyd George became Prime Minister in December 1916, and Romanones was given heart to take a harsher line toward Germany at the end of the year. Heightened Entente propaganda activities and resistance to the German declaration of unrestricted submarine warfare reflected a greater concern on the part of the Entente. Later, when the United States entered the war, even more economic pressure was exerted upon Spain. True to his initial course, Alfonso nevertheless continued to avoid actual participation in the conflict. In a struggle with Romanones (partly over Spanish entry into the war and partly over domestic issues), the King had succeeded in getting Romanones's resignation. Thereafter, the Germans seemed to relax, feeling Spanish neutrality was assured for the remainder of the war. But internal Spanish disturbances boded ill for the Germans. Instability of the monarchy and economic dislocations caused by the war as well as further Allied economic demands resulted in Alfonso's reorienting his foreign policy toward a pronounced pro-western bias.

FOOTNOTES FOR CHAPTER VI

[1]Just, "Neutralitaet," p. 366, taken from Hohenlohe telegram No. 288 of September 28, 1916, HHStA PA rot 895, Krieg 7, Spanien 1914-1916.

[2]Raymond Poincaré, Memoires trans. by Sir George Arthur (London: William Heinemann, 1926), p. 293.

[3]Ratibor to Foreign Office, September 5, 1916, Spanien 61. secr. Die Beziehungen zwischen Spanien und Deutschland, T136/ SA Reel 35/16.

[4]No signature, probably from Ratibor to Foreign Office, September 5, 1916, Ibid., SA Reel 35/16.

[5]Ratibor to Foreign Office, no date, probably September 1916 due to internal evidence and location of the document, Ibid., SA Reel 35/250-253.

[6]Ratibor to Foreign Office, September 5, 1916, Ibid., SA Reel 35/18.

[7]Holtzendorff to Foreign Office, September 8, 1916, Ibid., SA Reel 35/19-20.

[8]Kalle to Foreign Office, September 8, 1916, Ibid., SA Reel 35/21.

[9]Ratibor to Foreign Office, September 8, 1916, Ibid., SA Reel 35/no frame number indicated on the microfilm.

[10]Ratibor to Foreign Office, September 8, 1916, Ibid., SA Reel 35/30.

[11]Kalle to GHQ, September 17, 1916, Ibid., SA Reel 35/116.

[12]Ibid.

[13]Herr X at London to Berlin, October 23, 1916, Ibid., SA Reel 35/37-38.

[14]New York Times, September 13, 1916.

[15]Lancken to Foreign Office, September 13, 1916,

Spanien 61. secr. Die Beziehungen, SA Reel 35/56.

[16]Jagow to Gruenau, September 13, 1916, Ibid., SA Reel 35/56. The London Times noted on Tuesday, September 26, 1916 that Maura had delivered his speech just after an audience with the King and Romanones. Perhaps Jagow's assumption was correct and the Spanish were merely trying to placate the Entente. Nevertheless, Spanish editorial opinion continued to emphasize the need to remain neutral. See La Época, September 16, 1916.

[17]Lancken to Foreign Office, September 14, 1916, Ibid., SA Reel 35/65.

[18]Schubert at Bern to Foreign Office, September 25, 1916, Ibid., SA Reel 35/160. The Literary Digest in October 1916 saw Maura's speech as the beginning of Spanish adherence to the Entente cause. See Anonymous, "Spain Drifting to Allies," The Literary Digest, LIII (October 14, 1916), 942-943.

[19]Ratibor to Foreign Office, September 9, 1916, Spanien 61. secr. Die Beziehungen, SA Reel 35/42.

[20]Jagow to Lancken, September 10, 1916, Ibid., SA Reel 35/25.

[21]Jagow to Lancken, September 12, 1916, Ibid., SA Reel 35/43.

[22]Jagow to Ratibor, September 11, 1916, Ibid., SA Reel 35/31.

[23]Jagow to Ratibor, September 15, 1916, Ibid., SA Reel 35/70.

[24]Gruenau to Foreign Office, September 15, 1916, Ibid., SA Reel 35/94.

[25]Jagow to Ratibor, September 23, 1916, Ibid., SA Reel 35/135.

[26]Kalle to General Staff, September 11, 1916, Ibid., SA Reel 35/189-190.

[27]Ratibor to Foreign Office, October 3, 1916, Ibid., SA Reel 35/196.

[28]Jagow to Admiralty, September 16, 1916, Ibid., SA Reel 35/400.

[29]Jagow to Holtzendorff, September 16, 1916, Ibid., SA Reel 35/92.

[30]Holtzendorff to State Secretary, September 18, 1916, Ibid., SA Reel 35/133.

[31]Holtzendorff to Foreign Office, September 26, 1916, Ibid., SA Reel 35/142.

[32]Ibid.

[33]Ratibor to Foreign Office, September 15, 1916, Ibid., SA Reel 35/100.

[34]Ratibor to Foreign Office, September 16, 1916, Ibid., SA Reel 35/109.

[35]Ratibor to Foreign Office, September 28, 1916, Ibid., SA Reel 35/171.

[36]Holtzendorff to Foreign Office, September 29, 1916, Ibid., SA Reel 35/174.

[37]Jagow to Ratibor, September 27, 1916, Ibid., SA Reel 35/157.

[38]Gruenau to Foreign Office, October 10, 1916, Ibid., SA Reel 35/183.

[39]Willard to Lansing, October 14, 1916, U.S. Foreign Affairs, 1916 Supplement, The World War, pp. 776-777.

[40]Emmy-Ilse Grueneberg, "Die Handelsbeziehungen zwischen Deutschland und Spanien unter besonderer Beruecksichtigung der erzschaffenden und erzverarbeitenden Industrie," (Ph.D. dissertation, Berlin, Germany: The University of Berlin, 1927, p. 33 and 25 as cited in Gelos, p. 86-87. Also Kocherthaler to Foreign Office, September 1, 1916, Spanien 45. Die Finanzen Spaniens, T149/355/601-603.

[41]Kocherthaler to Foreign Office, September 1, 1916, Ibid.

[42]Gelos, p. 86-87.

[43]Kocherthaler to Foreign Office, September 1, 1916, Spanien 45. Die Finanzen Spaniens, T149/355/601-603.

[44]Stumm to Krupp von Bohlen, September 26, 1916, Spanien 44a. Marineangelegenheiten Spaniens T149/355/550. The influence of Military Attaché Kalle might have been of some importance in connection with the commercial arrangements. Kalle was the cousin of Wilhelm Ferdinand Kalle of the Chemical Factory Kalle and Company in Bierberich on the Rhine. After the war Kalle worked for the I.G. Farben Dye Works. There is no specific documentation connecting the

German business community and Kalle, but the importance of the chemical industry for Spanish imports and Kalle's attachments to German firms suggest he was foremost in promoting further German involvement in the Spanish market. See Marion Einhorn, Die Oekonomischen Hintergruende der faschistischen deutschen Intervention in Spanien, 1936-1939 (Berlin: Das Europaeische Vertrieb, 1975) p. 20.

[45]Ratibor to Foreign Office, November 2, 1916, Spanien 61. Die Politischen Beziehungen, T149/357/268.

[46]Krupp Firm to Foreign Office, November 16, 1916, Ibid., 289.

[47]Ratibor to Foreign Office, December 2, 1916, Ibid., 321.

[48]Krupp to Foreign Office, December 4, 1916, Spanien 44. Militaerische Angelegenheiten Spaniens, T149/355/553-554.

[49]Interior Secretary to Foreign Office, June 25, 1917, Spanien 61. Die Politischen Beziehungen, T149/357/425.

[50]Jagow to Polo, October 1, 1916, Spanien 61. secr. Die Beziehungen, SA Reel 35/181.

[51]Ratibor to Foreign Office, October 13, 1916, Ibid., SA Reel 35/222.

[52]Ratibor to Foreign Office, October 13, 1916, Ibid., SA Reel 35/224.

[53]Ibid.

[54]Jagow to Ratibor, October 15, 1916, Ibid., SA Reel 35/228.

[55]Zentralstelle fuer Auslandsdienst, Zeitungskontrolle, 1915-1918:Spanische Presse (Berlin: Druck von Julius Sittenfeld, Hofbuchdrucker, 1915-1917), vol. 38, col. 115.

[56]Ibid., col. 97.

[57]Ratibor to Foreign Office, September 25, 1916, Spanien 61. secr. Die Beziehungen, SA Reel 35/294-299.

[58]Ibid.

[59]Ratibor to Foreign Office, October, 1916, Ibid., SA Reel 38/218.

[60]Jagow to Polo, November 29, 1916, Spanien 61. Die Politischen Beziehungen, 357/308.

[61] Polo to Jagow, December 4, 1916, Ibid., 357/322 and Polo to Zimmermann, December 7, 1916, Ibid., 357/340.

[62] Zimmermann to Ratibor, November 16, 1916, Ibid., 357/191 and Ratibor to Foreign Office, November 29, 1916, Ibid., 357/315.

[63] Kalle to Pless, October 18, 1916, Spanien 61. secr. Die Beziehungen, SA Reel 35/6.

[64] Ratibor to Foreign Office, October 22, 1916, Ibid., SA Reel 35/27.

[65] Jagow to Ratibor, October 28, 1916, Ibid., SA Reel 35/43.

[66] Ratibor to Foreign Office, October 31, 1916, Ibid., SA Reel 35/63.

[67] Zimmermann to Lancken, November 3, 1916, Ibid., SA Reel 35/67, and Jagow to Ratibor, October 31, 1916, Ibid., SA Reel 35/58. The latter document states that Germany sought to issue the passes in view of the hardships suffered by the Spanish people. At least that was to be the view presented publicly.

[68] Ratibor to Foreign Office, January 14, 1916, Ibid., SA Reel 38/no frame number.

[69] Kocherthaler to Langwerth, December 6, 1916, Ibid., SA Reel 35/140 (Second Part). Even Ludendorff felt Germany had nothing to fear from Spain at the end of 1916. Erich Ludendorff, My War Memories (New York: Harpers, 1920), p. 372.

[70] Ratibor to Foreign Office, December 7, 1916, Deutschland 127. Die Spanische Mission in Berlin, T149/79/50. Hereafter cited Deutschland 127. Mission.

[71] Welczeck's inner Memorandum, December 16, 1916, Spanien 61. secr. Die Beziehungen, SA Reel 35 (Second Part)/153, and Ratibor to Foreign Office, December 17, 1916, Spanien 61. Die Politischen Beziehungen, 357/345-346.

[72] Zimmermann to Lancken, December 11, 1916, Spanien 61. secr. Die Bezienhungen, SA Reel 35/139 (Second Part).

[73] Wolfgang Steglich, Buendnissicherung oder Verstaendingungsfrieden, Untersuchungen zu dem Friedensangebot der Mittelmaechte vom 12. Dezember 1916 (Goettingen, Berlin, Frankfurt: Musterschmidt Verlag, 1958), p. 169, and the footnote references on pp. 238-239. The footnotes in this work suggest that Villalobar communicated with the Belgian King in La Panne so as to make a special peace offer to Belgium. Yet other statements indicate that a meeting took place only

between Villalobar and representatives of the Belgian King, probably on December 20, 1916 and again on January 3, 1917. The intervention of Villalobar, however, failed to lead to a special understanding with Belgium.

[74]Gruenau to Foreign Office, December 12, 1916, Spanien 61. secr. Die Beziehungen, SA Reel 35/146. (Second Part, Hofzug).

[75]Gruenau to Foreign Office, December 12, 1916, Spanien 55. Nr. 1. secr. Das Spanische Koenigshaus, T149/356/398 and Walter Goerlitz, The Kaiser and His Court (New York: Harcourt & Brace, 1964), pp. 223-224. See also Just, "Neutralitaet," p. 398. The last document is fuller than the German one and relates to the fear the Allies had that Alfonso would arrange a peace with his fellow monarchs, a peace unfavorable to the Entente. See in Just, Fuerstenberg, Telegram No. 557 of November 29, 1916, HHStA PA rot 895.

[76]William to Alfonso, December 13, 1916, Spanien 61. secr. Die Beziehungen, SA Reel 35/149 (Second Part of Roll).

[77]Lansing to Chargé Wilson, December 20, 1916, U.S. Foreign Relations, 1916 Supplement, The World War, pp. 102-103.

[78]Lansing to Wilson, December 27, 1916, Ibid., p. 116, and Memo of an Interview with Spanish Ambassador Riaño, Woodrow Wilson Papers, Microfilm Series 5A:Peace Conference Correspondence, Fr. 289.

[79]Times, January 1, 1917.

[80]Anonymous, "Spain as the Mediator," Literary Digest, LIV (March 1917), p. 698. For Alfonso's hope to assist in any general peace conference, see Lansing to Wilson, December 27, 1916, U.S. Foreign Relations, 1916 Supplement, p. 116., and the New York Times, December 31, 1916, p. 1.

[81]In September Kalle had delivered reports about the campaign in Rumania to Alfonso, see Gruenau to Foreign Office, September 16, 1916, Spanien 61. secr. Die Beziehungen, SA Reel 35/112. In December Alfonso requested yet further reports about the military situation on both the western and eastern fronts, Kalle to Foreign Office, December 16, 1916, Deutschland 127. Mission, 79/534.

[82]Ibid.

[83]La Época, December 10, 1916.

[84]Times, December 12, 1916.

[85]*El Imparcial* as quoted in the *Times*, December 23, 1916.

[86]*La Época*, December 26, 1916.

[87]*Times*, December 28, 1916.

[88]Sir Charles Petrie, *King Alfonso XIII and His Age* (London: Chapman & Hall, 1963), p. 131.

[89]*New York Times*, January 3, 1917.

[90]Ratibor to Foreign Office, January 5, 1917, Spanien 61. *secr. Die Beziehungen*, SA Reel 38/no frame number.

[91]Gruenau to Foreign Office, January 11, 1917, Ibid., SA Reel 38/no frame number.

[92]Ratibor to Foreign Office, January 11, 1917, Ibid., SA Reel 35/no frame number.

[93]Ibid.

[94]*New York Times*, January 21, 1917.

[95]Reichsschatzamt to Foreign Office, February 5, 1917, Ibid., SA Reel 38/no frame number.

[96]*New York Times*, February 13, 1917.

[97]Ratibor to Foreign Office, February 25, 1917, Ibid., SA Reel 38/no frame number.

[98]Ratibor to Foreign Office, March 4, 1917, Ibid., SA Reel 35/no frame number.

[99]Ratibor to Foreign Office, undated summary report about German publications in Spanish entitled: *Versand Statistik fuer die Taegliche Kriegsberichte sowie fuer die Veroeffentlichungen in Spanischen Sprache*, Ibid., SA Reel 38/no frame number--placed just after the March 4, 1917 missive of Ratibor to the Foreign Office.

[100]Ratibor to Foreign Office, January 10, 1917, Ibid., SA Reel 35/no frame number.

[101]Lancken to Foreign Office, January 24, 1917, Ibid., SA Reel 35/no frame number.

[102]Ratibor to Foreign Office, January 22, 1917, Ibid., SA Reel 35/no frame number.

[103]Ratibor to Foreign Office, February 15, 1917, Ibid., SA Reel 35/no frame number.

[104]Ratibor to Foreign Office, April 4, 1917, Spanien 67. Die Auswaertige Politik Spaniens, vol. 3, T149/78/265-268. Hereafter cited as Spanien 67. Auswaertige, followed by the frame number.

[105]Ratibor to Foreign Office, January 6, 1917, Spanien 61. secr. Die Beziehungen, SA Reel 38/no frame number.

[106]Ibid.

[107]Inner Memorandum January 19, 1917, Ibid., SA Reel 38/no frame number.

[108]Ratibor to Foreign Office, February 25, 1917, Weltkrieg Nr. 11q. Unternehmungen und Aufwiegelungen, vol. 1-3, T149/402/465. Hereafter cited Weltkrieg Nr. 11q. Aufwiegelungen, followed by the frame number.

[109]Gimeno to Ratibor, February 14, 1917, Germany, Auswaertiges Amt, Diplomatische Schriftenstuecke aus der Zeit vom 12. Dezember 1916 bis zum 19. Maerz 1917 (Berlin, 1920), pp. 68-69.

[110]Willard to Lansing, February 6, 1917, U.S. Foreign Relations, 1917 Supplement, The World War, pp. 120-121.

[111]New York Times, February 11, 1917.

[112]Wedel to Foreign Office, February 10, 1917, Spanien 61. secr. Die Beziehungen, SA Reel 38/no frame number. also, Just, "Neutralitaet," pp. 408-410. also see Wolfgang Steglich, Die Friedenspolitik der Mittlemaechte 1917/1918 (Wiesbaden: Steiner Verlag, 1964), vol. I, pp. 190-220.

[113]Zimmermann to Ratibor, February 5, 1917, Spanien 61. secr. Die Beziehungen, SA Reel 38/no frame number.

[114]New York Times, February 14, 1917.

[115]Ratibor to Foreign Office, February 20, 1917, Deutschland 127. Mission, 539.

[116]Ratibor to Foreign Office, March 26, 1917, Spanien 40. Allgemeine Angelegenheiten, T149/355/64. Cited hereafter as Spanien 40. Allgemeine, followed by the frame number, and Summary List of Spanish ships sunk, Memorandum of Admiralty to Foreign Office, August 24, 1918, T149/roll 359/87-90. Madariga, p. 316.

[117]Ibid., p. 65.

[118]New York Times, March 31, 1917, see in addition Gerald Meaker, The Revolutionary Left in Spain, 1914-1923 (Stanford, Calif.: Stanford Univ. Press, 1974), pp. 67-68.

[119]New York Times, March 25, 1917.

[120]Inner Memorandum, no date, Berlin, early 1917, Spanien 40. Allgemeine, 77.

[121]Thomas Bailey, The Policy of the United States Toward the Neutrals, 1917-1918 (Baltimore, Md.: Johns Hopkins Press, 1942), pp. 277-278.

[122]Ratibor to Foreign Office, February 21, 1917, Weltkrieg Nr. 11q. Aufwiegelungen, 496.

[123]Kalle to GHQ, March 1, 1917, Ibid., 483.

[124]Ratibor to Foreign Office, March 1, 1917, Ibid., 471.

[125]Polo to Zimmermann, no date, probably in March 1917 due to internal evidence, Ibid., 474.

[126]Holtzendorff to Foreign Office, March 3, 1917, Ibid., 475.

[127]Holtzendorff to Krohn, March 6, 1917, Ibid., 490.

[128]Ratibor to Foreign Office, March 9, 1917, Ibid., 495.

[129]Krohn to Admiralty, March 17, 1917, Ibid., 508.

[130]Zimmermann to Polo, March 19, 1917, Ibid., 505.

[131]Notes taken by Zimmermann in a conversation with Polo, March 26, 1917, Ibid., 521.

[132]Welczeck to Zimmermann, April 1, 1917, Ibid., 523.

[133]Zimmermann to Ratibor, April 7, 1917, Ibid., 527.

[134]Ratibor to Foreign Office, April 14, 1917, Ibid., 531.

[135]Ratibor to Foreign Office, June 21, 1917, Deutschland 127. Mission, 72 and Ratibor to Foreign Office, June 26, 1917, Ibid., 99.

[136]El Imparcial, January 10, 1917.

[137]Ibid.

[138]*El Imparcial*, January 31, 1917.

[139]Ibid., January 22, 1917.

[140]Quoted in Marquis of Cortina's *Terra Incognita* (Madrid: n.p., no date) pp. 106-107.

[141]*Times*, January 25, 1917.

[142]Romanones, *Notas de una Vida*, pp. 342-343.

[143]Ibid., p. 365.

[144]García Venero, *Santiago Alba: Monarquíco de Razón*, p. 155.

[145]*Times*, April 20, 1917.

[146]Willard to Lansing, April 18, 1918, Rcd. Grp. 159 State Dept., 763.72/3937, National Archives, Washington, D.C.

[147]War Dept. Chief of Staff, Record Group 165, 2072-122, September 14, 1918, The National Archives, Washington, D.C.

[148]Ratibor to Foreign Office, April 19, 1917, Spanien 57. *Ministerien*, 530.

[149]Ratibor to Foreign Office, April 19, 1917, Spanien 57. *Die Spanische Ministerien*, T149/356/530.

[150]*La Época*, April 20, 1917.

[151]García Venero, p. 307.

[152]Stanley G. Payne, *Politics and the Military in Modern Spain* (Stanford, Calif.: Stanford Univ. Press, 1967), p. 128.

[153]Ratibor to Foreign Office, June 21, 1917, Deutschland 127. *Mission*, 69-72.

[154]Ibid.

[155]Ratibor to Foreign Office, June 21, 1917, Ibid., 72-76. In addition, see *Die Frankfurter Zeitung, Der Grosse Krieg*, p. 6765. The reply of Prieto to the sinking of the *San Fulgencio* is contained in its entirety, and it reveals the mildness of the new government.

[156]Ratibor to Foreign Office, June 21, 1917, Deutschland 127. *Mission*, 80-81.

CHAPTER VII

DOMESTIC DISTURBANCE AND THE SUBMARINE PROBLEM

MAY 1917 - MARCH 1918

Spain Moves into the Entente Camp

In the summer of 1917 portions of the army leadership challenged the Spanish government, and a ministry more amenable to the military's demands for increased pay in the inflationary times came to power. Inflation also had affected industrial workers, most of whom were centered in Barcelona and other cities. Once the Government dissolved the Cortes and refused to call a constituent assembly, the Socialists and other leftists as well as the Catalan regionalists offered to join with the infantry to create a government more representative of the masses.

Conservative politician Antonio Maura, who had initially praised the movement as a true Spanish one, refused to cooperate with the illegal National Assembly meeting on July 19, 1917. Subsequently, the government dissolved the group, but the workers, impressed with the Workers and Soldiers Councils of Russia, became violent. In August 1917, a revolutionary general strike occurred, and those who earlier had called for the National Assembly and a new constitutional order now became frightened, advocating severe repression of the outbreaks. In October 1917, Spanish political leaders and the officers of the army once again closed ranks behind Manuel García Prieto, the leader of the conservative wing of the Liberals; domestic reform was thus stillborn.[1]

In the midst of these problems German submarines sought refuge in Spanish harbors, thereby initiating a strong campaign by the Allies to force Spain into a hostile attitude toward belligerent underwater craft. Indeed, what seemed to be a great German triumph in getting rid of Romanones eventually turned into the beginning of increased Allied pressure and influence. Perhaps most notable was the rising attention given Spain by the Allies and their more successful use of economic and propaganda tools. Allied policy toward Spain evidently shifted, and Spain could now function effectively as an ally of the Entente without formal association with the western belligerents. Through economic and diplomatic pressure, Spain was a "neutral ally" by early 1918.

The Germans sought to do all they could to aid the new government throughout April and May 1917. Hugo Kocherthaler in Brussels advised that García Prieto was truly interested in neutrality and the German representatives should do all in their power to come to terms with him.[2] Ratibor spoke with the new Prime Minister on April 25, 1917, when the latter related that Spain had to remain on good terms with the Allies due to her geographical position. At the same time, Spain sought to maintain good relations with Germany, and Prieto assured Ratibor that Spain would remain strictly neutral. In case of difficulty, Spain would even call on Germany. Ratibor replied that he would do everything possible to bring about the success of the new government.[3] Though there were some other ship losses that plagued the Spanish, Ratibor initiated a series of actions that were aimed toward winning support for the German side in public opinion.

German consuls visited the widows of sailors who had been on board the Spanish vessel San Patricio, sunk by U-boats.[4] In reply to a Spanish protest against the sinking of the San Patricio, the Germans were notably conciliatory, offering to give the Spanish flag a twenty-one gun salute for the violation.[5] Ratibor also argued he should continue to support the right wing of the Liberal Party in hope that after the war Germany could get more from it. Particularly, Germany needed a friendly Liberal government headed by Villanueva who was pro-German.[6] Even Reich Chancellor Theobald von Bethmann Hollweg praised Spain's noble traditions and faithful observance of neutrality.[7]

Developments seemed quite favorable, but there were some ominous possibilities. On June 9, 1917 Romanones's intrigues and opposition to García Prieto's acceptance of military demands for salary increases led to the Prime Minister's fall. Soon thereafter a crisis within the Liberal Party forced Romanones to abandon party leadership.[8] The King accepted the military's demands in June, and the left-conservative government of Eduardo Dato tried to restore order; the Germans feared the path for Allied influence was now wide open once again. Ratibor complained in late June that Alfonso was not aware of the seriousness of the situation. Ratibor really feared Dato could not possibly succeed and the Spanish monarchy was endangered, and to the Germans there could be no greater catastrophe than the fall of the monarchy which they regarded as the mainstay of their so-far successful policy.[9] By late June the idea of the army strike movement spread and infected workers' councils. Dato suspended constitutional guarantees and declared a state of martial law.[10]

The Allies, especially the French, blamed the disturbances upon Spain's ambiguous position in the war and upon María Cristina's favoritism for Austria. To them, Alfonso feared for his throne as a revolutionary result of the war; this attitude could clearly be seen in the King's concern for the Romanov family in Russia after March 1917.[11]

The Germans on the other hand saw Allied influence in the army and worker disturbances. Ratibor reported in July 1917 that foreign agents were responsible for the complicated domestic situation; the Spanish government, unfortunately, could react only lethargically. Ratibor saw the King as overwhelmed by Allied diplomatic pressure.[12] With the army disturbances, workers uprisings in Barcelona further excited German opinion. The Spanish Military Attaché in Berlin fueled German belief that Spanish difficulties lay in England and France. Major Valdivia, the Attaché, reported

French propaganda appealed to young soldiers against officers and to officers against the King. Valdivia felt the Allies were intent upon either Spanish entry into the war or revolution. Since war entry was an impossibility, only revolution remained as the Entente goal.[13] With the separatists' meeting in Barcelona on July 19, 1917, the Germans saw proof of this push toward "revolution." Ratibor reported the shift of the army toward the government and the closing of the Barcelona meeting.[14] By August 1917, a revolutionary general strike was called and the government found itself further embattled.

The Socialists and their workers union the UGT under the leadership of Pablo Iglesias, the bourgeois Catalan regionalists led by Francisco Cambo, and the anarchists and their union CNT joined to demand governmental reforms and control of high inflation. The bourgeois regionalists and the Socialists desired an orderly, peaceful change in the structure of government, but the anarchists were impatient, desiring violent, immediate confrontation with Madrid. Local disturbances in Valencia precipitated a revolutionary general strike, and while the Socialists carried out their promises made to the anarchists to participate in the movement, the bourgeois regionalists backed away and refused any part in the strike when it had become violent. The army in the meantime had gotten its demands for concessions in June 1917, and had lost its revolutionary fervor. Consequently, the army ruthlessly suppressed the outbreaks of violence from

August 13-18, 1917.[15]

The Germans saw the French as the culprits in Barcelona. A French supported newspaper supposedly proposed a revolutionary government to be led by Miguel de Unamuno and Alexander Lerroux. The English Ambassador, Sir Arthur Hardinge, also supposedly was to help support this move.[16] By August the Germans perceived the whole of the summer disturbances to have been a plot on the part of the English and French to regain the favorable position they had enjoyed under Romanones.[17]

Subsequently, the Allies and some historians have seen the Germans as instigators of the Barcelona disturbances. Subsequent newspaper accounts of German support for anarchists in Barcelona and Madrid would seem to indicate that the Germans had helped to foment disturbances in Spain.[18] It is true the Germans tried to halt Spanish exports useful to the Allies; there seems to be sufficient support for that view in German documents relating to espionage activities. But the Germans truly desired a stable monarchial Spanish government, and a careful reading of Ratibor's account of the disturbances modifies the view that the Germans had tried to aid the separatists in Barcelona. Indeed, there were strikes on the docks induced by the Germans, but those difficulties predated the August troubles.[19] And German diplomatic correspondence pointed toward fear of the fall of the monarchy. Naturally, one cannot account for individual actions at the time, but one can quite safely conclude that the Germans probably did not foment the disturbances nor did anything officially to further them.

Equally, one cannot accept the oversimplified view of Ratibor that the English and French were solely responsible for the disturbance. The domestic difficulties were due to internal political and economic forces whose origins lay in the modernization and urbanization of Spain; these two developments had been hastened by the economic effects of the war. What is of significance is that the Germans saw a decided weakening of the government and of the monarchy. To them this domestic change was caused by the Allies. In the light of attempts by German submarines to take refuge in Spanish harbors and of Spain's bowing to Allied demands to forbid submarine entry on pain of internment, the Germans saw a concerted effort by the Allies to turn previous pro-German Spain into a handmaiden of the Allies.

Beginning in early June 1917 and continuing through September, German-Spanish relations focused upon three submarines, the UC-52, the UB-23, and the UB-49. The Allies objected strenuously to the entrance and later exit of the UC-52, leading to a decree by Alfonso that threatened internment for such vessels. The Germans saw this as part of Allied pressure to weaken the monarchy and to push Spain back into the Allied camp, particularly as the decree went into effect on June 29, 1917, in the midst of Spain's domestic troubles. The UB-23 entered a Spanish harbor on June 29, 1917, and was duly interned. A few months later this submarine was sold to Spain and the proceeds used to bolster German propaganda there.

In September-October 1917 problems with the UB-49 brought German-Spanish relations to a crisis. This submarine entered a Spanish harbor and then escaped on October 6, 1917. Subsequently, the Allies put enormous pressure upon Spain to use this incident as an excuse to demand the recall of the German Naval Attaché presumably as a preview to further demands for the recall of Ratibor and the influential Military Attaché, Kalle.

In association with heightened economic pressure Allied propaganda efforts vastly improved, and a virtual press war challenged the Germans to a duel. By early March 1918, the Allies were virtually in control, having concluded favorable economic agreements with the Spanish, though significant details remained to be worked out. But the procession of events from June 1917 through March 1918 was almost ineluctable once the Allies set their minds upon it; Spain was definitely in the Allied camp without a declaration of war.

Once a German submarine, the UC-52, entered the Cádiz harbor in early June 1917, American and British authorities sought to get it interned.[20] The Germans were immediately aware of this pressure and attempted to bolster the Spanish in the face of it.[21]

The Spanish, in the meantime, placated both the Allies and the Germans. In a message to Berlin relayed by Polo, the Spanish set down generous terms for treating the vessel. The ship received repairs June 26-28, and was to leave for home directly without attacking anyone within twenty-four hours thereafter.[22] Chief of the Admiralty Staff Henning von Holtzendorff told the Foreign Office the vessel would obey Spanish requests in order to ease Spain's obvious difficulties with the Allies.[23]

The Germans were quite correct in assuming the Allies were putting pressure upon the Spanish for internment of the UC-52. The Allies saw the event as a repetition of the Cartagena Affair of June 1916, and the British in particular wanted all of the Allies to join in a vigorous protest.[24] By June 26, 1917, Spain insisted upon the departure of the UC-52 on pain of internment if the vessel did not leave by June 29, 1917.[25] The vessel finally left Cádiz at three o'clock in the morning of June 29, 1917.[26]

English and French pressure to forbid submarines to enter Spanish harbors was especially severe in July 1917. Questions in the House of Commons dealt with the issue, and the French Chamber of Deputies also focused upon violations of Spanish neutrality.[27] Subsequently, Alfonso issued a new royal decree that supplemented the one of November 1914. The three points contained in the decree were: (1) submarines of all the belligerent powers were forbidden to enter Spanish waters or ports; (2) if such vessels did enter Spanish waters or ports, then they would be interned for the duration of the war; and (3) the decree of November 1914 was yet in force respecting Spanish neutrality.[28]

But this was only the beginning of considerable pressure from the Allies. In the succeeding months, both the Americans and the British pressed Spain to do more to protect her neutrality. In early July 1917 the Allies quizzed Spain upon the number of Allied and neutral vessels sunk within Spanish territorial waters.[29] The Americans, staying slightly aloof from the French, desired precise proof of any attempts made in Spain to aid Germany directly.[30] American Ambassador Joseph Willard in Madrid wanted to base all Allied claims about Spanish aid to Germany upon British and French secret service investigations.[31] Indeed, the United States, once a neutral herself, yet tried to respect Spanish rights as a neutral, although France and Great Britain were not quite so circumspect.

The Spanish, in the meantime, resisted renewed pressure to take a more belligerent attitude toward Germany.[32] In reports about Entente efforts to control Spanish policy, particularly as the domestic troubles had become more severe, the Germans became frantic. Furthermore, press censorship was imposed, and German news reports were being suppressed while pro-Allied articles seemed to dominate the newspapers.[33] The Germans were further discomfited by a Swiss report that confirmed that the Allies were making demands.[34] The Germans were also convinced that military preparations in Portugal were a threat to Spain and were thus meant to bring the Spanish around to the Allied viewpoint.[35]

A further difficulty perplexed German relations with

Spain in July 1917. The Germans learned that Polo, the Spanish Ambassador at Berlin, had become quite jealous of Spanish Military Attaché Valdivia. While both were pro-German, the Germans had to keep Polo thinking he was the best informed of the Spanish delegation. On the other hand, Valdivia had better relations with the German Supreme Command. Often the Germans knew the Spanish considered Polo too pro-German, hoping Valdivia might be a useful corrective. Consequently, the Foreign Office had to walk its own tightrope in dealing with the Spanish delegation.[36]

Another crisis arose as the UB-23, a German underwater craft, entered a Spanish harbor, this time at La Coruña. The submarine was immediately interned and ordered to El Ferrol, a few miles away.[37] Interestingly, the submarine entered the harbor and anchored near an interned German merchant vessel, the _Belgrano_.[38] The Germans accepted the internment, and negotiations got underway to sell the submarine to Spain. By September 26, 1917, the sum of 1.348 million marks was agreed upon.[39] What is of interest, however, is that the Foreign Office directed that the money was to be used for German press propaganda in Spain.[40]

In the meantime, the Spanish renewed their personal diplomacy with the Germans. Prime Minister Dato told Ratibor the Allies were determined to drive the monarchy from Spain and Spain needed to mollify them. In addition, Spain would have a much easier time of it if the Germans did not protest the submarine decree of Alfonso.[41] The Germans also appealed directly to Alfonso, thanking him for his personal intervention and in permitting the UC-52 to leave Spain in June.[42] A Foreign Office memo to German Chancellor Kuehlmann suggested further economic aid to Spain and to the other neutrals by use of safe-conduct passages through the war zone for Spanish fruit ships, similar passes for shipments to America, and finally the founding of a company, the Hesperides, to purchase Spanish foodstuffs.[43] Nothing of great moment came from this suggestion, but the Germans were quite frightened that the Allies truly meant to destroy the Spanish monarchy and to create a republic.[44]

Another taste of the diversionary diplomacy of the Spanish King was revealed by the actions of his cousin in late August and September 1917. Alfonso Marie, the son of the King's peripatetic Aunt Eulalia, approached Germany once again, this time through the Swiss, holding out promises of a German-Spanish rapprochement. He asked if Germany would support Spanish occupation of Tangier, Gibraltar and further economic development in the peninsula. Furthermore, the Spanish evidenced interest in a commercial treaty with Germany. It is interesting that such a commercial treaty actually was negotiated after the war by the Weimar government.[45]

In the meantime, in September 1917 King Alfonso XIII expressed his recognition of Spanish economic dependence upon the Allies.[46] Both the Americans and British put considerable economic pressure upon Spain to accede to their desires.

Badly needed supplies were withheld, bringing Spain to agree to a commercial treaty with Great Britain by December 1917. In the Cortina Agreement England agreed to supply Spain with coal and to buy Spanish surplus fruit. Spain on its side agreed to supply England with all of its iron ore needs and to provide the necessary ship space for the task.[47] Americans began to withhold petroleum and cotton to get Spain to agree to supply the American Expeditionary Army with requisite mules, blankets, boots, and foodstuffs.[48] Therefore, German promises might be a useful counterweight in the negotiations in the fall of 1917 with the Allies.

The Germans responded to Alfonso Marie's suggestions in September 1917. A report from Bern indirectly revealed the status of the German-Spanish negotiations, when the Minister there reported that the King's cousin was greatly pleased that Germany promised to study the possibility of economic aid to Spain. Furthermore, the Spanish were happy that Germany was ready to accede to Spanish wishes about Tangier and Gibraltar.[49]

The actions of the King's cousin can be taken as his own personal initiative, but in light of previous activities on his part, that is unlikely. Actually, as Spain was negotiating at the same time what would become the Cortina Agreement with the English and an American-Spanish commercial agreement, one could speculate that King Alfonso sought to deflect the diplomatic and economic pressure being placed on him by the Allies through a feint toward the Germans.

Too, there may have been some suspicions at Madrid that the domestic disturbances really were Allied attempts to overthrow the monarchy. There is no direct evidence for this interpretation, but the previous actions of the King in trying to counterbalance the Allies with the Germans and the logic of his difficult situation in 1917 would argue strongly for it.

German espionage and sabotage efforts fared no better than economic activities by late 1917. On October 10, 1917, the Entente lodged a sharp protest against Spain for German espionage and propaganda activities. According to German sources, the Entente threatened to halt all coal shipments if the Spanish did not crack down on the Germans.[50] In addition, the German master spy for Spain, Arnold, was arrested by the British on his return from Buenos Aires.[51] The Allies also accused Germany of using the diplomatic pouch for espionage and propaganda.[52] Unfortunately for the Germans, the British had discovered that a letter Military Attaché Kalle had sent to his mother via the Diplomatic Pouch also contained secret messages to the Political Section of the Foreign Office. Thus, the Germans were shown to be violating the diplomatic pouch.[53]

The final entry of Spain in the Allied camp came during September 1917-March 1918. Another submarine crisis precipitated a barrage of Allied demands that Alfonso could not resist. In addition, the Allied propaganda work was functioning at peak efficiency by December 1917-March 1918.

and the Allies successfully removed or silenced Marine Attaché von Krohn and Embassy Secretary von Stohrer. With completion of the Anglo-Spanish Economic Agreement and of the U.S.-Spanish Agreement of March 1918, the process of creating a "neutral ally" out of Spain was complete. All that remained was for Spain to abandon its deferential attitude toward Germany and to demand the transfer of interned merchant vessels for Spanish ships sunk in the course of war. The crisis of the UB-49 precipitated those developments.

The UB-49 entered Cádiz on September 9, 1917, with a broken propeller shaft and was interned.[54] Not spectacular in itself, subsequent developments turned the affair into the key element that demonstrated Allied influence in Spain. The commander of this vessel told von Krohn, the Naval Attaché, that he wanted to break out of his internment and to return home.[55] Krohn apparently told the commander not to do it as it would cause too many political problems with the Spanish government.[56] But on October 6, 1917, the vessel slipped out of Cádiz harbor.[57] Ratibor reported the sudden departure of the vessel had caused an uproar in Spain.[58] The Allies joined in pressuring Spain to punish those responsible.[59] The Germans realized immediately the gravity of the situation. Ratibor sent a copy of Krohn's instructions to the submarine commander to the King to show that there was no premeditated attempt to get the vessel out of the Spanish port.[60] The British also demanded the recall of the Naval Attaché.[61] The Germans saw the demands to recall him as part of the concurrent negotiations between Spain and England and Spain and the U.S.A. for commercial treaties. To the Wilhelmstrasse the British and Americans had broken off their negotiations to get the removal of troublesome people at the German Embassy.[62] A formal note demanding von Krohn's withdrawl was presented in Berlin by an apologetic Polo on October 15, 1917. The Foreign Office did get assurances of safe-conduct passes for von Krohn and his family and seemed resigned to his recall.[63]

The Germans and Spanish argued for several months thereafter over whether or not the German commander had given his word of honor to the Spanish authorities at Cádiz that he would not escape. Of course the Spanish permitted the vessel to refuel, though the explosives were removed, and the crew remained on the submarine. The whole of Spanish comments from this point onward were based upon this point of "honor."[64] Probably the Spanish intended the vessel to escape. The real point of difficulty was the embarrassment caused Alfonso due to intense Allied pressure. Beginning with the Cartagena Affair in June 1916, and continuing through the summer of 1917, the Allies had become less and less patient with Spanish winking at German violations of Hispanic neutrality.[65]

The Foreign Office at Berlin seemed ready to recall von Krohn, but the military intervened. Admiral Mueller of the High Command wanted concrete reasons before von Krohn would be recalled.[66] In a lengthy message to Berlin, von

Krohn admitted he had engaged in a wide variety of activities that would inevitably displease the Allies. He said he was active in "information services," "Portuguese undertakings," and certain "destructions," (<u>Zerstoerungen</u>) all of which probably had violated Spanish neutrality.[67] In light of this situation, von der Bussche in the Foreign Office argued for immediate recall to avoid ill-feelings with Spain.[68] Ratibor, however, demonstrated his lack of diplomatic expertise once again and argued that the removal of von Krohn would set a precedent that might lead to his own recall.[69] Krohn added his voice to the cacophony arguing his recall would reveal German weaknesses that could later be exploited.[70] But the Spanish were adamant, demanding immediate recall.[71] The Spanish further threatened to cease representing German interests in Peru and Uruguay, if Germany did not act.[72] But Undersecretary von der Bussche's efforts were fruitless as Ludendorff declared himself forthrightly against the recall.[73]

The Allies in the meantime applied more pressure to get the Spanish to intern the crews of German merchant ships which they saw as centers of espionage activity.[74] The U.S.A. finally took this action by November 28, 1917.[75] The Germans also feared the Americans were putting pressure upon Spain to permit the crossing of American and Portuguese troops into France. There turned out to be nothing to this, but German diplomatic correspondence was taken up with it throughout the remainder of November and part of December.[76]

On December 11, 1917, Ratibor wrote a rather remarkable letter to the Foreign Office at Madrid. Ratibor abandoned his support for Krohn and gave sufficient reason, apparently to the military, so that von Krohn eventually was recalled. The letter described the shocking revelation that von Krohn had an affair with a French woman of the "demimonde" who was also in his pay as a German agent. Ratibor was really shocked that the good naval officer's affair was well known in the German colony and among the Spanish. He was also upset over the fact that von Krohn seemed completely under the lady's spell, and after the two finally had broken off their liaison, the scorned lady sent his love letters to Ratibor. The Ambassador discovered von Krohn had divulged state secrets to the woman. Ratibor sent the Naval Attaché off to take the water cure for his singed nerves.[77]

Interestingly, a recent biography of Gertrud Margarete Zelle, better known as Mata Hari, the nude dancer and German spy executed by the French in 1917, describes her meeting with von Krohn and Kalle at Madrid.[78] Contemporary and subsequent reports linked von Krohn and Mata Hari, but this recent biography of Miss Zelle suggests that von Krohn was friendly with a French female spy and not with Mata Hari. Regardless of who shared his amorous adventures, von Krohn had outlived his usefulness.

On a more serious note, the military now suggested a private letter be sent from the Emperor to Alfonso, in the hope such direct diplomacy among monarchs could settle the problem quickly.[79] A message from Ratibor crossed this one, and Ratibor reported the King had backed off from his demand of an immediate recall of the German Naval Attaché and had consented to let von Krohn rest for awhile at a resort outside Madrid so as not to make the connection between his removal and the recent submarine issue too obvious.[80] The matter rested thus while the Germans sought to maintain their prestige and not buckle under to what they knew were really Allied demands.

The Emperor, however, prepared his personal letter and the Foreign Office, at the same time, concocted an idea that appealed to the military, a mixed commission to investigate the circumstances of the departure of the German submarine.[81] In the meantime, the Anglo-Spanish Accord, an updated version of the "Cortina" Agreement of May 1917, which was not ratified until December 6, 1917, was signed. This agreement provided for specific shipments of English coal in return for Spanish iron ore.[82]

Just as the new year of 1918 began, the Germans sent a private letter from Emperor William to King Alfonso. The letter tied together the settlement of the escaped submarine question with the removal of von Krohn and further German economic aid after the war. The Emperor suggested that a mixed commission come to Berlin to investigate the case and eventually to settle it.[83] But Alfonso would have nothing of the German suggestion.

Once the Spanish Military Attaché Valdivia delivered the letter, he found himself roundly criticized by Alfonso for acting more like a German agent than a Spanish representative.[84] Valdivia, however, persevered, and he suggested a compromise was possible. Clearly, the Spanish Attaché noted, there was a misunderstanding due to unsatisfactory translations. The Cadiz officials had only thought the German submarine commander, Mellanthin, had given his word of honor not to escape. Therefore, to satisfy the Spaniards, a German submarine should be placed in drydock at the Austro-Hungarian port of Pola.[85]

But Alfonso was aloof and was not interested in Valdivia's further reports upon the general military situation in Europe.[86] The King formally rejected the idea of a mixed commission on January 17, 1918, and on the nineteenth wrote a letter with a very cool tone to Kaiser William. Alfonso merely stated he hoped future economic relations would develop, but the flight of the German U-boat had greatly strained relations between Germany and Spain. Alfonso suggested, however, that the problem could be ironed out, and in a rather sarcastic vein, he said that he had been forewarned something like this might happen.[87]

Several further attempts were made by the Germans to solve this vexing problem of Alfonso's supposedly wounded pride. The Germans officially agreed to set aside a submarine at the Austro-Hungarian port of Pola for the duration of the war. This was to be a sign to the Spanish of German goodwill and to demonstrate that a genuine misunderstanding occurred.[88] The Spanish took about a month to reply, and on March 5, 1918 they repeated their insistence upon the return of the submarine to Cádiz, whence it had escaped the previous year.[89] The Germans, of course, refused to do this.[90] Thus, by March 14, 1918 the whole matter of satisfying the Spanish over the departure of the German submarine was allowed to drop. Valdivia reported that the Allies had successfully insisted Alfonso remain firm in the case, thereby resulting in German failure to solve the problem satisfactorily.[91]

This submarine problem was only one of a great many difficulties the Germans had faced since early January, when Allied propaganda attacked the Germans in Spain and managed to shake the determination of the Ambassador. Ratibor reported on January 6, 1918 that severe attacks on Embassy personnel were appearing in the Spanish press. The government was doing nothing, out of fear of Entente agents, he surmised.[92] In the midst of German difficulties, Spanish domestic politics once again became important. Young army officers demanded new elections, threatening a coup d'etat otherwise. The King removed the young men from their posts and proposed calling new local elections as the army demanded.[93]

Domestic political considerations further clouded Spanish foreign policy. After the summer 1917 turmoil, the government of Eduardo Dato faltered, and in the fall of 1917 a new government, headed by Manuel García Prieto had tried to placate the army and the demands from regionalists and the urban proletariat for reform. The result was a promise for elections free from the chicanery normally practiced.

But the elections of February through March 1918 produced a totally new situation. The various elements demanding reform and regeneration had never been closely knit, but differences over the direction Spain should now take became crippling. García Prieto resigned on March 22, 1918, and Alfonso XIII found great difficulty in getting a new government. Threatening to abdicate and thereby creating a new crisis, the King persuaded Antonio Maura to head a national government made up of former Prime Ministers and of the regionalists led by Francisco Cambo.[94]

The King had never liked Maura, especially since the 1909 debacle and the "tragic week" of rioting over Maura's policies and the call-up of the army. The King told Albert Mousset, a French journalist, what he thought of Maura:

> He has a most formidable power of work and he is the most remarkable politician of this country, though he values himself too highly. He is only slightly traveled.[95]

Nevertheless, Maura was the only personality satisfactory to the military short of an outright military government which might eclipse the monarchy itself. With the new government political stability settled over Spain. Unfortunately for the Allies, the domestic crisis had monopolized Spanish attention, thus detracting from effects of the current spectacular revelations about German misdeeds by _El Sol_.[96]

The new government appeared stable, but the conflicting ambitions of the former Prime Ministers showed the seeds of future dissension. Eduardo Dato, the Minister of State, continually emphasized neutrality, but he too saw the need to get Spain on the winner's side, consequently he was one of the motivating forces behind the anti-German moves of the summer 1918. Obviously Romanones, the Minister for Grace and Justice, desired vindication for his previous policies, and he never ceased to continue his argument that Spain had to declare for the Allies. The Prime Minister, Antonio Maura, had earlier seemed pro-German, but his sympathies were really for an independent Spain, free from the difficulties of war, and he had to contend with both Dato and Romanones in the summer of 1918, finally accepting the demands of both men to pursue a harsher policy toward Germany.

Meanwhile, Allied propaganda activities developed apace. Ratibor protested to the Spanish about the personal attacks upon him in the Spanish press.[97] Ratibor had heard that during a ministerial council meeting on January 23, 1918, the government painted the Germans as being responsible for the outbreaks of unrest the previous summer.[98] Very strong protests were made through Polo at Berlin about the press attacks on the German Embassy and its personnel. Interestingly enough, these were the first notes sent in Spanish rather than French.[99] Some of the offending newspapers were seized, but others continued the attacks. By the end of the month stories began to appear that accused German Legation Secretary von Stohrer of spy activities.[100]

With the continued attacks upon Spanish ships, notably the Giralda, the Germans became less legalistic and quite conciliatory. In a note to Polo on January 31, 1918 the

Germans said they had issued orders to submarine commanders to treat Spanish vessels with special regard.[101] The Spanish, of course, had protested strongly against this sinking and against subsequent ones.[102] The sinking of the _Ceferino_ also caused great excitement in Spain and subsequent German conciliation. The Spanish demanded an explanation for the destruction of the _Ceferino_ and for the sinking of an Italian ship, the _Duca di Geneva_, in Spanish territorial waters.[103] Polo was told that the submarine commanders had exceeded their instructions; the German government thus replied quite quickly and in a conciliatory manner.[104]

The most spectacular press campaign against the Germans probably came from French sources. By February 21, 1918, the French paper _Le Matin_ reported the Spanish paper _El Sol_ had documents to prove that the Second Secretary of the German Legation, Dr. von Stohrer, had sent money to anarchists in Spain, ostensibly to stir up the August 1917 rebellion.[105] The Germans also sent von Krohn home on February 21, 1918, and the London _Times_ reported this organizer of German "submarine piracy" was now out of Spain.[106] Ratibor became quite excited at the revelations later printed in _El Sol_, particularly the word for word letters that obviously had been stolen from Embassy files.[107] A copy of a letter allegedly sent from Dr. Stohrer to Miguel Pascual, an anarchist and syndicalist, according to police records, was printed in the London _Times_.[108] In the American publication, _Literary Digest_ of April 20, 1918, a summary of the newspaper accounts of German activities appeared. One of the secretaries at the German Embassy, Herr Grimm, allegedly received Miguel Pascual in April 1915. Later the Second Secretary of the Embassy, von Stohrer, also spoke with Pascual. Allegedly, the Germans supplied Pascual with funds to organize anarchist and syndicalist groups to attack Romanones. According to a Times report quoted by the Literary Digest, the Spanish government dealt quite tolerantly with the allegations. The Times said the Spanish government seemed inclined to "dampen the matter down. It has confiscated the Sol (the Spanish newspaper that made the allegations) and all other papers, including the Época, which ventured on comment, and stopt (sic) telegrams for London and Paris dealing with the subject."[109] The implication was that the Germans had inspired the general strike of August 1917. Spanish government officials seized all issues of El Sol that made these revelations.[110]

In Berlin reaction to these spectacular charges was sanguine, apparently nothing to get very excited over.[111] The Marquis of Villalobar commented in Brussels that the whole thing was Ratibor's fault anyway. Villalobar had always taken a dim view of Ratibor's use of "second class" publications to attack Romanones. Now the Ambassador was only getting his due.[112]

The Foreign Office was far more interested in the upcoming election results for the Cortes; von der Bussche too felt that the personal attacks on Ratibor were indeed the Ambassador's own fault.[113] Nevertheless, the Spanish did take heed of German protests, and in mid-March 1918, Polo presented a list of newspapers that had been punished for the slanders against the Germans.[114] Eventually, even El Sol was hauled into court because of the charges it had made, and von Stohrer personally visited Romanones and assured the latter that the German had no intention of killing the former Prime Minister.[115] Von Stohrer also wrote to Alfonso denying all of the allegations directed against him.[116]

In the meantime, the Austrians approached Alfonso to negotiate an end to the war. Alfonso and his government acted as couriers between Emperor Karl at Vienna and President Woodrow Wilson from February 18 to April 21, 1918. Spain somewhat unenthusiastically carried out the exchange; Alfonso was not pleased in his role as postman. Prince Fuerstenberg reported on March 13, 1918 that Spain wanted its part in the exchange to be kept secret as it feared economic reprisals from the Germans. Actually Spain was negotiating for better economic terms with the Americans and French; consequently the Spanish position was tenuous at best.[117]

Clearly, Spain was now solidly within the Allied camp and the phrase "neutral ally" became an appropriate appellation. The Germans were faced with a negative attitude in regard to the escape of the UB-49, with a hostile press and severe charges of interfering in Spain and violating Spanish neutrality, and with a far more hostile and demanding attitude whenever Spanish ships were sunk. Ratibor himself seemed depressed by the experiences of the previous few months, and on March 26, 1918 he said that promises of future German economic concessions could have no further effect.[118] The recent economic agreements with Great Britain in December with the United States and France in early March precluded use of economic pressure as a lever in German-Spanish relations.[119] The Germans did comfort themselves that with the elections in February and March their effort at maintaining neutrality had not done badly. With government changes in March, the finally stabilized national government under Antonio Maura at least was firmly in the neutral camp, though few ministers of the new government were pro-German.[120] Germans now began to worry that the Allies would repeat their actions in regard to Holland and Latin American nations and seize German merchant ships. They did not have long to wait to see such a policy.

In the interim American press influence began to be felt in Spain. The Committee for Public Information, headed by George Creel, directed an American businessman, Frank J. Marion, to supply "pro-American" movies to Spain.[121] The Americans' propaganda view was similar to the one taken in regard to economic and political matters; the United States was to maintain a distance from the French and English. The only purpose of the press activities was to acquaint Spain with the United States.[122] But Irene Wright, an American student at Sevilla, offered her services to the American government. She described the need for propaganda to counteract German work.[123] The U.S. Ambassador, Joseph E. Willard, objected to any propaganda campaign, but the activities of Marion and of the Naval Attaché, Captain Burton C. Decker, had already begun with some success.[124]

Wright was the moving force, suggesting picture displays in windows of the Singer Sewing Machine Company, and by May 1918 directing a news service that supplied the Spanish Fabra Agency with North American propaganda.[125] Direct means were also used. A memo from the CPI Office in Madrid dated June 19, 1918, ordered that a payment of five hundred pesetas be made to the editor of a "friendly" newspaper so he would print news favorable to the United States.[126] The Diario Palentino apparently was the paper mentioned in the memo.[127]

Clearly, the high moral tone taken by President Woodrow Wilson was not always followed. Even in the face of the opposition of Ambassador Willard to the propaganda of the American contingent in Spain, the United States sought to supplement British and French propaganda which had been so successful in attacking von Stohrer, Ratibor, von Krohn, and Kalle.

Ratibor squirmed under the renewed Allied propaganda campaign. As early as April 1918, his picture along with Spanish anarchists was published by El Parlamentario, thus suggesting that the Germans really were behind anarchist agitators.[128] Extra editions of the paper were later published, but Ratibor's protests succeeded, and the paper was seized by Spanish authorities.[129] Further propaganda attacks on the Germans appeared in El Sol throughout May; one was a facsimile of a purported letter that attributed the war solely to the Kaiser and written by Kaiser William II.[130]

But in Berlin the Germans did not take the propaganda attacks too seriously. Like the view taken earlier about sensationalism in the Stohrer revelations, Chancellor von Kuehlmann said that remonstrances with Polo would be made. It was recognized that the Spanish could not be forced to forego freedom of the press, and the only effective way to fight the attacks was to use the German information service.[131]

Ratibor, however, could not leave well enough alone. He sought the culprits responsible for the earlier Stohrer revelations. He claimed the French Naval Attaché and Romanones himself were responsible for bribing Miguel Pascual into making his comments to El Sol.[132] Ratibor further stated his intentions to use this information in a new "press war" against the Allies and Romanones.[133] But the Foreign Office would have nothing of what amounted to a campaign of revenge and ordered Ratibor to stick to a more mundane repudiation of points made by the pro-Entente press.[134] Ratibor did happily report by late June that Niceto Alcalá Zamora's newspaper, El Día, severely criticized Romanones and pointed out that Romanones did not represent the viewpoint of the majority of Spanish Liberals. Another paper, La Nación, owned by the Marquis of Polavieja, also defended the pro-German Liberal view. These papers revealed Romanones's private financial interests in coal and other items shipped from England. Ratibor was quite delighted that Romanones's "double-dealings" could now be revealed.[135]

Other attempts to meet the increased Allied propaganda efforts were publications of lists of French and British spies. These reports allegedly uncovered French intelligence activity in which Spanish telegraph operators on board steamers were bribed to radio the locations of German U-boats to Allied naval contingents.[136]

Back in Berlin, the Foreign Office also tried to stem the tide of Entente influence in Spain by complaining of Allied activities. On July 1, 1918, the Foreign Office presented Polo with a lengthy list of Entente violations of Spanish neutrality and asked that they be stopped. Particularly, the Germans were incensed at Allied opening of German diplomatic mail.[137] But Spain responded slowly to German remonstrances.

Meanwhile, pro-German papers were regularly seized as they criticized Entente activities. Ratibor did manage to get Prime Minister Maura to bring up the subject of a more evenhanded censorship law at the next ministerial council meeting.[138] A few days later, Ratibor's efforts were rewarded. A new censorship law was passed, and for the moment, German interests seemed protected once again.[139]

Interestingly enough, Spain did try to placate the Germans in the summer of 1918. Each point of complaint made at Madrid was eventually answered. The Spanish promised to "watch the mails" to avoid Entente seizures of it.[140] The

Cortes also passed a new "spy" law that attempted, on paper at least, to restrict the intelligence activities of the belligerents.[141] The only real beneficiary of the legislation was Germany, thus revealing that Spain truly desired to maintain her neutrality and hoped to use Germany as a counterweight to the enormous economic pressures from the Entente. At least the Germans interpreted the new law in that sense.[142]

The Allies soon managed to circumvent the press and spy laws, creating totally new propaganda papers such as Los Aliados.[143] A few days later two more new papers appeared, Figaro and Jornado.[144] Ratibor complained that Allied news reports were not censored while those of the Germans were.[145] With Romanones strongly influencing Development Minister Santiago Alba, Ratibor reported that the spy law was of no consequence for the Central Powers. Its intent and possible positive effects for the Germans were ignored by the Spaniards.[146] New remonstrances were made by the Foreign Office in Berlin, but the military situation had changed by the first week of August. Germany definitely had lost the war, and it was only a matter of time before the end.[147] Entente supported newspapers became "unbridled" in their denunciation of Germany and of the Germans, according to Ratibor, and Allied pressure to force Spain to seize interned German ships found a ready hearing in the cabinet meeting rooms.[148]

The problem of the loss of Spanish ships due to the submarine war had been a vexing one since the war had started.

The first Spanish ship had not been sunk until August 1915, and Spanish remonstrances never grew very strong. Only later, in 1916, did both King Alfonso and public opinion become actively concerned. The King used the incidents to recover political influence lost to Romanones and to get the transfer of ten ships to Spain. This offer was not publicized until the fall of 1916, and by then Romanones had mounted a campaign to force Germany to break relations with Spain. Thus, the ship transfer offer was never carried out, partly because of the conciliatory effect it would have had. Romanones opposed it, and then Spain could not really carry out the terms set for the transfer. Too, since the seriousness of the German offer was open to doubt, the Foreign Office probably wanted to use it to score propaganda victories in Spain. The only concessions made were offers to spare fruit ships that sailed with special passes issued by the ambassadorial or consular offices. In addition, one German submarine was sold to the Spanish government after the ship had been interned in 1917.

As Spanish economic troubles mounted and as Allied economic agreements were signed with Spain, there were more urgent reasons to seize the estimated eighty-four interned German ships. But the Spanish delayed constantly in seizing them. The Allies urged the Spanish on during the summer of 1918, and examples of German vessels seized and interned in Argentina, Chile and Holland gave added nerve to Madrid. Indeed, as the direction of Spanish policy swung toward a pro-Allied neutrality in the spring of 1918, the Germans became acutely aware of the danger to their interned vessels.

The economic agreements Spain signed with both the French and Americans contained extra clauses that postponed the toughest negotiating points which revolved around Spain providing extra ship space for the Allies. Spain accepted the favorable terms of the agreement, but she was reluctant in doing what was obviously necessary to provide the space for the Allies, that is, to seize the interned German ships. The reasons for this attitude were not hard to find.

Germany had recently defeated the Russians as shown by the Treaty of Brest-Litovsk. German arms on the Western front were still strong, and Germany was yet capable of a new offensive which could turn the tide of the war. In keeping with an opportunistic approach to diplomacy, King Alfonso preferred not to anger the Germans. Only when it became obvious the Germans were defeated did the Spanish relent and demand the transfer.

The Spanish, however, were yet solicitous of German feelings, possibly out of concern for the enormous influence that the Allies exerted. An Allied victory would reveal Spain to be at the total mercy of France and England. Hence, even a weakened Germany would be a useful counterweight to the Allies. Also, Spain had refused to be rushed by the Allies as shown in previous pressure that the Entente had attempted to exert.

Throughout April 1918, the Germans began receiving

hints of secret clauses in the U.S.-Spanish Agreement of March. Newspaper reports suggested that the Allies now demanded that Spain provide new ship space.[149] The Spanish government discussed forcing the use of all available vessels, thus greatly arousing German suspicions.[150] Information filtering down to Ratibor indicated that at a ministerial council meeting use of interned German and Austro-Hungarian ships was mentioned to ease the lack of Spanish bottoms. Antonio Maura, apparently Ratibor's informant, rejected this suggestion and helped to persuade the council to turn to other devices to get the needed ship space.[151]

The Germans began an inter-office debate that focused upon economic aid given Spain since the war had begun. An inter-office memo detailed the offers made and those actually carried out.[152] Evidently, the Germans hoped to counter the Allied economic impact by reminding the Spanish what the Imperial Government had either done or had promised to do. Information arriving from the pro-German Spanish Legation Councillor, Count Pradere, indicated the need for Germany to reach an economic agreement with Spain. The Germans now began to think in terms of promises for aid after the war in case Spain retained its neutrality during the conflict.[153] But by April 21, 1918, the Germans learned through the Transatlantic Company, a pro-German firm, that the March agreements specified that in two months another agreement would be negotiated concerning the use of Spanish ship space.[154] The navy urged severe measures to deny such possible extra aid to the Allies.[155]

FOOTNOTES FOR CHAPTER VII

[1]Carr, pp. 500-505.

[2]Lancken to Langwerth, April 24, 1917, Spanien 57. Ministerien, 537.

[3]Ratibor to Foreign Office, April 25, 1917, Ibid., 538.

[4]New York Times, May 23, 1917.

[5]Ibid., June 3, 1917.

[6]Ratibor to Foreign Office, May 4, 1917, Spanien 57. Ministerien, 540-541.

[7]Times, May 16, 1917.

[8]Zimmermann to Gruenau, July 3, 1917, Spanien 61. Die Politischen Beziehungen, 357/438.

[9]Ratibor to Foreign Office, June 24, 1917, Spanien 40. Allgemeine, 102-103. See also Ratibor to Foreign Office, June 26, 1917, Ibid., 101.

[10]Ratibor to Foreign Office, July 4, 1917, Ibid., 85.

[11]Paul Cambon, Correspondence, 1870-1924 (Paris: B. Grasset, 1940-1946), pp. 182-183 and Anatole Nekludoff, Diplomatic Reminiscences Before and During the World War, 1911-1917 (London: Murray, 1920), p. 503.

[12]Ratibor to Foreign Office, July 4, 1917, Spanien 40. Allgemeine, 89.

[13]Lorenz to Lersner, July 20, 1917, Deutschland 127. Mission, 550.

[14]Ratibor to Foreign Office, July 24, 1917, Spanien 40. Allgemeine, 107.

[15]Meaker, pp. 82-87.

[16]Bassewitz to Foreign Office, August 18, 1917, Spanien 40. Allgemeine, 123.

[17]Bassewitz to Foreign Office, August 20, 1917, Ibid., 124.

[18]*Times*, March 8, 1917. See also Gerald Brenan's *The Spanish Labyrinth* (Cambridge: Cambridge Univ. Press, 1960), p. 69. A more recent examination of the role that gangsters, especially Richard Stahlmann, led by the Germans during the war played in the 1917 disturbances and later ones is to be found in Jorge Subirato Centura's "La Verdadero personalidad del 'Baron de Koenig'," *Cuadernos de Historia Economíca de Cataluna* (1971) V:103-118.

[19]Stein to Foreign Office, September 9, 1917, Weltkrieg Nr. 11q. *Aufwiegelungen*, 191-195. See also War Ministry to Foreign Office, September 9, 1915, Ibid., 284.

[20]Gracey to Lansing, June 12, 1917, U.S. *Foreign Relations*, 1917 Supplement 2, vol. 2, pp. 1289-1290.

[21]Ratibor to Foreign Office, June 14, 1917, Spanien 61. *Die Politischen Beziehungen*, 357/412.

[22]Polo to Zimmermann, June 19, 1917, Ibid., 357/414.

[23]Von Holtzendorff to Foreign Office, June 20, 1917, Ibid., 357/423.

[24]Willard to Lansing, June 22, 1917, U.S. *Foreign Relations*, 1917 Supplement 2, vol. 2, pp. 1290-1291.

[25]Ratibor to Foreign Office, June 26, 1917, Spanien 61. *Die Politischen Beziehungen*, 357/437.

[26]Willard to Lansing, June 29, 1917, U.S. *Foreign Relations*, 1917 Supplement 2, vol. 2, p. 1291.

[27]*Times*, July 27, 1917.

[28]Ibid., 1292. For the text of the decree, see the *American Journal of International Law*, Supplement II, 1917, p. 177.

[29]Lansing to Willard, July 2, 1917, U.S. *Foreign Relations*, Supplement 2, vol. 2, p. 1292.

[30]Lansing to Willard, July 5, 1917, Ibid., p. 1292.

[31]Willard to Lansing, July 7, 1917, Ibid., p. 1292.

[32]Willard to Lansing, July 8, 1917, Ibid., p. 1293.

[33]Lersner to Foreign Office, July 15, 1917, Spanien 40. *Allgemeine*, 93.

[34]Romberg to Foreign Office, July 19, 1917, Spanien 61. <u>Die Politischen Beziehungen</u>, 357/454.

[35]Kalle to Foreign Office, July 24, 1917, Spanien 70. <u>Beziehungen zu Portugal</u>, T149/78/501.

[36]Zimmermann to Lersner, July 27, 1917, Deutschland 127. <u>Mission</u>, 550.

[37]Willard to Lansing, July 31, 1917, U.S. <u>Foreign Relations</u>, 1917 Supplement 2, vol. 2, p. 1293.

[38]<u>New York Times</u>, August 1, 1917.

[39]State Secretary of the Reichsmarineamt to Foreign Office, September 26, 1917, Spanien 61. <u>Die Politischen Beziehungen</u>, 357/511.

[40]Eckhardt to Welczeck, September 20, 1917, Spanien 46. <u>secr. Subventionierung</u>, 196.

[41]Ratibor to Foreign Office, August 9, 1917, Spanien 40. <u>Allgemeine</u>, 112.

[42]Foreign Office to Ratibor, August 20, 1917, Spanien 61. <u>Die Politischen Beziehungen</u>, 357/498.

[43]Welczeck to Kuehlmann, August 22, 1917, Ibid., 357/499-501.

[44]Ibid.

[45]<u>New York Times</u>, May 10, 1926. See also Wesendonk to Foreign Office, August 31, 1917, Spanien 55. <u>Das Spanische Koenigshaus</u>, T149/355/740-741.

[46]Willard to Lansing, September 21, 1917, U.S. <u>Foreign Relations</u>, Supplement 2, vol. 2, p. 1208.

[47]Gelos, <u>Neutralitaetspolitik Spaniens</u>, p. 95.

[48]Lansing to Willard, December 1, 1917, U.S. <u>Foreign Relations</u>, Supplement 2, vol. 2, p. 1216.

[49]Romberg to Foreign Office, October 1, 1917, Spanien 55. <u>Das Spanische Koenigshaus</u>, T149/355/745-746.

[50]Ratibor to Foreign Office, October 10, 1917, Spanien 61. <u>Die Politischen Beziehungen Zwischen Spanien und Deutschland</u>. T149/357/521.

[51]Kalle to Foreign Office, October 13, 1917, Weltkrieg Nr. 11q. <u>secr. Aufwiegelungen</u>, T149/402/556.

[52]Understate Secretary to Lersner, October 16, 1917, Spanien 61. Die Politischen Beziehungen, T149/357/538.

[53]Lersner to Welczeck, November 23, 1917, Ibid., 607.

[54]Gracey to Lansing, September 17, 1917, U.S. Foreign Relations, 1917 Supplement 2, vol. 2, p. 1294.

[55]Krohn to Foreign Office, October 4, 1917, Spanien 61. Die Politischen Beziehungen, 357/516.

[56]Ibid.

[57]Willard to Lansing, October 6, 1917, U.S. Foreign Relations, 1917 Supplement 2, vol. 2, p. 1295.

[58]Ratibor to Foreign Office, October 7, 1917, Spanien 61. Die Politischen Beziehungen, 357/517.

[59]Lansing to Willard, October 9, 1917, U.S. Foreign Relations, 1917 Supplement 2, vol. 2, p. 1295.

[60]Ratibor to Foreign Office, October 9, 1917, Spanien 61. Die Politischen Beziehungen, 357/518.

[61]Ratibor to Foreign Office, October 10, 1917, Ibid., 357/519.

[62]Kalle to Foreign Office, October 12, 1917, Ibid., 357/559.

[63]Inner Memorandum by Bussche, October 16, 1917, Ibid., 357/527.

[64]Note to Polo from Madrid, shown by Polo to Germans and recorded by them, October 15, 1917, Ibid., 357/543.

[65]Ratibor to Foreign Office, October 15, 1917, Ibid., 357/547.

[66]Gruenau to Foreign Office, Hofzug, October 16, 1917, Ibid., 357/535.

[67]Lersner to Foreign Office, no date, probably October 1917 due to the location in the archives and internal evidence, Ibid., 357/536.

[68]Bussche to Gruenau, October 16, 1917, Ibid., 357/549.

[69]Ratibor to Foreign Office, October 18, 1917, Ibid., 357/563.

[70]Krohn to Admiralty, October 18, 1917, Ibid., 357/565.

[71] Bussche to Gruenau at the Hofzug, October 19, 1917, Ibid., 357/556.

[72] Welczeck to Langwerth, October 20, 1917, Ibid., 357/561.

[73] Lersner to Foreign Office, October 23, 1917, Ibid., 357/578.

[74] Chargé Wilson to Lansing, November 13, 1917, U.S. Foreign Relations, 1917 Supplement 2, vol. 2, p. 1298.

[75] Willard to Lansing, November 28, 1917, Ibid., p. 1215.

[76] Bussche to Lancken, December 7, 1917, Spanien 61. Die Politischen Beziehungen, 357/618. Also Willard to Lansing, November 6, 1917, Department of State Record Group 159, 763.72/7599, National Archives, Washington, D.C.

[77] Ratibor to Foreign Office, December 11, 1917, Ibid., 357/622-623.

[78] Sam Waagner, Mata Hari (New York: Appleton Century, 1965), pp. 170-171.

[79] Lersner to Legation Secretary, Pless, December 12, 1917, Deutschland 127. Aufwiegelungen, 532.

[80] Ratibor to Foreign Office, December 12, 1917, Spanien 61. Die Politischen Beziehungen, 357/624.

[81] Welczeck to Simon, December 18, 1917, Ibid., 357/627.

[82] Willard to Lansing, December 12, 1917, U.S. Foreign Relations, 1917 Supplement 2, vol. 2:1218.

[83] Foreign Office to Ratibor, January 2, 1918, Spanien 61. Die Politischen Beziehungen, 357/632.

[84] Lersner to Foreign Office, January 11, 1918, Ibid., 357/655.

[85] Lersner to Foreign Office, January 11, 1918, Ibid., 357/656.

[86] Berckheim to Foreign Office, January 11, 1918, Ibid., 357/659.

[87] Alfonso XIII to Kaiser William, January 19, 1918, Ibid., 357/710.

[88]Holtzendorff to Foreign Office, February 4, 1918, Ibid., 357/694-695.

[89]Polo to Foreign Office, March 5, 1918, Ibid., 357/767.

[90]Valdivia to Alfonso XIII, March 7, 1918, Ibid., 357/775.

[91]Foreign Office to Lersner, March 14, 1918, Ibid., 357/802-803.

[92]Ratibor to Foreign Office, January 6, 1918, Ibid., 357/638.

[93]Lersner to Foreign Office, January 8, 1918, Spanien 40. Allgemeine, 139. Also, Ratibor to Foreign Office, January 12, 1918, Ibid., 142.

[94]Carr, pp. 505-506, see also Romanones, Notas, pp. 372-374.

[95]Albert Mousset, Histoire d'Espagne, p. 528.

[96]Willard to Lansing, #1127, Willard Family Papers, Box 115, March 9, 1918, Manuscript Division, Library of Congress, Washington, D.C.

[97]Ratibor to Foreign Office, January 19, 1918, Spanien 61. Die Politischen Beziehungen, 357/673.

[98]Ratibor to Foreign Office, January 23, 1918, Ibid., 357/679.

[99]State Secretary to Polo, January 28, 1918, Ibid., 357/687.

[100]Ratibor to Foreign Office, January 29, 1918, Ibid., 357/688.

[101]Foreign Office to Polo, January 31, 1918, Ibid., 357/684.

[102]New York Times, February 2, 1918. See also Ratibor to Foreign Office, February 8, 1918, Spanien 61. Die Politischen Beziehungen, 357/720.

[103]Frankfurter Abendblatt, February 23, 1918. See the formal demands in Polo to Foreign Office, February 24, 1918, Spanien 61, Die Politischen Beziehungen, 357/756-760.

[104]Pro-memoria to Polo, February 24, 1918, Spanien 61. Die Politischen Beziehungen, 357/744.

[105] New York Times, February 21, 1918. Von Stohrer later was Germany's Ambassador to Spain during World War II. Stohrer wrote the Foreign Office on July 8, 1942 that Germany had succeeded in keeping Spain neutral during the First World War through the army juntas. Whether this reference meant that the juntas were merely happy occurrences or that Germany had instigated them is not clear. Probably the latter inference is correct. For Stohrer's statement that Germany was responsible for the disturbances see Einhorn, Die oekonomischen Hintergruende der faschistischen deutschen Intervention in Spanien, p. 19.

[106] Times, February 21, 1918.

[107] Ratibor to Foreign Office, February 27, 1918, Spanien 61. Die Politischen Beziehungen, 357/755.

[108] Times, March 8, 1918.

[109] Anonymous, "Autocracy Flirts with Anarchy," Literary Digest (April 20, 1918) LVII:23.

[110] Times, March 9, 1918.

[111] Foreign Office to Ratibor, March 1, 1918, Spanien 61. Die Politischen Beziehungen, 357/756.

[112] Lancken to Foreign Office, March 1, 1918, Ibid., 357/761.

[113] Bussche to Ratibor, March 6, 1918, Ibid., 357/770.

[114] Polo to Foreign Office, mid-March 1918, no date, Ibid., 357/793-795.

[115] Welczeck to Lersner, March 20, 1918, Ibid., 357/813-814.

[116] Ibid.

[117] For Fuerstenberg's observations see Just," Neutralitaet," p. 413, taken from HHStA PA rot Krieg 25029. For the complete text of the exchange between the Emperor Karl and Wilson, see Gelos, Neutralitaetspolitik Spaniens, Anhang I, pp. 172-187. By August even the Germans sought to open avenues of discussion with Americans through the intermediary of Alfonso. See brief mention of this German attempt in Albrecht Philipp, Die Ursachen des Deutschen Zusammenbruchs im Jahre 1918 (Berlin: Deutsche Verlagsgesellschaft fuer Politik und Geschichte, 1925), p. 221.

[118] Ratibor to Foreign Office, March 26, 1918, Spanien 61. Die Politischen Beziehungen, 357/820.

[119]Bailey, The Policy of the United States Toward the Neutrals, 1917-1918, p. 289. A good summary of the economic negotiations between the U.S. and Spain in 1917-1918 can be found in Shirley Jackson's "The United States and Spain," p. 213.

[120]Bussche to GHQ, March 24, 1918, Spanien 57. Ministerien, 587.

[121]James Mock and Cedric Larson, Words that Won the War: The Story of the Committee on Public Information, 1917-1918 (Princeton, N.J.: Princeton University Press, 1939), p. 264. See also George Viereck, Spreading Germs of Hate (New York: Liverwright, 1930), p. 204 and Shirley Jackson, "The United States and Spain, 1917-1918," p. 241. Further useful background information upon the slow start of American propaganda in Spain is to be found in Joseph Mehl, Jr., "Intelligence Reporting by American Observers from the the European Neutrals, 1917-1919," (Ph.D. dissertation, The American University, 1962), esp. pp. 56 and following. Mehl effectively chronicled the bad feeling between Ambassador Willard and the attachés who tried to expand their propaganda and intelligence activities. Hereafter the first book mentioned above will be cited as Mock, Words.

[122]Mock, Words.

[123]Ibid., p. 265.

[124]Ibid., pp. 266-267.

[125]Ibid., p. 268.

[126]Ibid., p. 270.

[127]Ibid., p. 273.

[128]Ratibor to Foreign Office, April 24, 1918, Spanien 61. Die Politischen Beziehungen, 358/4.

[129]Ratibor to Foreign Office, May 3, 1918, Ibid., 358/9.

[130]Ratibor to Foreign Office, May 10, 1918, Ibid., 358/17.

[131]Kuehlmann to Berckheim, June 4, 1918, Ibid., 358/35-37.

[132]Ratibor to Foreign Office, June 5, 1918, Ibid., 358/42.

[133]Ibid.

[134]Representative of the Undersecretary of State to Ratibor, June 10, 1918, Spanien 40. Allgemeine, 148.

[135]Ratibor to Foreign Office, June 21, 1918, Deutschland 127. Aufwiegelungen, 64-66.

[136]Ratibor to Foreign Office, June 27, 1918, Spanien 61. Die Politischen Beziehungen, 358/66-67.

[137]Bussche to Polo, July 1, 1918, Ibid., 358/56.

[138]Ratibor to Foreign Office, July 1, 1918, Ibid., 358/69.

[139]Ratibor to Foreign Office, July 4, 1918, Ibid., 358/75.

[140]Ratibor to Foreign Office, July 13, 1918, Ibid., 358/86 and 92.

[141]Ratibor to Foreign Office, July 8, 1918, Ibid., 358/79.

[142]Bussche to Lancken, July 23, 1918, Ibid., 358/100.

[143]Ratibor to Foreign Office, July 23, 1918, Ibid., 358/108.

[144]Bassewitz to Foreign Office, August 6, 1918, Ibid., 358/354.

[145]Ratibor to Foreign Office, July 23, 1918, Ibid., 358/108.

[146]Ratibor to Foreign Office, August 3, 1918, Ibid., 358/135.

[147]Hanson Baldwin, The World War: An Outline History (New York: Harpers, 1962), p. 147 and A. Cruttwell. A History of the Great War (Oxford: Clarendon, 1936), p. 549 also see Cyrill B. Falls, The Great War (New York: Putnam, 1959), p. 376 and Basil H. Liddell-Hart, The Real War, 1914-1918 (Boston: Little Brown, 1930), p. 429 and finally Carlton Hayes, A Brief History of the Great War (New York: MacMillan, 1920). p. 324.

[148]Ratibor to Foreign Office, August 12, 1918, Spanien 61. Die Politischen Beziehungen, 358/166.

[149]Voelkische Zeitung report from Rotterdam, originally dated April 6, 1918, received in Berlin April 21, 1918, Weltkrieg Nr. 28. Druck der Entente gegen Spanien, T149/146/42. Hereafter cited as Weltkrieg Nr. 28. Druck.

[150]Ratibor to Foreign Office, April 10, 1918, Ibid., 37.

[151]Ratibor to Foreign Office, April 10, 1918, Ibid.

[152]Inner Memorandum, April 14, 1918, Spanien 61. Die Politischen Beziehungen, 357/821-825.

[153]Fromann at Stuttgart to Foreign Office, April 16, 1918, Ibid., 358/2.

[154]Holtzendorff to Foreign Office, April 21, 1918, Weltkrieg Nr. 28. Druck, 41.

[155]Ibid.

CHAPTER VIII

SHIP TRANSFER NEGOTIATIONS

APRIL - NOVEMBER 1918

Neutral Ally

As the details of the Spanish-American and French-Spanish agreements became known, Germany began to realize how far Spain had moved toward the Allied camp. By late April 1918 Ratibor reported the extensive financial help France had proffered Spain. For a counterproposal he suggested making more funds available to build German-owned wharves and ships in Spain, all to be used in the postwar period. He reported that the German colony was quite enthusiastic about the idea.[1] The Foreign Office, however, was cool to such suggestions as it had its eye set on the Allied pressure to get Spain to seize German ships. The subject of economic aid was then set aside in favor of a program to deflect any forcible seizure of those vessels.

Secretary Hilmar von dem Bussche-Haddenhausen instructed Ratibor to protest officially about the possible use of German interned vessels for Spanish transport, threatening Spain with suspension of safe-conduct passes for certain agricultural shipments.[2] If relations were broken, von der Bussche advocated pushing the zone for unrestricted submarine attacks to the very coastline of Spain.[3] Thusly, Germany hoped to resist American and French blandishments to seize German vessels. At the same time the Germans, learning that the Americans also were putting considerable pressure upon Spain, suggested America would not respect Spanish territorial waters even if the March agreements were carried out in their entirety.[4]

In May the Spanish were faced with yet more Allied pressure. The American navy refused to permit Spanish ships loaded with vitally needed supplies to leave, thereby causing Spain no small amount of distress and forcing them to accede to Allied demands for more use of Spanish ship bottoms.[5] The Germans suspected the Spanish would be forced to seize German ships. The Allies had recently taken Dutch vessels and used them for Atlantic transport.[6]

In a conversation with Ambassador Ratibor, King Alfonso sought to reassure the Germans of his interest in their cause. He still hoped to see the success of German arms in the recently begun offensive of July 15, 1918 in the west. Clearly, with German military power still a reality, the King felt it necessary to court Berlin once more. He also promised to disavow Allied charges that Spanish vessels had been German submarine targets, with the exception of the recent sinking of the Atzexi Mendi, subtly suggesting German caution for his continued favor.[7] This vessel's destruction resulted in Allied pressure to force Spain to protest vigorously.[8] The Germans thus realized that they should be more careful in submarine warfare, particularly if they wished to manipulate Spain and to counter the Allies.[9]

Seeking desperately to neutralize Spain, the German Foreign Office revived plans for economic aid, directing Richard Klimsch of the bank firm Urquijo and Company to arrange a loan of 100 million marks to be used over a five-year period for the purchase of Spanish goods.[10] In addition, the Foreign Office informed Polo that Germany would loan large sums without guarantees.[11] In an inter-office memorandum, the Germans proposed to use the commercial company Hesperides as a device to purchase Spanish foodstuffs and transport them to Germany after the war.[12] But the suggestion was really stillborn as Spanish financial circles indicated it was hopeless to try to stem the tide of Allied gold.[13]

While the Germans talked of economic aid, they continued to remonstrate with Polo about the unneutral character of the U.S.-Spanish economic agreement.[14] German blandishments were to no avail, however, as summer approached. By early June, the Spanish government nationalized all shipping. Freight rates were lowered and stabilized in the "national interest." All available ship bottoms were used to import needed raw materials such as corn, cotton, and petroleum.[15] German vessels were not seized, but such a step was near.

Obviously the Spanish had to walk a tightrope between the Allies and the Germans, and since Americans prevented Spanish vessels from leaving North American ports with valuable and needed cargoes, the Germans saw clearly that tension had arisen between Spain and the Allies over secret clauses in the agreements. The Spanish now attempted to meet the emergency by controlling their entire merchant marine. In addition, the Americans and Allies through economic means sought to force Spain to protest activities of German submarines around the Iberian peninsula.[16]

Through July and early August, American and English delegations arrived in Madrid to work out the details of the secret clauses, but the King continued to resist their pressures until such a time as the military balance had obviously shifted totally against Berlin. Ratibor insisted that measures were needed to counter the influence of the Entente, but he was not specific.[17]

A letter from the Ambassadorial Councillor, José de Landecho, revealed that Spain wanted neutrality, but of a pro-Entente variety. Landecho made clear what the Germans already knew; namely, that the Spanish could stand up to the Americans and Allies only with strong German victories on the battlefield.[18] The Germans were somewhat heartened by the fact that Allied negotiators had left rather early, indicating the Spanish had not submitted.[19]

A few days later the German Foreign Office presumed that no agreements had been reached to provide the Allies with a specific number of ships or with transfers of the interned German ones.[20] But Spain did agree to sell considerable quantities of food, clothing, and draft animals to

France, thereby freeing Allied bottoms that might have conveyed such items to France.[21]

The German Admiralty sensed that Spain might demand the use of interned German ships immediately, and instructions were forwarded to Ratibor to make preparations to scuttle the vessels.[22] Meanwhile, Alfonso, finally convinced of imminent German defeat, at long last took a far harsher attitude toward Germany. Romanones had also played his part in convincing Alfonso by August 7, 1918 of the seriousness of the Central Powers' position. Both Berlin and Vienna were on the verge of collapse due to the failure of the July offensive.[23]

Consequently, in August when a German submarine, the UC-56, was interned at Santander, the commander and crew were unceremoniously removed from their vessel and moved inland. Normally, the Spanish showed great respect to German naval officers.[24] Similar treatment occurred with other German underwater craft that heretofore had operated in Spanish waters with impunity.[25] Spain became extremely truculent over the sinking of the _Sardinero_, a Spanish ship carrying grain for Switzerland. The Spanish also refused to handle German diplomatic mail.[26] Polo officially remonstrated and pointed out the seriousness of the situation in light of the recent sinkings.[27]

Pressure mounted inside Maura's cabinet to seize German interned vessels. Minister of State Eduardo Dato had intimated to U.S. Ambassador Joseph Willard as early as

April 5, 1918, that Spain would soon have to decide for either the Allies or the Central Powers.[28] With the attacks upon Spanish ships and with worsening of Spain's supplies of foodstuffs, Dato continued to remonstrate with Berlin, quietly pleading for Ratibor's assistance in convincing Berlin of the seriousness of Spain's economic situation.[29]

In May the King began to think of the possibility of using the interned German ships to meet both Spain's needs and the demands of the Allies.[30] The U.S. Ambassador along with the British and French kept up the pressure to get Spain to act in providing ship space.[31] On July 17, 1918, Count Romanones wrote a letter to Prime Minister Maura recounting recent sinkings and suggesting that Germany's military position was now unfavorable. Therefore, he strongly proposed a cabinet meeting to demand satisfaction from the Germans.[32] Dato, in a letter to Maura on July 30, 1918, insisted that the Spanish government had to deal with the problem before or during the first week of August. He recounted in detail the patience Spain had hitherto shown, and the moment to act had now arrived.[33]

The cabinet meetings of Thursday, Friday, and Saturday, August 8, 9, 10, 1918 were stormy. Those who had supported a more active policy against Germany in April 1917 reiterated their hopes, and those who wanted to avoid any hint of violating Spain's strict neutrality defended their view with vigor. Romanones related he argued for five hours for a policy of open, benevolent neutrality for the Allies and a break with Germany. He even threatened to resign if agreement were not immediately forthcoming.[34] Maura reported to his son that the meeting was punctuated with "gnashing and clawing."[35] González Besada, Minister of Finance, reported that the cabinet divided up into contending groups, but Maura held them together.[36] Maura even convinced Romanones not to resign but to await the results of the moderate policy finally formulated.[37]

During these three days, the cabinet decided to demand a German interned vessel for each future Spanish ship that might be sunk. Interestingly, Romanones told a French newspaperman in a private interview after the war that Maura preferred to accept German safe-conduct passes but that the sinkings of July forced the Prime Minister to adopt a policy much like that recommended by Romanones in April 1917.[38] Publicly, the ministers reiterated their stand on strict neutrality but also said they would vigorously defend their rights against the Germans.[39]

German Embassy Secretary Bassewitz reported that a charged atmosphere dominated Madrid and that Spain was quite serious in its view.[40] The loss in July of the _Ramón de Larinaga_, carrying American oil, and the _Esuguiza_, loaded with Egyptian cotton for Barcelona, especially excited Spanish ire.[41] The Germans intercepted the text of the decision confirming their worst suspicions: Spain would now seize interned ships to cover for Spanish losses.

On August 12, 1918, in a spate of internal messages,

the Germans discussed the text of the note Polo would soon present. The Spaniards said specifically that in the future Spain would "substitute" an interned German vessel for each Spanish ship sunk. The German vessel would be used in exactly the same way as the sunken Spanish ship.[42] To the Germans this meant that Spain was serving notice that sinkings in the interdicted zone, declared in February 1917 around Great Britain, would be considered diplomatic breaches; heretofore Spain had accepted imperious German announcements that Spain had no recourse if her vessels went into the zone.[43]

The Germans sought to determine their line of policy before the note was formally presented. The Foreign Office in Berlin wanted to take a conciliatory course by replying that Germany would try to spare Spanish ships sunk outside the zone. Any vessels sunk accidently would be subject to negotiation; restitution would be made if the Germans were at fault. The Foreign Office conveyed these thoughts to Chief of the Admiralty Staff Reinhardt Scheer and the German Minister in Brussels, von der Lancken. With luck von der Lancken would inform Villalobar for transmission to Madrid and the King himself. The Foreign Office saw a real danger that Spain might now be drawn into the war against Germany and attributed the more belligerent Spanish attitude to the failing German war situation and to the sinking of Spanish vessels laden with badly needed supplies.[44]

The Germans availed themselves of Polo's pro-German

attitude to get him to ask his government to postpone an immediate answer to the Spanish note for at least a time. The Spanish diplomat was able to get a six week extension, first because of a recent change in the leadership of the navy to Admiral Scheer and second because of the desire of the German Foreign Office to convince the military to avoid a break with Spain.[45] The fears of the difficulty of convincing the Admiralty of the need to placate the Spanish were well-founded. The Foreign Office initially was cautious, reflecting the view of the Admiralty when Polo read the message out loud to the German State Secretary.

The Germans were not willing to accede to all of the Spanish demands. Three basic rejoinders were made by the Admiralty: there could be no sparing of ships sunk in the interdicted zone; Germany would provide safe-conduct permits for ships carrying needed supplies for Spain only; and finally, the Germans were willing to observe Spanish territorial waters and to refrain from warlike activity there. Also, Germany might spare ships caught outside the zone, and even substitute ships sunk there by mistake or accident, but Germany expected an investigation of any such accident or misfortune before restitution would be made.[46] While seeming to be firm, the Germans hinted they would also replace vessels lost in those areas outside of the interdicted zone, the first time they had been willing to do this. But the military remained adamant about sinkings within the zones around the British Isles.

Polo advised the Germans in a friendly way. He suggested that more concessions would be necessary to make a good impression in Spain. Recent sinkings and the obvious decline of German arms combined with failure to halt the influx of American troop transports had changed Spanish opinion. He hinted that the United States was behind demands for seizure of German vessels and that to get that added ship space the Americans were threatening to occupy the Canary Islands.[47]

This suggestion for concessions came at the same time that Ratibor learned Spain did not plan to negotiate with Germany over future sinkings. Foreign Minister Dato planned to seize German vessels "automatically" for Spanish ships attacked and sunk.[48] Ratibor was instructed by von der Bussche to negotiate with Alfonso for safe-conduct escorts for Spanish necessities. This policy of negotiation with the King had been successful in the past, so there might be a chance it would work again.[49] In addition, Polo was told the war situation was not too serious for Germany. Hopefully, this would influence him favorably and this view would get back to Madrid.[50]

The Germans hoped initially to conduct all negotiations in secret, but as a result of newspaper reports the contents of the Spanish note and the German reply were soon known.[51] At first Minister of State Dato tried to deny that Spain had made any demands upon Germany. The pro-Allied press however argued that the government sought to bring about a break with Germany, thus revealing that the Spanish note was more like an ultimatum.[52] The firm Spanish position was out in the open and Germany now had a threat to her prestige were she to bow to Spanish demands.[53]

German efforts to stem the Allied influence were of little avail. Ratibor reported great uncertainty among pro-German elements at the Spanish court, largely because the thirty Spanish protests lodged against Germany for sinkings had remained unanswered and created an atmosphere of distrust and fear.[54] The Military Attaché added his voice to those of the Foreign Office in calling for concessions.[55] The note, officially published on August 22, 1918, announced that for every German sinking of a Spanish ship in the future an interned German vessel would be put to Spanish use.[56] In the meantime, the German Admiralty issued orders to submarine commanders to avoid sinking Spanish ships.[57]

This major crisis continued from the end of August until October 14, 1918. The Germans pretended they had not been forced to transfer their ships when in fact they had no choice but to give seven vessels to Spain on October 14, 1918. The main point of disagreement--the possibility of restitution for vessels sunk inside the interdicted zone--was resolved when Germany agreed to these transfers for those outside the zone or for those the Germans regarded as "unjustly sunk." In the meantime, even the Germans argued rather legalistically that they had served notice that any vessel around the British Islands were liable to be sunk.

If a Spanish ship went into this zone and were sunk, it would be a just sinking. But if special permission were given for a particular ship to go through the zone and it were accidentally torpedoed, then this would be an "unjust" sinking. To avoid quarrels over precisely what ships were "justly" or "unjustly" sunk, Alfonso proposed that a set number of ships be transferred, thus meeting Spanish needs. Romanones sought out the Military Attaché, Kalle, and assured him Spain did not desire a break with Germany; indeed, the bulk of the Spanish government communicated through several channels the desire to avoid an actual break leading to war. Once a Spanish ship was sunk in the interdicted zone on October 8, 1918, Spain served notice that she would seize enough German ships to equal the tonnage lost since the August declaration, although the demand was moderated by letting Germany specify which ships would be transferred. The word seizure was not used and Prime Minister Antonio Maura described the event as a peaceful transfer. Thus, by means of a diplomatic slight of hand, Spain effectively took seven German ships in retaliation for her losses since the war had begun. Entente pressure was enormous, to be sure, but Spain genuinely needed extra transport.

On August 22, 1918, Ratibor spoke with Alfonso, hoping to get the King to change Spanish intentions. The King emphasized once more he had no desire to fight Germany. Commercial difficulties of supplies for Spanish industry were the government's primary focus. He also admitted that the Entente had put continuous pressure upon him to enlarge his contributions to transatlantic shipping. Ratibor still thought Alfonso personally was pro-German but that the King and his government were acting at the behest of the Entente.[58] To counter the interventionists and to bolster the pro-German elements at the King's court, the Ambassador suggested a conciliatory approach. Indeed, even transferring more ships might serve as a symbol of how far Germany would go to satisfy the needs of an old friend.[59] Basic support for the view that Spain still wanted neutrality came from Brussels; Villalobar reported pretty much in the same vein as had Ratibor, and emphasized Spain's desire to maintain her neutrality and her need for extra ship space.[60]

This information gave German Councillor Welczeck and other Foreign Office experts considerable encouragement to follow an official policy of appeasement toward Spain. Welczeck argued that Spain's note had never mentioned the interdicted zone, and that consequently, it would be possible to transfer ships to Spain and thereby avoid any further unpleasantries.[61] Major Valdivia, the Spanish Military Attaché in Berlin, discussed the situation with Welczeck, and both seemed pleased that a break could be avoided.

But events moved much faster than the Germans had expected. On August 31, 1918, in consideration of an official note from Spain about the July sinking of the *Ramón de Larrinaga*, Germany was faced with a new situation. The Admiralty insisted that this vessel had sunk in the interdicted zone; therefore there would be no recognition of the need to compensate Spain for the loss. Due to the "unjust" sinking of the Sardinero, a Spanish grain ship which Berlin had allowed to sail to France with foodstuffs for Switzerland and which was torpedoed, the Admiralty was willing to permit at least one German vessel to be transferred.[62]

The sinking of the steamer Caraso, carrying coal from England to Spain, resulted in a special ministerial council meeting on August 31, 1918.[63] Discussion of the Ramón de Larrinaga, the Caraso and another vessel sunk earlier, the Atzeri Mendi, provided for an especially stormy council meeting, according to American Ambassador Joseph Willard.[64] Ratibor reported the meeting in the same way.[65] The Spanish decided to take a German ship for the sinking of the Atzeri Mendi and another for the loss of the Caraso.[66] Ratibor also reported Alfonso still was warm and friendly, apparently trying to calm Ratibor and take German ships at the same time.[67]

In the midst of the crisis, the Foreign Office had to conduct its diplomatic battle on two fronts. First the Admiralty had to be assured that transfers of ships and a conciliatory attitude were necessary. Secondly, Germany had to avoid the loss of prestige involved in any actual seizure. Councillor Welczeck suggested to the Admiralty that a special convoy be organized to provide Spain with coal, but he was met with a rebuff.[68] The Foreign Office did ignore Admiralty demands that the Ambassador be instructed to scuttle the ships.[69]

Ratibor saw the situation from a fresh perspective by September 4, 1918. He analyzed the situation as one in which the Spanish were forced by the Entente to get more ships. Thus, an offer from Germany would relieve the pressure upon them and provide a way out of their difficulties with the Entente.[70] American documents suggest the extent of this pressure upon Spain. Willard told American Secretary of State Robert Lansing on September 5, 1918 that Spain could be forced to continue her opposition to Germany by making exceptions for bunkering regulations dependent upon a pro-Entente view.[71]

In the meantime, Alfonso Marie, the King's cousin, briefly and accurately sketched the situation for the Germans and the best policy for Germany to follow. A delaying tactic would be best; when the military situation improved, Spain would come closer to Germany. Current Entente military successes were responsible for pressures to replace pro-German diplomats, especially Polo, with pro-Allied ones. Don Alfonso said technical problems such as the press law and the German need to continue the submarine war made it difficult to alter the current situation. However, Don Alfonso himself was not able to go to Spain to counter current tendencies due to Madrid's pro-Entente view.[72]

From another direction, the Foreign Office received militant advice from the Admiralty, which now argued that war with Spain would be preferable, since it would deprive the Allies of the territorial waters around Spain--waters useful for troop and munitions' transport.[73] The Admiralty stated flatly that any ship seizures for vessels sunk in the zone would lead to war. The Admiralty further informed the Military Attaché in the same sense on September 7, 1918.[74] But Kalle reported (as had Ratibor a few days earlier), that Spain now found itself pushed into a corner and would like to get out.[75]

Prince Fuerstenberg, the Austro-Hungarian Ambassador, told the King a break with Germany would also mean a break with the Dual Monarchy. The Foreign Office persisted in its moderate course.[76] It sent a radio message to Ratibor telling him that a seizure of ships would not be viewed as a *casus belli* under any conditions.[77] Understate Secretary Langwerth then sought to convince the Chancellor and the Admiralty of the need to avoid war with Spain. Langwerth noted that the Admiralty had not really given up the idea of ordering the Naval Attaché to disable German ships. However, the Foreign Office considered that this would inevitably lead to war. To meet the Admiralty's objections to a moderate course, the Foreign Office suggested Spain should send naval experts to Germany. They would work out the problems of tonnage and then transfer what Spain needed, thereby avoiding a seizure and a possible escalation of bad feelings and war.[78]

This controversy between the Foreign Office and the navy was not a complete secret. An article appeared in the

Dutch press and was preserved in the German documents. This publication said that the German navy's attitude toward Spain had become unduly bellicose. Chancellor Kuehlmann's announced desires for a negotiated peace in the summer of 1918 could not be squared with the Admiralty's belligerence. Consequently, the postwar situation would depend greatly upon German attitudes toward Spain.[79] Furthermore, recent scuttlings in Chile did not assure the neutrals of German sincerity in desiring peace.[80]

In the meantime a rather remarkable conversation took place between Military Attaché Kalle and Count Romanones, convincing the Germans further of a need for conciliation. The former Prime Minister assured Kalle that there should be no break in relations between Spain and Germany. Romanones seemed to be making a plea to convince the Germans of Spanish need; Entente pressure was not the only reason for Spanish insistence. In an analysis of Romanones's remarkable appeal, Kalle suggested Romanones really wanted to avoid the opprobrium that might fall on his head were Spain actually to be dragged into the conflict. Romanones, as Minister of Grace and Justice in Maura's cabinet, could be accused of having engineered this latest move. Consequently, Kalle regarded the appeal as an attempt to get the Germans to hand over extra ship space and thus avoid a clash and a consequent breaking of relations.[81] Romanones was trying to avert the blame for any untoward results and make clear that such would be sole responsibility of Eduardo Dato, the Foreign Minister in Maura's cabinet.[82]

Count Romanones may have tried to keep his record clear and to challenge Dato, the leader of the left wing Liberals. Possibilities that Romanones would become the Prime Minister were great, therefore he could not afford to be accused of bringing Spain into the war when the nation's domestic structure was so delicate. Participation in the war undoubtedly would have destroyed the monarchy, especially since the weaknesses of the Spanish government had become clear in the summer of 1917. This interpretation might be questioned, however, as Romanones was a prime factor in getting the cabinet to make the demands of August 8, 1918. More accurately, he may have thought that a bold stroke such as this would convince the Germans to give way more quickly, and, if anything, the Count could claim credit for the sudden capitulation. But the negotiations dragged on for the remainder of September; curiously, Romanones mentioned nothing of this meeting in his memoirs, possibly because he was unsuccessful in bringing the Germans around through his secret efforts.

As Romanones pleaded for conciliation, the question of disablement of the interned German vessels reappeared. The Foreign Office felt any precipitate action would mean a definite break in relations and perhaps war. Consequently, the Foreign Office instructed Ratibor to scuttle the interned ships only upon direct orders from the Wilhelmstrasse.[83] Understate Secretary von der Bussche told Admiral Reinhardt

Scheer the Embassy would not permit disablement.[84] Between September 10-24, 1918, the Admiralty argued with the Foreign Office over the need to make preparations to destroy the vessels, but the adamant attitude of Ratibor and the Foreign Office forced the Admiralty to admit that the decision to initiate disablement proceedings was completely up to the Ambassador, a tacit admission that the disablement would never occur.[85] Thus, part of the struggle with the Admiralty concluded successfully.

But the German-Spanish battle over the question of ships inside and outside the interdicted zone still remained. From September 11-28, 1918 negotiations were intense, but the agreement, finally reached, permitted transfer of a set list of German ships for Spanish ships which had been sunk. The Germans apparently wanted to postpone any actual transfers; with the sinking of a Spanish ship in early October 1918, the Spanish took advantage of the agreement and did "transfer" seven ships; they were not "seized." The reality of the situation was recognized by the American representative in Madrid when Joseph Willard remarked in a cable to Washington that he believed recent German-Spanish negotiations would "result in a seizure of German ships once the Cortes assembled by October 15. But such a seizure would follow an understanding between the German Ambassador and the Spanish government."[86] The American Ambassador did not realize the extent of the tortuous negotiations that had already preceeded this agreement.

In a note to Maura of September 9, 1918, Ratibor emphasized Germany's firm position. The Ambassador, following the instructions of the Wilhelmstrasse, charged that some 38,000 tons of shipping were in the service of the Entente, and a seizure of those vessels would increase the space needed for foodstuffs and other necessities. Ratibor had doubts about the attitude of Dato, the Minister of State, and so had the note transmitted directly to Maura, the Prime Minister. Ratibor's note also complained about censorship directed against German views and about the failure of the Spanish to allow publication of the conciliatory reply of Germany at the end of August.[87] Maura ostensibly was pleased at the direct transmission of the message to him, but he rejected the idea that Spain should seize vessels allegedly in the service of the Entente.[88]

In the meantime, the Admiralty reported to Berlin that the July and August sinkings were in the forbidden zone. The _Ramón de Larrinaga_, sunk July 13, 1918, was in the interdicted area and belonged to a company with its headquarters in Liverpool, the Taja firm. Similarly, the coal ship _Caraso_ was accompanied by an enemy warship, which in the German view made the Spanish vessel an enemy vessel.[89] The only satisfaction the Germans were willing to give Spain was a transfer of one ship for the sinking of the _Sardinero_, the Swiss grain ship which they felt had been sunk unjustly.[90]

Germany's formal reply to the August 14 Spanish note was actually delivered on September 11, 1918, and in this memorandum Germany reviewed its favorable policy toward Spain during the past few years. It regretted that Spanish vessels had been sunk in the course of the submarine war. Germany offered to give special safe-conduct passes to Spanish vessels, agreed to the transfer of German coal to Spain through Dutch harbors, and expressed regret that Spain had been previously unable to take advantage of these offers. Germany also offered to purchase Spanish agricultural products, although it knew Entente interests forbade shipments to Germany or to other neutrals. However, Germany promised to recompense Spain for all losses occasioned by mistakes or outside of the forbidden zone, while charging, nevertheless, that several ships had been sunk due to mines or other causes and not by German torpedoes. Finally, and perhaps most importantly, Germany pointed out that great quantities of Spanish ship space were being taken up by the shipment of Allied war materials. Due to technical reasons its submarines could not follow usual search and seizure rules. Germany emphasized that it would not give up submarine warfare, the only means of naval defense left to it. Germany did concede that submarine commanders had orders to observe the sanctity of Spanish territorial waters and to spare Spanish vessels outside of the interdicted zone. In the sinkings of other Spanish vessels, Germany was willing to enter into new discussions. But the only ship transfers to be permitted would be for those unjustly sunk. Any other seizures would cause a protest and serious consequences.[91]

In response to the formal presentation of the memorandum of September 11, 1918, Eduardo Dato, the Foreign Minister, expressed misgivings that the German concessions really did not meet the problem of future sinkings, suggesting instead that he and the Ambassador discuss a specific list of German interned vessels that might be transferred, postponing the adjudication process for later negotiations between the two governments. Ratibor rejected this suggestion, proposing instead negotiations over each case in the future and between naval experts of the respective countries.[92]

Ratibor saw the Foreign Minister as trying to destroy German prestige and in any future haggling over details about ship transfers, Dato would demand more from the Germans. Yet Dato did suggest that a certain number of vessels be transferred to Spain in order to avoid problems with the Entente which might itself seize such vessels, if the ships were merely chartered for Spanish use. On the contrary, Ratibor believed the Entente had agreed to a ship by ship transfer from Germany to Spain; consequently, the Ambassador saw Dato as pushing Germany as far as he could, following a personal policy of getting as many vessels transferred to Spanish registry as possible, if not forcing Germany to a break in relations.[93]

On the same day, Ratibor suggested a break in relations if German vessels were seized outright, thereby forcing the Spanish government to fear not only the Entente but also the Germans.[94] Ratibor continued his personal diplomacy against Dato (and what Ratibor saw as the Foreign Minister's close relations with Romanones), suggesting that Germany make an offer of five ships for chartering to avoid a diplomatic break. This accession to Dato's demands would undermine his position. The idea would be to avoid loss of prestige with a direct seizure.[95] The Foreign Office at Berlin seemed receptive to Ratibor's idea. Foreign Secretary Hintze told Ratibor that Germany might possibly offer Spain some ships in hope of restraining them in the future.[96]

In a memo delivered to Spain on September 14, 1918 Germany gave a veiled approval to the ship transfer plan. First, any ship "unjustly" sunk after August 14, 1918 outside of the interdicted zone would mean chartering of a German ship interned in Spanish harbors to Spain, but only after diplomatic negotiations had been consummated. Germany hoped to satisfy itself that Spain would never present Berlin with a _fait accompli_.[97] Ratibor pressed further with his argument to prevent the Entente from forcing a break in relations between Germany and Spain. Only an immediate listing of ships that _could be_ chartered would really satisfy the Spanish. A voluntary chartering would, therefore, save face for the Germans.[98] But Berlin hoped to stave off the inevitable; the Foreign Office told Ratibor to ask Spain to send naval experts to Berlin to work out the differences over the sinking of Spanish ships.[99] The idea seemed to be that a negotiation with naval experts might cover the actual charters of German ships for Spanish ones sunk in the *forbidden zone*.

King Alfonso entered the picture on September 17, 1918. He suggested to the Austro-Hungarian Ambassador, Prince Fuerstenberg, that Germany present Spain with a pair of ships at one time. This would avoid the problem of negotiating over whether or not any specific ship were sunk in the interdicted zone.[100] Ratibor was apparently delighted, and he reiterated his earlier suggestion of a charter list.[101] The Foreign Office on the same day told Polo in Berlin that Germany would accept a chartering for those ships sunk in the interdicted zone. The Germans wanted simply to avoid a *fait accompli*. Foreign Secretary Hintze told Polo that in the public presentations the Germans must maintain their viewpoint. But through other channels Hintze emphasized that the Spanish government and the Spanish King were to understand that Germany would eventually transfer some ships.

Thus, by September 17, 1918, the Foreign Office had come around to what was really the only policy left to them. In effect the Spanish could seize German ships, but only with the consent of the Germans as to precisely which ships. The implication was that Germany would not protest such seizures though the vessels sunk could have been in the interdicted zone. The loss of prestige in any unilateral Spanish seizure and attempts to maintain Spanish neutrality were uppermost in German minds.[102]

Interestingly enough, while this was going on, the Americans reported that the British and French said they did not really want Spain in the war. On September 17, 1918, Joseph Willard, the U.S. Ambassador in Madrid, reported to Washington that the French and British chargés each told him that they did not want Spain actually to go to war with Germany. Spanish exports might be interrupted more than they were if Spain were actively in the war.[103] It was ironic that the Germans had finally caved in to Spanish demands out of fear, partly at least, that Spain might be close to a break with Germany.

On September 20, 1918, Alfonso talked with Military Attaché Major Kalle about the ship crisis. The King said he was pleased that ships would now be transferred without regard to the circumstances of their sinkings. The King also said he knew that military and strategic necessity led the Germans to engage in such sinkings, but in a similar vein, economic necessity now led Spain to seize German ships. Kalle replied that any direct seizure would lead to a break in relations. At this the King merely turned to a discussion of the war situation, which was quite unfavorable for the Germans. Kalle remarked that the King always made policy on the basis of battlefield fortunes, and now he felt Germany definitely had lost. The King concluded the interview by suggesting that the ship question should be settled peacefully and quickly.[104] Also, Alfonso said he hoped the policy would be extended in the interdicted zone.[105] In essence, the Germans were adhering to their original view of no compensation for ships sunk inside of the interdicted zone; but they would allow chartering for all vessels sunk outside the zone, without quarreling about the circumstances of the sinking.

To make their offer a reality, the Germans drew up a list of five vessels suitable for chartering to make up for Spanish losses, ostensibly outside of the interdicted zone. The Germans would put these ships at the disposal of the Ambassador to offer in the event of an imminent seizure, free to offer one or all five as he saw fit.[106] At the same time, Hintze further emphasized to Ratibor that even with a seizure of ships, there would be no break in relations.[107]

The German Foreign Office clearly created an impression that there would be no transfers for ships sunk in the interdicted zone. The reality was that a list of ships was now prepared, and when a threatened seizure occurred, Germany would acquiesce. The navy, naturally, resisted any "chartering" or transfer of German merchant vessels to the Spanish, but the Kaiser personally ordered that the transfers be prepared.[108] The Spanish seemed willing to go along with what was essentially a game of words. Ratibor saw the Spanish acceptance of no outright seizures as a great success for German diplomacy; in reality it was a considerable concession from Germany to Spain.[109] Perhaps the Germans learned Spain had asked Wilson what would be offered Spain were she to enter the war. Willard was told to tell Spain that the United States would support Madrid in the event of a war with Germany.[110]

By the end of September 1918 the six week time limit was up, but the Germans suddenly sought to buy time. Ratibor made public threats that any seizures would mean war, even though the Germans had now already made concessions. The reason for German truculence was the feeling that the Foreign Office had given away all bargaining points. The Wilhelmstrasse tried to smooth over Admiralty objections by pointing out that the list of five ships could perhaps purchase time until some formula could be reached so that sinkings in the forbidden zone could be dealt with. Until then, the concomitant loss of prestige from the imminent seizure of German ships could be avoided by making use of the special list.[111] By September 24, 1918, Dato totally refused to send any naval experts and to negotiate over safe-conduct passes.[112] Thus, the Germans were pushed closer and closer to a public statement of their offer of five ships.

In the meantime, the London Times reported Germany had actually offered seven ships to Spain.[113] Hintze asked that the report be suppressed, although the Spanish as well as the whole world evidently knew what the Germans were planning. Thus, the Germans on September 26, 1918 authorized Ratibor to tell Spain officially of the offer of five ships at whatever was an appropriate moment.[114] This was something of a useless maneuver as the Germans at Berlin had already told Polo of their intentions. Thus, the Spanish were ready to take at least five ships.[115] The German public, however, was told that Berlin planned to give Spain only one ship and no more.[116]

In the meantime, the Foreign Office had to fight the last part of its internal war with the Admiralty. The Chief of the Admiralty, Reinhardt Scheer, objected to any concessions at all on September 10, 1918, and he reiterated his objections in November.[117] In Scheer's view, any circumvention of submarine warfare would lead to a breakdown of the German war effort.[118] Other voices in the Admiralty as well as in the Supreme Command joined with Scheer a day later.[119] Hintze, however, had gotten the Kaiser to agree to an order suggesting five ships that could be chartered.[120] Evidently the Kaiser always saw Spain in a highly favorable light, and therefore gave his consent. Admiral Scheer obeyed the order, but he did not like the idea.[121] The Admiral related his reminiscences of the ship question in his memoirs, stating that after September 10, 1918, the problem with Spain became serious. He did not describe the complexity of the negotiations throughout September, but he alluded to the quarrels among the army Supreme Command, the Foreign Office, and the navy. He emphasized, as did contemporaries, that the blockaded area was sacrosanct, yet Germany would do all that was necessary to avoid making Spain an enemy.[122]

Thus, the Foreign Office was able to accomplish its purpose. Even if Spain seized ships for those sunk inside the zone, Germany was ready to meet the challenge, and the military had to go along. All that was lacking were triggering events that would give the Spanish excuses actually to take German vessels. Such events occurred in October.

On October 5, 1918, Ratibor's worst fears were realized. A total of five ships were sunk from August 10 to October 5, 1918, when three more vessels went under. The Mercedes, the Vila Valero, and the Conde Vilfredo were sunk or torpedoed and severely damaged from October 1-5. Ratibor feared a Spanish seizure of German vessels.[123] Berlin desperately tried privately the tactic of enlarging their list of ships that might be offered to Spain for purposes of conciliation, thus avoiding outright seizures.[124] A Spanish ministerial council was held on October 8, 1918 and ship seizures were imminent.[125]

The German expectations were confirmed when an official message arrived from Madrid on October 9, 1918. The Spanish were cordial, explaining that they had to take some vessels but that they had no desire to give offense to Germany. Indeed, the message emphasized that the German Ambassador in Madrid could select the vessels to be transferred.[126] In an official reply to the Spanish, the Germans reiterated their point that they could not recognize transfers for ships sunk in the interdicted zone, but nothing stronger was mentioned. Indeed, the tone of the note was that Spain might take substitutes for vessels sunk in the forbidden zone, and the Germans would not protest vigorously. In a cordial manner reflecting the Spanish position, Germany officially offered five vessels to Spain. The note emphasized the need for "monarchial powers" to remain united in the face of challenges from the republics, a constant theme in German communications with Spain.[127] The note ended with a positive emphasis, stating that Germany wished to meet the needs of Spain and to avoid Spanish entry into the war.[128]

In a note of October 10, 1918, the Spanish indicated they would seize at least 15,000 tons of shipping for the recent sinkings of the Caraso, the Atzeri Mendi, the Francoli, the Mercedes, and the María. The naming of these ships was significant as the list contained vessels that had been sunk inside the interdicted zone. This use of pressure forced the Germans to act, and a time limit was set. If Ratibor did not name the ships to be transferred, then Spain would choose the vessels herself.

Consequently, the empty assertion of Germany to distinguish between open sea and interdicted zone sinkings was shoved aside, and the Germans had to accept the situation.[129] In a telegram to Ratibor, von der Bussche said he had told Polo he rejected the reasoning used by Maura that there was no difference between open sea and interdicted zone sinkings, but Germany would only mildly protest the seizure of vessels for sinkings inside of the zone.[130] Between October 10-15, 1918 Ratibor tried to suggest that five other ships could be offered so that the Spanish would not announce they were seizing ships for sinkings inside of the restricted zone.[131] But the attempt was fruitless. The Spanish pressed the Germans further by October 11, 1918 demanding the immediate naming of vessels to be transferred, but the only concession the Spanish were willing to make was a statement after the transfer that this was not a seizure but a friendly arrangement between Spain and Germany.[132] By October 14, 1918, Ratibor gave the Spanish a list of six ships to be "chartered" for the duration of the war, and one extra ship was offered for the "unjustified" sinking of the Mercedes.[133]

Thus, the Germans somewhat legalistically ceded two vessels for the sinkings of the Sardinero and the Mercedes, both of which had been "unjustly" sunk. The other five were mere charters to maintain Spanish goodwill. But the Spanish saw the vessels as necessary repayment for sinkings in the forbidden zone. All told, the German merchant vessels the Eriphia, the Siegfried, the Klio, the Matilda, the Irmfried, and Rudolf were offered.[134] Later, other names of vessels were reported, and apparently confusion existed between the Admiralty and the Ambassador as to precisely which ships were to be offered, but the exact names were insignificant; a total of more than 16,000 tons of shipping was now in Spain's hands. The Spanish kept their side of the bargain. Prime Minister Antonio Maura stated in an official note that this was not a seizure but a friendly arrangement with Germany. He also made public the fact Ratibor had designated the ships to be used now by Spain.[135]

Ratibor summarized the tedious negotiations in a telegram on October 18, 1918, pointing out that Spain would make compensation for the transfers in the future. But what was of greatest significance, from the German standpoint, was the fact that the Germans had not totally accepted the Spanish viewpoint in the affair. Nor had Spain accepted the German view in its entirety. Ratibor saw the situation as one in which the Spanish did not have to back down from their decision of the previous August. Thus, the tremendous pressure from the Entente could be borne by the Spanish. Germany, too, did not have to make sharp protests that could have led to a break in relations, and war. Clearly, Ratibor saw the event as a victory for German diplomacy.[136]

The Entente probably agreed that Spain was still too pro-German, for the Spanish government immediately was faced with Entente protests. The pro-Entente press saw the transfer as a victory for the Germans.[137] The British intimated to the Spanish that any peace settlement would mean the transfer of all German merchant vessels to the Entente and not to the neutrals. Ratibor and the Spanish then discussed the possibility of selling the vessels directly to Spain, thereby keeping them out of British hands, although apparently this never was done.[138] On November 6, 1918, Great Britain informed Spain that the vessels would be seized by the Entente once they sailed into the open sea. Thus, the British saw the transfers as a demonstration of a pro-German stance by the Spanish.[139] The cabinet in London insisted the peace conference at the end of the war would determine the status of such vessels transferred from Germany to neutrals.[140] The American view was the same.[141]

In January 1919, however, the English and the Spanish

came to an agreement about the permanent disposition of the seven ships transferred in October 1918. In return for giving up claims to extra ships for losses sustained during the war, Spain was allowed to keep the seven vessels, renamed España I through VII.[142] Formal American assent for Spanish use of the ships was given on January 22, 1920.[143]

In the meantime, the war ended and the Spanish government changed; Manuel García Prieto, the right wing Liberal became Prime Minister. Diplomatic representation of Spain in Berlin also changed. The policy of neutrality was condemned by Count Romanones.[144] The previous Foreign Minister, Eduardo Dato, resigned due to opposition to the apparent conciliatory attitude of the Maura government to the Germans in the ship question.[145] The government seemed weakened in the meantime; the Allies had won the war and Romanones's policy was, as a consequence, totally vindicated, thus his influence soared.[146] In a report from the German Overseas Company, the new direction for Spanish foreign policy was to be that of 1902 to 1910, that is, pro-Allied. The community of interests between Spain and the Western Powers in the Mediterranean was now the focus of attention as it was in the earlier period. The Germans congratulated themselves at least on preventing Romanones from coming to influence and to power any sooner.[147]

By December 5, 1918, Romanones created his own government with a decidely anti-German cast.[148] Romanones promptly announced his intention to expel Ratibor and the whole German contingent and to remove Polo de Bernabé from Berlin.[149] The Ambassador at Madrid, Ratibor, was formally asked to leave on December 14, 1918.[150]

Romanones sought to win influence with Wilson at Paris. On December 19, 1918, Romanones went to Paris and visited Wilson seeking approval to keep the ships taken in October.[151] Evidently, Wilson admitted the moral right of neutrals to be at the Versailles Peace Conference, but lamented that he could not agree to Spain's presence.[152] Thus, Spain returned to the policy that Romanones had advocated in the prewar years and from 1915 to 1917, but she did not participate in the peace conference.

On January 9, 1919, virtually the entire entourage of the Germany Embassy left Spain. Ratibor and his family along with Military Attaché Major Kalle, Legation Secretary von Stohrer, Naval Attaché Stefan, and the Naval Intendant Councillor Grimm all were declared _personae non gratae_. Thus, the personal feud between Ratibor and Romanones had an ending with a slight twist. Though Ratibor had helped in bringing Romanones down in 1917, it was Romanones now who was vindicated and who managed to remove Ratibor.[153]

FOOTNOTES FOR CHAPTER VIII

[1]Ratibor to Foreign Office, April 29, 1918, Spanien 61. Die Politischen Beziehungen, 358/8.

[2]Zimmermann to Ratibor, April 27, 1918, Weltkrieg Nr. 28. Druck, 43.

[3]Ibid.

[4]Ratibor to Foreign Office, April 30, 1918, Ibid., 48.

[5]Ratibor to Foreign Office, May 5, 1918, Ibid., 48.

[6]Ibid.

[7]Ratibor to Foreign Office, May 7, 1918, Spanien 55. Koenigshaus, 771.

[8]Ratibor to Foreign Office, May 7, 1918, Weltkrieg Nr. 28. Druck, 52.

[9]Lersner for Ludendorff to Foreign Office, May 12, 1918, Ibid., 72.

[10]Langwerth to Lersner, May 22, 1918, Ibid., 78-79.

[11]Welczeck to Lersner, May 22, 1918, Spanien 61. Die Politischen Beziehungen, 358/29.

[12]Langwerth Inner Memorandum, May 22, 1918, Spanien 45. Finanzen, 621-623.

[13]Deutsche Bank to Foreign Office, May 16, 1918, Ibid., 621.

[14]Welczeck to Lersner, May 22, 1918, Spanien 61. Die Politischen Beziehungen, 358/29.

[15]Ratibor to Foreign Office, June 2, 1918, Weltkrieg Nr. 28. Druck, 81. And Spain, Cortes, Congreso de los diputados, Diario de las Sesiones de Cortes, 1838-1923 (Washington, D.C. Microcard Editions, 1971), Ap. 2, Number 21, May 21, 1918, pp. 1-4, read by Augusto González Besada.

[16] Ratibor to Foreign Office, June 26, 1918, Ibid., 91.

[17] Ratibor to Foreign Office, June 30, 1918, Ibid., 98-99.

[18] Landecho to Welczeck, July 13, 1918, Ibid., 100-101.

[19] Ratibor to Foreign Office, July 13, 1918, Ibid., 101.

[20] Welczeck to Admiralty Chief of Staff, July 23, 1918, Spanien 61. Die Politischen Beziehungen, 358/97.

[21] Lersner to Foreign Office, July 27, 1918, Ibid., 358/107.

[22] Scheer to Foreign Office, August 7, 1918, Ibid., 358/269.

[23] Bassewitz to Foreign Office, August 7, 1918, Ibid., 358/149.

[24] Ratibor to Foreign Office, August 8, 1918, Ibid., 358/157.

[25] Bassewitz to Foreign Office, August 9, 1918, Ibid., 358/158.

[26] New York Times, August 10, 1918. See also Foreign Office to Madrid, August 10, 1918, Spanien 61. Die Politischen Beziehungen, 358/147.

[27] Polo to Bussche, August 10, 1918, Spanien 61. Die Politischen Beziehungen, 358/161.

[28] Willard to Lansing, #1205, Willard Family Papers, Box 115, April 5, 1918, Manuscript Division, Library of Congress, Washington, D.C. Hereafter cited Willard Family Papers.

[29] Eduardo Dato to Antonio Maura, Archivo Maura, in Appendix V, Rafael Olivar Bertrand, "Repercusiones en España de la primera guerra mundial," p. 35.

[30] Willard to Lansing, Confidential, Willard Family Papers, Box 115, May 2, 1918.

[31] Willard to Dato, Willard Family Papers, Box 115, June 3, 1918 and Hardinge to Dato, July 10, 1918 in Bertrand, "Repercusiones," Appendix VI, pp. 36-37.

[32] Romanones to Maura, Archivo Maura, Ministry of Grace

and Justice, July 17, 1918, Appendix IX in Bertrand, "Repercusiones," pp. 39-40.

[33]Dato to Maura, July 30, 1918 in Appendix XIII in Bertrand, "Repercusiones," pp. 42-43.

[34]Romanones, Notas de Una Vida, pp. 380-381.

[35]Maura to his son in García Venero, Santiago Alba, p. 154.

[36]García Venero, pp. 156-157.

[37]Ibid., p. 154.

[38]Mousset, Espagne dans la Politique Mondiale, pp. 203-205.

[39]New York Times, August 12, 1918.

[40]Bassewitz to Foreign Office, August 11, 1918, Spanien 61. Die Politischen Beziehungen, 358/36-37.

[41]Ibid., 59-60.

[42]Bussche to Lersner, August 12, 1918, Spanien 32. Ueberlassung von deutschen Schiffe an Spanien. T149/359/24. Hereafter cited as Spanien 32. Ueberlassung. The losses of Spain were considerable as shown by independent accounts, upwards of 60,000 tons or $18 million in value. See Edgar Turlington, Neutrality: The World War Period (New York: Columbia University, 1936), p. 26.

[43]Bussche to Lersner, August 12, 1918, Spanien 32. Ueberlassung, 24. The exact same point was made in a book published in 1930; indeed, the whole exchange of wireless messages between Madrid and Berlin were snatched out of the air and decoded in Paris. The entire story was not known, but a large part of it was. See the book based on French archival material: Louis Guichard, The Naval Blockade, p. 246.

[44]Bussche to Lancken, August 12, 1918, Spanien 32. Ueberlassung, 27.

[45]Bussche to Chief of the Admiralty Staff, August 14, 1918, Ibid., 44.

[46]Bussche to Berckheim, August 14, 1918, Ibid., 39-40.

[47]Polo to Welczeck, August 16, 1918, Spanien 61. Die Politischen Beziehungen, 358/175.

[48]Ratibor to Foreign Office, August 16, 1918, Spanien 32. Ueberlassung, 63.

[49]Bussche to Ratibor, August 16, 1918, Ibid., 50-53.

[50]Bussche to Polo, August 17, 1918, Spanien 61. Die Politischen Beziehungen, 358/173.

[51]New York Times, August 19, 1918.

[52]Ibid., August 20, 1918.

[53]Ratibor to Foreign Office, August 21, 1918, Spanien 61. Die Politischen Beziehungen, 358/188.

[54]Ratibor to Foreign Office, August 22, 1918, Spanien 32. Ueberlassung, 106.

[55]Berckheim to Foreign Office, August 22, 1918, Ibid., 72.

[56]New York Times, August 22, 1918.

[57]Handwritten note of Captain Zencker, August 21, 1918, Spanien 32. Ueberlassung, 66.

[58]Ratibor to Foreign Office, August 27, 1918, Ibid., 114-115.

[59]Ratibor to Foreign Office, August 27, 1918, Ibid., 116.

[60]Lancken to Foreign Office, August 27, 1918, Ibid., 110-111.

[61]Welczeck to Bussche, August 28, 1918, Ibid., 77.

[62]Welczeck to Bussche, August 31, 1918, Ibid., 127.

[63]Ratibor to Foreign Office, August 31, 1918, Spanien 61. Die Politischen Beziehungen, 358/258.

[64]Willard to Lansing, September 1, 1918, U.S. Foreign Relations, 1918 Supplement 1, vol. 2, pp. 1719-1720.

[65]Ratibor to Foreign Office, September 1, 1918, Spanien 32. Ueberlassung, 131.

[66]Willard to Lansing, September 1, 1918, U.S. Foreign Relations, Supplement 1, vol. 2, pp. 1720-1721.

[67]Ratibor to Foreign Office, September 2, 1918, Spanien 61. Die Politischen Beziehungen, 358/262.

[68]Welczeck to Bussche, September 4, 1918, Ibid., 358/241.

[69]Bussche to Welczeck, September 4, 1918, Ibid., 358/235.

[70]Ratibor to Foreign Office, September 4, 1918, Spanien 32. Ueberlassung, 157.

[71]Willard to Lansing, September 5, 1918, U.S. Foreign Relations, 1918, Supplement 1, vol. 2, p. 1722.

[72]Internal Memorandum from Luzern, September 6, 1918, Spanien 61. Die Politischen Beziehungen, 358/390. Evidently Alfonso wanted to remove Polo, so the Americans had learned. See Lang to Milstaf, Record Group 165, 2266-S-29, September 5-6, 1918, Cablegram #78. The National Archives, Washington, D.C.

[73]Welczeck to Bussche, Report of a Conversation with Admiralty Officer Captain Horn, September 6, 1918, Spanien 61. Die Politischen Beziehungen, 358/122.

[74]Admiralty to Foreign Office, September 7, 1918, Ibid., 358/271.

[75]Berckheim to Foreign Office, September 7, 1918, Ibid., 358/273.

[76]Ratibor to Foreign Office, August 7, 1918, Ibid., 358/303.

[77]Welczeck to Ratibor, September 7, 1918, Spanien 32. Ueberlassung, 146.

[78]Langwerth to Chancellor Hertling, September 7, 1918, Ibid., 142-145.

[79]Summary of newspaper reports of the Aktenpost, The Hague, September 7, 1918, in Spanien 61. Die Politischen Beziehungen, 358/266.

[80]Hintze to Scheer, September 7, 1918, Ibid., 358/260.

[81]Kalle to GHQ, September 13, 1918, Spanien 32. Ueberlassung, 201.

[82]Ibid.

[83]Hintze to Ratibor, September 9, 1918, Ibid., 358/126.

[84]Bussche to Scheer, September 9, 1918, Ibid., 358/270.

[85]Admiralty to Foreign Office, September 24, 1918, Spanien 32. Ueberlassung, 290.

[86]Willard to Lansing, September 28, 1918, U.S. Foreign

Relations, 1918 Supplement 1, vol. 2, p. 1727.

[87]Ratibor to Foreign Office, September 9, 1918, Spanien 32. Ueberlassung, 189.

[88]Ratibor to Foreign Office, September 11, 1918, Ibid., 194.

[89]Admiralty to Foreign Office, September 9, 1918, Spanien 61. Die Politischen Beziehungen, 358/322.

[90]Stumm to Berckheim, September 11, 1918, Spanien 32. Ueberlassung, 154-155. For the point that the Sardinero carried goods intended for Switzerland, see James W. Garner, International Law and the World War (London: Longmans Green, 1920), p. 174.

[91]Ratibor to Foreign Office, September 11, 1918, Spanien 32. Ueberlassung, 202-210.

[92]Ratibor to Foreign Office, September 11, 1918, Ibid., 194-195.

[93]Ratibor to Foreign Office, September 12, 1918, Ibid., 223.

[94]Ratibor to Foreign Office, September 12, 1918, Ibid., 224.

[95]Ratibir to Foreign Office, September 13, 1918, Ibid., 226.

[96]Hintze to Ratibor, no date, probably September 1918, Ibid., 247.

[97]Memorandum to Spain, September 14, 1918, Ibid., 185-186.

[98]Ratibor to Foreign Office, September 15, 1918, Ibid., 248-249.

[99]Stumm to Lersner, September 16, 1918, Ibid., 227.

[100]Ratibor to Foreign Office, September 17, 1918, Ibid., 257.

[101]Ibid.

[102]Hintze to Ratibor, September 17, 1918, Ibid., 243-244.

[103]Willard to Lansing, September 17, 1918, U.S. Foreign Relations, 1918 Supplement 1, vol. 2, p. 1725. See also Pingaud, Histoire Diplomatique, vol. III, pp. 41-42.

[104]Kalle to GHQ, September 20, 1918, Spanien 32. Ueberlassung, 264.

[105]Ibid.

[106]Gatzke to Foreign Office, September 22, 1918, Ibid., 293.

[107]Hintze to Ratibor, September 23, 1918, Ibid., 275.

[108]Hintze to Gruenau, GHQ, and the Admiralty, no date, probably late September 1918, Ibid., 280-281.

[109]Ratibor to Foreign Office, September 22, 1918, Spanien 32. Ueberlassung, 269.

[110]Willard to Lansing, September 23, 1918, U.S. Foreign Relations, 1918 Supplment 1, vol. 2, pp. 1725-1726.

[111]Welczeck to Lersner, September 23, 1918, Spanien 32. Ueberlassung, 250-251.

[112]Ratibor to Foreign Office, September 24, 1918, Ibid., 303-304.

[113]Internal Note of State Secretary Hintze, September 25, 1918, Ibid., 297.

[114]Hintze to Ratibor, September 26, 1918, Ibid., 302. Also see Guichard, Naval Blockade, p. 249.

[115]Ratibor to Foreign Office, September 27, 1918, Spanien 32. Ueberlassung, 314-315.

[116]Bussche to the Neutral Countries' Representative, September 28, 1918, Ibid., 310.

[117]Scheer to Hintze, September 21, 1918, Ibid., 268.

[118]Ibid.

[119]Admiralty to Hintze, September 22, 1918, Ibid., 282-283.

[120]Gruenau to Foreign Office, September 26, 1918, Ibid., 301.

[121]Scheer to Foreign Office, September 27, 1918, Ibid., 310.

[122]Reinhardt Scheer, Germany's High Seas Fleet in the World War (London: Caswell, 1920), pp. 337-338.

[123] Ratibor to Foreign Office, October 8, 1918, Spanien 32. Ueberlassung, 351.

[124] Foreign Office to Seekriegsleitung, October 8, 1918, Ibid., 349.

[125] Inner Memorandum, no date, Berlin, probably around October 8, 1918 due to its location in the documents. Spanien 61. Die Politischen Beziehungen, 358/409.

[126] Polo to Bussche, October 9, 1918, Spanien 32. Ueberlassung, 356-357.

[127] Bussche to Polo, October 9, 1918, Ibid., 360-361.

[128] Ibid.

[129] Maura to Hintze, October 10, 1918, Spanien 61. Die Politischen Beziehungen, 358/411-413.

[130] Bussche to Ratibor, October 10, 1918, Spanien 32. Ueberlassung, 367.

[131] Bussche to Ratibor, Ibid., 371.

[132] Ratibor to Foreign Office, October 12, 1918, Ibid., 389-397.

[133] Ratibor to Foreign Office, October 14, 1918, Ibid., 413.

[134] Ibid.

[135] Ratibor to Foreign Office, October 15, 1918, Ibid., 412.

[136] Ratibor to Foreign Office, October 18, 1918, Ibid., 445.

[137] Ratibor to Foreign Office, October 17, 1918, Ibid., 425.

[138] Ratibor to Foreign Office, October 21, 1918, Ibid., 440.

[139] Ratibor to Foreign Office, November 6, 1918, Spanien 61. Die Politischen Beziehungen, 358/440.

[140] Ratibor to Foreign Office, November 8, 1918, Ibid., 358/442.

[141] Willard to Lansing, November 9, 1918, U.S. Foreign Relations, 1918 Supplement, vol. 2, p. 1728.

[142]Deutsche Ueberseeische Bericht fuer Februar 1919, March 4, 1918, Spanien 40. Allgemeine, 281-282. Later in Paris the Reparations Commission was charged with the final disposition of the vessels. See U.S. Foreign Relations, 1919, The Paris Peace Conference, vol. 8, p. 536.

[143]Lansing to Willard, #15, Willard Family Papers, Box 115, January 22, 1920.

[144]New York Times, October 30, 1918.

[145]Ratibor to Foreign Office, October 30, 1918, Spanien 61. Die Politischen Beziehungen, 358/431.

[146]Ratibor to Foreign Office, November 10, 1918, Spanien 55. Spanische Staatsmaenner, T149/356/63.

[147]Report for October from the Deutsche Ueberseeische Bank to the Foreign Office, November 1918, Spanien 40. Allgemeine, 205.

[148]Ratibor to Foreign Office, December 5, 1918, Spanien 57. Ministerien, 615.

[149]New York Times, December 9, 1918 and Ratibor to Foreign Office, December 9, 1918, Deutschland 127. Mission, 580.

[150]New York Times, December 14, 1918.

[151]Ratibor to Foreign Office, December 19, 1918, Spanien 55. Spanische Staatsmaenner, 111.

[152]Bassewitz to Foreign Office, December 30, 1918, Ibid., 113. Also see Romanones, Notas de una Vida, pp. 383-384.

[153]Times, January 13, 1919.

CONCLUSION

German policy toward Spain evolved through four major phases, each corresponding in large measure to the policies of King Alfonso XIII, who conducted an independent course and who exploited the war to Spain's benefit. Though the King had tried before the war to get concessions for his adherence to the Triple Entente, he was unsuccessful, and in German-Spanish relations from 1914 through 1916, the Wilhelmstrasse attempted to attract Spain to the Central Powers, using an extensive propaganda network and shrewd offers of postwar rewards. German military victories also persuaded Alfonso XIII to listen to proposals from Berlin.

The King, however, was at heart a Francophile, and in 1915, while he consulted the Germans about benevolent neutrality for their cause, he continued the major lines of his prewar negotiations with the Allies, trying to transfer the internationalized city of Tangier to Spain. Once again, Alfonso's project was rejected, and he turned to Berlin, seeking guarantees for German investments and aid in Spanish military preparations. The German Military Attaché was happy to promise help, but nothing came of the plans as Germany was too far away and too involved in the war to provide economic and military assistance. Throughout the fall of 1915, the King had to contend with increasing economic problems wrought by shortages due to the war and with a cabinet crisis resulting in the formation of a new government on December 9, 1915. Count Romanones, a declared enemy of Germany, headed the new cabinet.

While Romanones and Alfonso had similar feelings about the war, the two differed markedly in their approach to the conflict. Romanones was determined to proclaim benevolent neutrality for the Allies, but the King was equally determined to avoid any provocation of the Germans who could mobilize public opinion and possibly topple his crown. From December 1915 through August 1916, the King tried to control the overzealous policies of his Prime Minister, and the Germans were his assistants.

Through several channels, the King convinced Berlin to send a submarine to Cartagena harbor on June 22, 1916, including a letter acceding to Alfonso's requests to participate in any forthcoming peace conference and offering Spain use of interned German vessels for domestic commerce. Actually, the value of this spectacular demonstration of the King's influence with Kaiser William II was to counter Romanones's growing power. The Germans were not really sincere in offering Alfonso a place at a future peace table; they too were interested in the gains to be had from publicity as a result of the visit. The Wilhelmstrasse feared Romanones and wanted to assure themselves that Spain would remain neutral, preferably strictly neutral. But both their hope and that of the King were dashed when, in the summer of 1916, the French and British apparently decided to force Spain toward a declaration of benevolence for the Entente, and Romanones was their willing accomplice.

From September 1916 through April 1917, Spanish adherence to the Entente seemed a foregone conclusion. The French and British assiduously cultivated Romanones in late August and early September 1916, convincing him of the need for Spain to enter the war or to break with Germany so that Spain might have a place at the peace table. When a new British Prime Minister, David Lloyd George, came to power in December 1916, British troops prepared for service in Spain. A crisis in German-Spanish relations thus developed.

From September through November 1916, Romanones challenged German sinkings of Spanish vessels, and King Alfonso XIII continuously assured Germany that Spain would never depart from neutrality and would not break relations with Berlin. The Germans ultimately were able to break through Spanish press censorship and print notices of their good intentions and offers of safe-conduct passes for Spanish fruit ships. By November 1916 the German campaign seemed successful, and a break was avoided. But more ships were sunk, and Romanones's mood became even more truculent in late December 1916, when he gave an interview proclaiming he would, in the future, insist upon Spanish rights and vigorously protest any more losses on the high seas.

Another crisis evolved from December to April 1917.

Kaiser William II communicated with Alfonso XIII intimating directly Spain could expect even more losses were she to adhere to current American peace proposals and to Romanones's policies. In January 1917 the German Embassy also stepped up its propaganda campaign against the Spanish Prime Minister.

Indeed, Spain had gone further down the road of benevolence for the Entente than the Germans realized. Romanones had initiated talks with Sir Edward Grey in the fall of 1916 for a special economic agreement with Great Britain. The British were to guarantee Spain supplies of coal; probably these negotiations were concomitants of the proposals to break relations with Germany. Throughout January 1917 into February and March these negotiations proceeded, though they halted once Romanones left office.

After the Germans declared unrestricted submarine warfare around the British Islands on February 1, 1917, Spanish losses soared geometrically and domestic inflation and scarcities of foodstuffs increased. Alfonso XIII was stunned that the Germans would go this far, but he told the Americans he would not yet permit Spain to enter the war. Subsequent attacks upon Spanish ships, however, precipitated action; Romanones attempted to break relations with Germany on April 19, 1917. The Prime Minister failed to get his entire cabinet to back his plans, and, certainly, the King was adamantly opposed to the move. Thereafter, Romanones resigned, and the Germans seemed to have won a signal victory.

The third phase of German-Spanish relations was

punctuated by greater discord as Spain shifted into the Entente camp. Turmoil caused by soldiers and workers in the summer of 1917 came close to revolution, and the Spanish conservative ruling classes realized the impossibility of participation in the conflict. Accidental developments further drove Spain toward the Entente. Damaged German submarines put in at Spanish harbors for repairs, thereby exciting cries of outrage from the Allies. Too, Allied propaganda had improved markedly by the summer of 1917, and all violations of Spanish neutrality were mercilessly exposed. The Spaniards were forced to declare that any future submarines entering Spanish harbors would be interned. When one of the vessels escaped, further pressure from the Allies resulted in ejection of the German Naval Attaché. Spain had also begun conversations with the U.S. for guarantees of cotton and coal supplies, leading to an agreement in March 1918. The Anglo-Spanish negotiations were completed in December 1917, and Spain was thus drawn into the Entente camp. But there was no formal break with Germany. Indeed, by March 1918 one could say that Spain was a "neutral ally."

Alfonso XIII was not able to stop this drift toward the Allies, indeed, his pro-French and pro-British personal feelings may have predominated by the fall of 1917, and the possibility of countering German propaganda may have given him heart. But the entrance of the United States into the war and the possibilities of an Allied victory may have accelerated Spain's tendencies toward the Entente. Also by early 1918 there was some evidence that the Germans may have played a role in the turmoil of 1917, possibly leading the King to opt for the Allies in order to preserve his crown. But once the economic agreements were made, Spain's economy was more closely than ever before tied in with that of the Entente, therefore Spain had, for all practical purposes, abandoned neutrality.

The fourth and final phase of German-Spanish relations remained quite delicate, particularly as German military power was still evident in the spring of 1918, but once the offensive of July failed, the Spanish government became truculent, though not without some regard for appearances. Domestic politics, in which the traditional fixed elections resulted in alternating liberal and then conservative governments, began to disintegrate, and in March 1918, Spain faced a ministerial crisis which was solved by the creation of a National Government headed by the conservative Antonio Maura and consisting of former Prime Ministers, particularly Romanones. Conflicting ambitions among the former chief executives resulted in stormy cabinet meetings, and in early August 1918, demands for indemnities for losses suffered in the submarine war. For any future sinkings, Spain would take an interned German vessel. But the Spanish backed down from actually seizing any German ship outright. Indeed, negotiations between the Spanish and Germans were polite though legalistic, and in the end the Germans were allowed to save face. Germany merely transferred ships she had selected and ostensibly gave them to Spain voluntarily. Ultimately, the vessels came under the Spanish flag and were never returned to Germany. This was Spain's small reward for her pro-Allied benevolent neutrality in the last few months of the war.

Clearly, German-Spanish relations proceeded upon Alfonso XIII's desire to maintain neutrality and upon German hope to keep Spain strictly neutral. Both were successful to some degree. Both were working toward similar goals, and Alfonso was skillful in convincing the Germans he was on their side when the occasion demanded. He also ably convinced the Entente he had their interests uppermost, yet countering Romanones and successfully maintaining neutrality until the Count had to resign. The Germans profited from an excellent propaganda network and informational and intelligence organization. The Wilhelmstrasse maintained a balanced perspective regarding Spain, remaining unruffled even in the last days of the war when Maura's cabinet made severe demands. Though the Germans failed to keep strict Spanish neutrality from the beginning to the end of the war, yet they fended off Spanish absorption into the Entente until early 1918.

Spain, therefore, conducted an independent foreign policy throughout the First World War. Exploitation of the two power blocs continued in wartime, although the conditions of 1914-1918 were not quite the same as those between 1898-1914. Major political and social changes accelerated with the war, and Spain's economy improved markedly, but Alfonso XIII still played a major role in diplomatic affairs, and he successfully balanced the economic attraction of the Entente by negotiations with the Germans.

Spanish independence did not serve the country well when it came time to discuss the peace conference. Alfonso had repeated many times during the war that Spain, as Europe's largest and most important neutral, should serve as the catalyst for eventual peace. But once the war ended, the Allies had no further use for Spain. The competition between the two power blocs had created conditions in which Spanish policy became important. Since Germany was defeated, Spain no longer counted. Possibly, Spanish independence may have been regarded as duplicity by the Entente. In the end, Spain was not permitted to participate in the peace discussions in Paris and in Versailles.

Though Spain later joined the League of Nations, she turned inward from 1919 through the 1930s. Internal dissensions, exacerbated by the war, continued until a military dictatorship assumed control in the twenties. Further difficulties resulting from continued modernization of the Spanish economy led to the removal of Alfonso in 1931 and the Second Republic. Spanish liberals and conservatives were quite correct in assuming that Spain should not enter the First World War. Had she done so, social disturbances would have come sooner.

Later, in the 1930s, smaller nations again became significant as pawns in diplomatic games. Unfortunately for

Spain, international quarrels from 1936-1939 coincided with disruption of the Spanish social structure.

SELECTED BIBLIOGRAPHY

A. Primary Sources

1. Microfilmed German Documents

Deutschland 127. *Die Spanische Mission in Berlin*, vol. 15: ACP 79/526-604.

Spanien 32. *Ueberlassung von deutschen Schiffen an Spanien*, vols. 2-3: ACP 359/22-507.

Spanien 40. *Allgemeine Angelegenheiten Spaniens*, vols. 50-51: ACP 355/1-335.

Spanien 44. *Militaerische Angelegenheiten Spaniens*, vol. 26: ACP 355/474-563.

Spanien 44a. *Marineangelegenheiten Spaniens*, vol. 8: ACP 355/564-580.

Spanien 45. *Die Finanzen Spaniens*, vols. 15-16: ACP 355/581-627.

Spanien 46. *Die Spanische Presse*, vols. 4-5, ACP 355/628-684.

Spanien 46. *secr. Subventionierung Spanischer Zeitungen*, vols. 3-5: ACP 356/124-309.

Spanien 55. *Kronpraetendant Don Carlos und seine Familie*, vol. 1: ACP 355/797-812 and ACP 356/1-34.

Spanien 55. *Das Spanische Koenigshaus*, vols. 21-22: ACP 355/685-796.

Spanien 55. Nr. 1 *secr. Das Spanische Koenigshaus*, vol. 1: ACP 356/310-400.

Spanien 55. Nr. 2 *Spanische Staatsmaenner*, vols. 10-11: ACP 356/35-123.

Spanien 55. Nr. 3 *Spanische Generaele*, vol. 3: ACP 74/57-109.

Spanien 55. Nr. 4 *Spanische Journalisten*, vol. 1: ACP 74/110-162.

Spanien 56. Verlaengerung des Handelsvertrages mit Deutschland, vol. 3: ACP 74/373-448.

Spanien 57. Die Spanische Ministerien, vols. 12-14: ACP 356/401-643.

Spanien 58. Die Diplomatische Vertretung Spaniens im Auslande, vol. 7: ACP 356/644-695.

Spanien 60. Parlamentarische Angelegenheiten Spaniens, vols. 8-9: ACP 356/696-821.

Spanien 61. Die Politischen Beziehungen zwischen Spanien und Deutschland, vols. 5-12: ACP 357/1-833 and vols. 13-18: ACP 358/1-620.

Spanien 61. secr. Die Beziehungen zwischen Spanien und Deutschland, vol. 1: SA Reel 34, vols. 2-3: SA Reel 35, vols. 4-7: SA Reel 38.

Spanien 65. Beziehungen zu Frankreich, vols. 10-11: ACP 358/621-703.

Spanien 67. Die Auswaertige Politik Spaniens, vol. 3: ACP 78/243-273.

Spanien 69. Umtriebe der Bourbons in Spanien, vol. 1: ACP 78/274-344.

Spanien 70. Beziehungen zu Portugal, vol. 2: ACP 78/439-502.

Spanien 74. Eisenbahnen, vol. 1: ACP 358/783-828.

Weltkrieg Nr. 11q. secr. Unternehmungen und Aufwiegelungen in Spanien, vols. 1-3: ACP 402/178-287.

Weltkrieg Nr. 28. Druck der Entente gegen Spanien, vol. 1: UM 146/28-146.

2. Collected Documents

Diaz Plaja, Fernando. Francófilios y Germanófilios. Los Españoles en la Guerra Europea. Barcelona: Dopesa, 1973.

France. Commission de Publications des Documents relatifs aux Origines de la Guerre du 1914. Documents Diplomatiques Francais, 1871-1914. 36 vols. 2nd and 3rd series used. Paris: Imprimerie Nationale, 1929.

Germany. Auswaertiges Amt. Diplomatische Schriftenstuecke aus der Zeit vom 12. Dezember 1916 bis zum Maerz 1917. Berlin, 1920.

________. Auswaertiges Amt. Die Deutsche Dokumente zum Kriegsausbruch. Charlottenberg: Deutsche Verlagsgesellschaft fuer Politik und Geschichte, 1919.

________. Lepsius, Johannes, et. al., eds. Die Grosse Politik der Europaeischen Kabinette, 1871-1914. 40 vols. Berlin: Deutsche Verlagsgesellschaft fuer Politik und Geschichte, 1924.

________. Philipp, Albrecht. Die Ursachen des Deutschen Zusammenbruchs im Jahre 1918. Berlin: Deutsche Verlagsgesellschaft fuer Politik und Geschichte, 1925.

Great Britain. British and Foreign State Papers, 1916. vol. CX. London: H. M. Stationery Office, 1920.

________. Gooch, G. P. and Harold Temperley, eds. British Documents on the Origins of the War, 1898-1914. 11 vols. London: H. M. Stationery Office, 1927.

________. Keltie, J. Scott, ed. The Statesman's Yearbook, 1914. 51st Annual Publication. London: MacMillan, 1914.

Riaño y Gayangos, Juan. Papers, 1885-1929. Manuscripts Division, Library of Congress, Washington, D.C.

Russia. Pokrovsky, M. M. and Otto Hoetzsch, eds. Die Internationalen Beziehungen im Zeitalter des Imperialisimus, Dokumente aus den Archiven der Zarischen und den Provisorischen Regierung. vols. 6 and 7. Berlin, 1934.

Spain. Cortes, Congreso de los Diputados. Diario de las sesiones de Cortes, 1838-1923. Madrid: Corero Impr. de J. A. García, 1874. Microfiche, Washington, D.C.: Microcard Editions, 1971.

________. Instituto de Reformas Sociales. Sección Segundo. Informes de los Inspectores del Trabajo sobre la Influencia de la Guerra Europea, 1912-1918. Tomo Primero. Madrid: Imp. de la Sucesora de M. Minnesa de los Rios, 1918.

________. Instituto de Reformas Sociales. Informes de los Inspectores del Trabajo sobre la Influencia de la Guerra en las Industrias Españoles durante el año 1915. Madrid: Imp. de la Sucesora de Minnesa de los Rios, 1916.

United States. Department of Foreign and Domestic Commerce. Spanish Finance and Trade. Arthur N. Young. Special Agent Series No. 202. Washington, D.C.: U.S. Government Printing Office, 1920.

________. Department of State. Papers Relating to the Foreign Relations of the United States, 1914 Supplement, The World War. Washington, D.C.: U.S. Government Printing Office, 1928.

________. Papers Relating to the Foreign Relations of the United States with the Address of the President to Congress, December 7, 1915. Washington, D.C.: U.S. Government Printing Office, 1924.

________. Papers Relating to the Foreign Relations of the United States 1915 Supplement The World War. Washington, D.C.: U.S. Government Printing Office, 1928.

________. Papers Relating to the Foreign Relations of the United States with the Address of the President to Congress December 5, 1916. Washington, D.C.: U.S. Government Printing Office, 1925.

________. Papers Relating to the Foreign Relations of the United States 1916 Supplement The World War. Washington, D.C.: U.S. Government Printing Office, 1929.

________. Papers Relating to the Foreign Relations of the United States 1917 Supplement 1 The World War. Washington, D.C.: U.S. Government Printing Office, 1931.

________. Papers Relating to the Foreign Relations of the United States 1917 Supplement 2 The World War. vols. 1-2. Washington, D.C.: U.S. Government Printing Office, 1932.

________. Papers Relating to the Foreign Relations of the United States 1918 Supplement 1 The World War. vols. 1-2. Washington, D.C.: U.S. Government Printing Office, 1933.

________. Papers Relating to the Foreign Relations of the United States 1919 The Paris Peace Conference. vols. 1 and 3. Washington, D.C.: U.S. Government Printing Office, 1942-1943.

________. Record Group 45: Naval Records Collection of the Office of Naval Records and Library. Subject File 1911-1927. National Archives, Washington, D.C.

________. Record Group 59: State Department Decimal File 1910-1929. File 862.20252: German Military Activity in Spain. National Archives, Washington, D.C.

________. Record Group 63: Records of the Committee on Public Information. Files CPI-23-A1. National Archives, Washington, D.C.

________. Record Group 120. Records of the American Expeditionary Forces General Headquarters. File G-2-B: "German Methods" Folders 532 (1) 541 G-2. Military Attaché Reports-Madrid. National Archives, Washington, D.C.

________. Record Group 159. Department of State. National Archives, Washington, D.C.

________. Record Group 165. Modern Military Records. National Archives, Washington, D.C.

Willard, Joseph E. Papers. Embassy Correspondence. Boxes 113-116. Manuscripts Division, Library of Congress, Washington, D.C.

Wilson, Woodrow. Papers. Manuscript Division, Library of Congress, Washington, D.C.

3. Memoirs and Diaries

Bertie, Lord of Thane. The Diary of Lord Bertie, 1914-1918. ed. by Lady Algernon Gordon Lennox. London: Hodder and Stoughton, 1924.

Buelow, Berhard von. Memoirs. 3 vols. London: Putnam, 1932.

Cambon, Paul. Correspondence, 1870-1924. Paris: Grosset, 1946.

Chapman Huston, Desmond and Princess Pilar of Bavaria. Every Inch a King: Alfonso XIII. New York: Dutton, 1932.

Churchill, Winston. Great Contemporaries. London: Thornton Butterworth, 1937.

Cortina, Marquis of. Terra Incognita (Recuerdas de una mission oficial en Londres. n. d.

Creel, George. How We Advertised America. New York: Harper, 1920.

Eulalia, Princess of Spain. Memoirs of Her Royal Highness the Princess Eulalia. Trans. by Phyllis Mégoy. London: Hutchinson and Co., 1936.

García Calderon, José. Diario Intimo, 12 Septiembre 1914-3 de Mayo 1916. Perambulo por Alberto Jochamowitz. Lima: Universidad Nacional Mayor de San Marcos, 1969.

Gilbert, Martin, ed. Winston Churchill. Companion volume III, Part i. Boston: Houghton-Mifflin, 1973.

Goerlitz, Walter. The Kaiser and His Court. New York: Harcourt and Brace, 1964.

Hardinge, Sir Arthur. A Diplomatist in Europe. London: Jonathan Cape, 1927.

Hohenlohe-Schillingsfuerst, Chlodwig. Denkwuerdigkeiten des Fuersten Chlodwig zu Hohenlohe-Schillingsfuerst. Stuttgart: Deutsche Verlagsanstalt, 1907.

House, Colonel Edward M. ed. by Charles Seymour. Intimate Papers of Colonel Edward M. House. 4 vols. London, Boston, New York: Houghton-Mifflin, 1926-1928.

Lancken-Wakenitz, Oskar Freiherr von der. Meine Dreissig Dienstjahre (1888-1918). Berlin, 1931.

Lerroux, Alejandro. Mis Memorias. Madrid: Afrodisio Aquado, S.A., Editores Labreros, 1963.

________. La Pequeña Historia. Buenas Aires: Editorial Cimera, 1945.

________. La Verdad a mi País, España y la Guerra. Madrid: Liberia, 1915.

Ludendorff, Erich. My War Memories. New York: Harpers, 1920.

Maura, Antonio. Treinta y Cinco Años de Vida Publica. vol. 1: Ideas, Políticos, Doctrinas de Gobierno y Campaña Parlamentarias. Recopiladas por José Ruiz Castillo. Madrid: Biblioteca nueva, 1918.

Nekludoff, Anatole. Diplomatic Reminiscences Before and During the World War, 1911-1917. London: Murray, 1920.

Nicolai, Walter. Nachrichtendienst, Presse und Volksstimmung. Berlin: E.S. Mittler, 1920.

________. Geheime Maechte: Internationale Spionage und Ihre Bekaempfung im Weltkriege und Heute. Leipzig: Koehler, 1923.

Papen, Franz von. Memoirs. Trans. by Brian Connel. New York: Dutton, 1953.

Poincaré, Raymond. The Memoirs of Raymond Poincaré. Trans. by Sir George Arthur. London: William Heinemann, 1926.

Reynoso, Francisco de. The Reminiscences of a Spanish Diplomat. London: Hutchinson, 1933.

Romanones, Conde de. Las Responsibilidades políticas del antiguo régimen de 1875 a 1932. Madrid: Renacimienta, n. d.

________. Notas de una Vida, 1912-1931. Madrid: Espasa-Calpo, 1947.

________. Obras Completas. vol. III. Madrid: Editorial Plus-Ultra, 1949.

Rosen, Friedrich. Aus meinem diplomatischen Wanderleben. 2 vols. Berlin: Transmare, 1932.

Scheer, Reinhardt. Germany's High Seas Fleet in the World War. London: Caswell, 1920.

Talbot, Hayden. An Interview with the King of Spain. New York: ITT Corp., 1924.

Tirpitz, Alfred P. F. von. My Memoirs. New York: Dodd and Mead, 1919.

Wickham-Steed, Henry. Through Thirty Years, 1892-1922. New York: Doubleday and Co., 1925.

4. Newspapers and Chronicles

El Debate, 1917-1919.

Deutscher Geschichtskalendar: Der Europaeischer Krieg in aktenmaessiger Darstellung. Leipzig: Verlag von Felix Meiner, 1914-1919.

La Época, 1914-1919.

Frankfurter Zeitung. Der Grosse Krieg. Eine Chronik von Tag zu Tag. Urkunden, Depesche und Berichte der Frankfurter Zeitung. Heft 71. Nr. 71-80. 1917.

Frankfurter Zeitung und Handelsblatt, 1914-1920.

Gaceta de Madrid, 1914.

Great Britain. Series 1. Daily Foreign Press Review, January-February 1916. London: H. M. Stationery Office, 1916.

El Imparcial, 1914-1919.

El Mundo, 1914-1918.

New York Times, 1914-1919.

Schulthess' Europaeischer Geschichtskalendar, 1914-1918. Munich: C.H. Beck'sche Verlagsbuchhandlung, 1921.

El Socialista, 1914-1919.

El Sol, 1917-1919.

The Times, 1914-1919.

Vorwaerts, 1918.

Zentralstelle fuer Auslandsdienst. Zeitungskontrolle, 1915-1918: Spanische Presse. Berlin: Druck von Julius Sittenfeld, Hofbuchdrucker, 1915-1918.

B. SECONDARY SOURCES

1. Books

Absagen, Karl H. Canaris. Trans. by Alan H. Broderick. London: Hutchinson, 1956.

Albertini, Luigi. The Origins of the War of 1914. Trans. by Isabella M. Massey. London, New York: Oxford Univ. Press, 1952.

Albrecht-Carrie, René. A Diplomatic History of Europe Since the Congress of Vienna. New York: Harpers, 1958.

Alengry, Jean. Les Relations Franco-Espagnoles et l'Affaire du Maroc. Paris: La Vie Universaire, 1920.

Almagro, Don Melchor Fernandez. Historia del Reinado de Don Alfonso XIII. Barcelona: Montaner y Simon, 1933.

Bailey, Thomas A. The Policy of the United States Toward the Neutrals, 1917-1918. Baltimore, Md.: Johns Hopkins, 1942.

Baldwin, Hanson. The World War: An Outline History. New York: Harpers, 1962.

Becker, Jeronimo. Historia de las Relaciones Exteriores de España durante el Siglo XIX. Madrid: J. Rates, 1924.

________. Los estudios geográficos en España. Madrid: J. Rates, 1917.

________. España y Marruecos, sus relaciones diplomáticas durante el siglo XIX. Madrid: Tipolitografia, R. Peant, 1903.

Bello, Luis. España durante la Guerra. Política y Acción de los Alemanes, 1914-1918. Madrid: Editional Europa, 1920.

Bergamini, John D. The Spanish Bourbons: The History of a

Tenacious Dynasty. New York: Putnam, 1974.

Blasco Ibañez, Vicente. Alfonso XIII Unmasked: The Military Terror in Spain. New York: Dutton, 1924.

Brenan, Gerald. The Spanish Labyrinth. Cambridge: Cambridge University Press, 1960.

Cameron, Rondo. France and the Economic Development of Europe 1800-1914. Princeton, N.J.: Princeton Univer. Press, 1961.

Carlgren, W.M. Neutralitaet oder Allianz: Deutschlands Beziehungen zu Schweden in den Anfangsjahren des ersten Weltkrieges. Stockholm: Alinquist and Wiksell, 1962.

Carr, Raymond. Spain, 1808-1939. Oxford: Clarendon, 1966.

Carter, Joseph. 1918, Year of Crisis, Year of Change. Englewood Cliffs, N.J.: Prentice Hall, 1968.

Cecil, Lamar. The German Diplomatic Service, 1871-1914. Princeton, N.J.: Princeton Univ. Press, 1976.

Churchill, Winston. The World Crisis. 4 vols. London: Thornton Butterworth, 1924.

Cordero Torres, José. Relaciones exteriores de España. Madrid: Movimiento, 1950.

Cortes Cavanilla, Julian. Alfonso XIII y la guerra del 14. Madrid: Alce, 1976.

Craig, Gordon A. From Bismarck to Adenauer. Baltimore, Md.: Johns Hopkins Press, 1958.

________. Germany, 1866-1945. New York: Oxford University Press, 1978.

Cruttwell, A. A History of the Great War. Oxford: Clarendon, 1936.

Einhorn, Marion. Die oekonomischen Hintergruende der faschistischen deutschen Intervention in Spanien 1936-1939. East Berlin: Das Europaeische Buch, VVA, 1975.

Espíno Moltó, Víctor. Alfonso XIII y la Guerra: Espejo de neutrales. Madrid: Rev. de Arch., Biblioteca y Museo, 1918.

Esposito, Vincent J. A Concise History of World War I. New York: Praeger, 1964.

Falls, Cyrill. The Great War. New York: Putnam, 1959.

Feldman, Gerald. Army, Industry and Labor in Germany, 1914-1918. Princeton, N.J.: Princeton University Press, 1966.

Fischer, Fritz. World Power or Decline. The Controversy over Germany's Aims in the First World War. Trans. by L. Farrar and R. Kimber. New York: Norton, 1974.

Flier, Marius van der, et al. The Netherlands and The World War. Oxford: Clarendon Press, 1923-1928.

Friedensburg, Ferdinand. Das Erzproblem der deutschen Eisenindustrie. Berlin: Duncker und Humboldt, n.d.

García Venero, Maximiano. Melquiades Alvarez: Historia de un Liberal. Madrid: Editorial Alhambra, 1954.

________. Santiago Alba: Monarquicó de razón. Madrid: Aguilar, 1963.

Garner, James W. International Law and the World War. London: Longmans Green Co., 1920.

Gay de Montella, Rafael. Diez Años de política internacional en el Mediterraneo, 1904-1914. Madrid: Francisco Beltran, n.d.

Gelos, Ferreira de vaz, Lillian. Die Neutralitaetspolitik Spaniens waehrend des ersten Weltkrieges. Hamburg: Institut fuer Auswaertige Politik, 1966.

Gottlieb, Wolfram. Studies in Secret Diplomacy during the First World War. London: G. Allen and Unwin, 1957.

Guichard, Louis. The Naval Blockade, 1914-1918. Trans. by Christopher R. Turner. New York: Appleton, 1930.

Halpin, Paul G. The Mediterranean Naval Situation, 1908-1914. Cambridge, Mass.: Harvard University Press, 1971.

Hantsch, Hugo. Leopold Graf Berchthold, Granseigneur und Staatsmann. Graz: Verlag Styria, 1963.

Hayes, Carlton. A Brief History of the Great War. New York: MacMillan, 1920.

Hecksher, Eli, et al. Norway, Sweden, Denmark and Iceland in the World War. New Haven, Conn.: Yale University Press, 1930.

Herre, Paul. Die Kleinen Staaten Europas und die Entstehung des Weltkrieges. Munich: C.H. Beck'sche Verlag, 1937.

Hills, George. Rock of Contention: A History of Gibraltar.

London: Robert Hale, 1974.

Holborn, Hajo. A History of Modern Germany, 1840-1945. New York: Alfred A. Knopf, 1969.

Huber, Lewis. [Murray Bookchin] The Spanish Anarchists: The Heroic Years 1868-1936. New York: Free Life Editions, 1977.

Irwin, Will. Propaganda and the News or What Makes You Think So? New York: Whittlesey House, 1936.

Katz, Friedrich. Deutschland, Diaz und die Mexikanische Revolution; die Deutsche Politik in Mexiko, 1870-1920. East Berlin: Deutscher Verlag der Wissenschaften, 1964.

Kern, Robert and R. Dolkart, eds. Caciques: Oligarchial Politics and the System of Caciquismo in the Luso-Hispanic World. Albuquerque, N.M.: The University of New Mexico, 1974.

Kern, Robert W. Liberals, Reformers and Caciques in Restoration Spain, 1875-1909. Albuquerque, N.M.: The University of New Mexico, 1974.

________. Red Years Black Years: A History of Spanish Anarchism, 1911-1937. Philadelphia, Pa.: Institute for the Study of Human Issues, 1978.

Liddel-Hart, Basil H. The Real War, 1914-1918. Boston: Little-Brown, 1930.

Madariaga, Salvador de. Spain, A Modern History. New York: Frederick A. Praeger, 1958.

Maiski, Ivan M. Neuere Geschichte Spaniens, 1808-1917. East Berlin: Ruetten und Loening, 1961.

May, Ernest R. The World War and American Isolation. Cambridge, Mass.: Harvard University Press, 1959.

Meaker, Gerald. The Revolutionary Left in Spain, 1914-1923. Stanford, Calif.: Stanford University Press, 1974.

Mock, James R. and Cedric Larson. Words that Won the War: The Story of the Committee on Public Information, 1917-1919. Princeton, N.J.: Princeton University Press, 1939.

Mousset, Albert. Elements d'une bibliographie des livres, brochures et tracts imprimés ou publiés en Espagne de 1914 à 1919 et relatifs à la guerre mondiale. Madrid: Biblioteca Nueva, 1919.

________. L'Espagne dans la politique mondiale. Paris: Bossard, 1923.

________. Histoire d'Espagne. Paris: Societe d'Editions Francaises et Internationales, 1947.

________. La Política exterior de España, 1873-1918. Madrid: Biblioteca nueva, 1918.

Muehlen, Norbert. The Incredible Krupps. New York: Henry Holt and Company, 1959.

Oliviera, Antonio Ramos. Politics, Economics, and Men of Modern Spain, 1808-1946. London: Victor Gollancz, Ltd., 1946.

Payne, Stanley G. Politics and the Military in Modern Spain. Stanford, Calif.: Stanford University Press, 1967.

________. Politics and Society in 20th Century Spain. New York: Watts, 1976.

Pérez y Gómez, Antonio. Don Juan de la Cierva, Ministro de Alfonso XIII (1864-1938). No City: Academia de Alfonso X El Sabio, 1965.

Peterson, H. C. Propaganda for War. The Campaign against American Neutrality, 1914-1917. Norman, Oklahoma: The University of Oklahoma, 1939.

Petrie, Sir Charles A. King Alfonso XIII and His Age. London: Chapman and Hall, 1963.

Pilapil, Vicente. Alfonso XIII. New York: Twayne Publishers, 1969.

Reemtsen, Reemt. Spanisch-deutsche Beziehungen zur Zeit des ersten Dreibundesvertrages 1882-1887. Berlin: Verlag Emil Ebering, 1938.

Renouvin, Pierre. La Crise europeene et la premiere guerre mondiale. Paris: Presses universitaires de France, 1948.

Ribas, Antonio Fabra. La Semana Tragica, El Caso Maura, El Krausismo. Madrid: Seminarios y Ediciones, 1975.

Riste, Olav. The Neutral Ally: Norway's Relations with Belligerent Powers in the First World War. Oslo: Universitetsforlaget, 1965.

Schulte, Henry F. The Spanish Press, 1470-1966: Print,

Power and Politics. Chicago: University of Illinois Press, 1968.

Sencourt, Robert. King Alfonso, A Biography. London: Faber and Faber, 1942.

Smith, Arthur L. The Deutschtum of Nazi Germany and the U.S. The Hague, The Netherlands: Nyhoff, 1965.

Sontag, Raymond. European Diplomatic History, 1871-1932. New York and London: Century Co., 1933.

Squires, James D. British Propaganda at Home and in the U.S. from 1914-1917. Cambridge: Cambridge University Press, 1935.

Steglich, Wolfgang. Buendnissicherung oder Verstaendigungsfrieden. Berlin: Frankfurter Musterschmidt Verlag, 1958.

________. Die Freidenspolitik der Mittelmaechte 1917-1918. Wiesbaden: Steiner, 1964.

Taylor, A.J.P. The Struggle for Mastery in Europe. Oxford: Clarendon Press, 1954.

Tuchmann, Barbara. The Zimmermann Telegram. New York: Bantam, 1971.

Turlington, Edgar. Neutrality: The World War Period. New York: Columbia University Press, 1936.

Ullmann, Joan C. The Tragic Week, A Study of Anticlericalism in Spain, 1875-1912. Cambridge, Mass.: Harvard University Press, 1968.

Vagts, Alfred. The Military Attaché. Princeton, N.J.: Princeton University Press, 1967.

Viereck, George S. Spreading Germs of Hate. New York: Liverwright, 1930.

Waagner, Sam. Mata Hari. New York: Appleton Century, 1965.

Wiehler, Rudolf. Deutsche Wirtschaftspropaganda im Weltkrieg. Berlin: Mittler, 1922.

Wright, Gordon. Raymond Poincaré and the French Presidency. New York: Octogon Books, 1967.

Yahuda, A.S. King Alfonso and the Jews. London: Jewish Forum, 1941.

Zeman, Z. A. B. _Diplomatic History of the First World War_. London: Weidenfeld, 1971.

2. Articles and Dissertations

Anonymous. "Decree Governing the Treatment of Submarines in Spanish Waters," _American Journal of International Law_. XI (October 1917) Supplement II:175-177.

________. "L'Espagne Francophile," _Bulletin Hispanique_. XIX (1917):134-135.

________. "La Prensa Española y la Guerra," _Bulletin Hispanique_. XIX (1917):123-133.

________. "Spain as the Mediator," _Literary Digest_. LIV (March 1917):698.

________. "Autocracy Flirts with Anarchy," _Literary Digest_. LVII (April 1918):23.

________. "Spain Drifting to the Allies," _Literary Digest_. LIII (October 1916):942-943.

Barker, William R. "England and the European Neutral-Belligerents 1914-1917," Ph.D. dissertation, University of Southern California, 1937.

Bertrand, L. "Mon Enquête en Espagne," _Revue des Deux Mondes_. XXXI (January 15, 1916):240-281.

Bledsoe, Gerie. "Spain and the League of Nations," Ph.D. dissertation, Florida State University, 1968.

Boerlitz, E. "Das Deutschtum im Spanien," _Zeitschrift fuer Auslandkunde: Organ des Verbandes Deutschland-Spanien_. I (1919):1-10.

Boyd, Ernest. "Cosas de España," _Foreign Affairs_. IV (January 1926):321-329.

Cancio, Rita M. "The Function of María Cristina of Austria's Regency (1885-1902) in Preserving the Spanish Monarchy," Ph.D. dissertation, St. Louis University, 1955.

Cunningham, Charles. "Spain and the War," _American Political Science Review_. XI (August 1917):421-447.

Friedman, Isaiah. "German Intervention on Behalf of the Yishuv 1917," _Jewish Social Studies_. 33(1971):23-43.

Galvan, Manuel de. "Spain and the World War," _Current History Magazine_. VII (October 1917):58-62.

González, N. "Entender a Alfonso XIII," Razón y Fé. (1970): 258-283.

Griffith, Sanford. "The German Myth in Spain," Outlook. CXVI (July 4, 1917):364-365.

Grueneberg, Emmy-Ilse. "Die Handelsbeziehungen zwischen Deutschland und Spanien unter besonderer Beruecksichtigung der erzschaffenden und erzverarbeitenden Industrie," Ph.D. dissertation, University of Berlin, 1927.

Harrison, R. J. "Catalan Business and the Loss of Cuba," Economic History Review. 52 (August 1974):431-438.

Hasenclever, Adolf. "Zur Geschichte der spanisch-franzoeschischen Beziehungen vor Ausbruch des Weltkrieges," Berliner Monatshefte. XIV (September 7, 1936):718-730.

Jackson, Shirley. "The United States and Spain, 1898-1918," Ph.D. dissertation, Florida State University, 1967.

Just, Harald. "Neutralitaet im Ersten Weltkrieg," Mitteilungen des Oesterreichischen Staatsarchiv. XIX (Vienna 1965):363-435.

Klinger, Wallace R. "Spain's Problem of Alliances," Ph.D. dissertation, University of Pennsylvania, 1944.

Lamy, E. "Choses d'Espagne," Revue des Deux Mondes. XXXIV (July-August 1916):241-258.

Lantier, Raymond. "L'Attitude des Intellectuels," Mercure de France. CXIII (January 1916):10-20.

________. "L'Espagne y la Litterateur de Guerre," Mercure de France. CXVI (July 1916):11-15.

Lopez, Santiago Roldan. "La Consolidation de la vía nacionalista del capitalismo español durante la guerra mundial," Anales de economía. (July-September 1971): 17-91.

Lutz, Ralph. "Studies of World War Propaganda," Journal of Modern History. V (1933):496-516.

Mehl, Joseph M. Jr. "Intelligence Reporting by American Observers from the European Neutrals, 1917-1919," Ph.D. dissertation, American University, 1962.

Moos, Ferdinand. "Politik und Wirtschaft in Spanien," Die Neue Zeit. (February 27, 1918):488-492.

Mousset, Albert. "L'Espagne dans la Conflit Actuel," La Grand

Revue (April 1915):180-188.

Olivar Bertrand, Rafael. "Repercusiones en España de la primera guerra mundial," Cuadernos de Historia Diplomática. III (1956):3-45.

Pardo de Tavera, T. H. "Spain and the Great War," Century Magazine. XCV (January 1918):360-365.

Pelasco, Edmundo. "Die Spanische Sozialisten und der Krieg," Die Neue Zeit. (May 26, 1916):239-242.

Pijoan, José. "Spain: Before, During, and After the War," The Nineteenth Century and After. 9 (October 1921): 667-682.

Pilapil, Vicente. "Spain in the European State System," Ph.D. dissertation, Catholic University of America, 1964.

Pingaud, Albert. "L'Espagne dans le Conflit Actuel," Revue des Deux Mondes. 101 (May 1931):194-202.

Reval, G. "L'Oeuvre Humanitaire de S. M. le roi d'Espagne," Revue des Deux Mondes. XXXV (October 1916):842-843.

Soeffner, Walter. "Die deutsch-spanischen Handelsbeziehungen von 1871-1926," Ph.D. dissertation, University of Leipzig, 1926.

Stadelmann, R. "Friedensversuche in den ersten Jahren des Weltkrieges," Historische Zeitschrift. CLVI (1937): 485-545.

Trice, Thomas G. "Spanish Liberalism in Crisis: A Study of the Liberal Party during Spain's Parliamentary Collapse, 1913-1923," Ph.D. dissertation, University of Wisconsin, 1974.

Vincent-Smith, John. "Britain, Portugal and the First World War, 1914-1916," European Studies Review. IV (July 1974):207-238.

Ventura Subirate, Jorge. "La verdadera personalidad de 'Baron de Koenig'," Cuadernos de Historia Economíca de Cataluna. V (1971):103-118.

Whealey, Robert H. "Opportunities and Disappointments in the Spanish Foreign Ministry Archives," Archives. XII (Autumn 1975):68-73.